KNUPPELDIK TRUST
POSBUS 14066
SINOVILLE 0129
012 567 2082

Fit for a king

English Version of "Knuppeldik aan Koningskos"

Fit for a king is a recipe book compiled by the outstanding confectioners and cooks of the Pretoria Officers' Women's Club. Each recipe bears evidence of careful planning and excellent insight — not only for experienced bakers, but also for beginners or even for males risking their skills in culinary art. Humour features promenently and is as delightful as the delicious dishes — especially "Knuppeldikkie" cropping up ever so often to evoke a smile.

I also regard this work as a practical guide with the valuable hints and sound ideas. This recipe book is indeed a show-piece and a must in every kitchen.

I sincerely hope that the funds raised by the sale of this book can be used to the benefit of the South African Police Comforts Fund and the South African Police Care of the Aged Fund.

My personal congratulations to the compilers and my best wishes for a wonderful success with this ambitious project.

Mrs Snow Cruywagen
(Wife of the Administrator of the Transvaal)
August 1985

Fit for a king

English Version
of "Knuppeldik aan
Koningskos"

Tried and
tested recipes
from the ladies of the
Pretoria Police Officers' Women's
Club.

In aid of
SA Police Comforts Fund, 02 200024 0006
SA Police Care of the Aged Fund, 02 2001950003
SA Police Widows and Orphans Fund, 02 2001020005
and any other SAP Benevolent Fund

> *For health and strength and daily food,*
> *We praise Thy Name, O Lord!*

© Copyright Reserved
Copyright Pretoria Police Officers' Women's Club
Set in 10 on 11 point Souvernir Light
Set, printed and bound by:
CTP Book Printers
Cape Town

First edition, first print 1989
First edition, 2nd print 2003
ISBN 0 620 10218 7

Acknowledgements:
Col. Buks van Staden – photography
Pierre Victor – artist
Col. Tiaan Crafford – technical advisor
Brig. D. Botha
Elise Malan – flowers and styling

Contents

Metric Conversions (Tables of weights
and measures) 6
Preface 7
Beverages 9
Dips 19
Starters — Entrèes 29
Savouries and Snacks 41
Soups 57
Fish 63
Meat 73
Minced Meat dishes 101
Venison 121
Barbecues 127
Chicken dishes 147
Vegetables 165
Desserts 179
Rusks and Bread 219
Salads and Salad Dressings 233
Cakes 253
Biscuits 273
Tarts 317
Sweets 345
Microwave Recipes 353
Preserves 375
Champagne Breakfasts 385
Alphabetical list of recipes 393

METRIC CONVERSIONS

The cups, tablespoons and teaspoons are adapted to the metric system.

The liquid content of the metric cup of 250 ml is approximately two tablespoons more than the imperial cup.

The metric tablespoon (2½ t) on the other hand is smaller than the imperial tablespoon which contains 3 teaspoons.

1 Tsp — 12.5 ml	¼ c — 60 ml
2 Tsp — 25 ml	⅓ c — 80 ml
4 Tsp — 50 ml	½ c — 125 ml
¼ t — 1.5 ml	¾ c — 190 ml
1 t — 5 ml	1 c — 250 ml
1 pint — 600 ml	1 bottle — 750 ml

ABBREVIATIONS

bot — bottle
dsp — dessertspoon
t — teaspoon
Tsp — tablespoon
lb — pound
g — gram
kg — kilogram
ml — millilitre
(— litre
pkt — packet
hr — hour
mins — minutes
c — cup

DRY INGREDIENTS

1 cup flour — 120 g — 250 ml
1 cup butter — 250 g — 250 ml
1 cup sugar — 200 g — 250 ml
1 Tsp — 12.5 ml
1 t — 5 ml

180 °C — 350 °F

Substitutes

SELF-RAISING FLOUR: Sieve 480 g (4 x 250 ml unsifted measures) flour, 30 ml cream of tartar and 15 ml bicarbonate of soda together four times.

MILK: For every 250 ml milk required, mix 250 ml cold water with 60 ml milk powder.

YEAST:	1 cake (20 g) compressed or fresh yeast is equivalent to 1 packet (10 g) of 12,5 ml active dry or granular yeast.
SOUR MILK:	Add 20 ml lemon juice or vinegar to 250 ml milk.
SOUR CREAM:	Add 20 ml lemon juice or vinegar to 250 ml cream.

Preface

For the Pretoria Officers' Women's Club this recipe book is the realisation of a dream, because recipes tested through the years are here at the disposal of all involved in the preparation of food.

We are convinced that this recipe book will be a best-seller — it must surely be with all the outstanding and sensible cooks amongst the South African Police ladies.

A more appropriate name could not have been selected. *Fit for a king ("Knuppeldik aan Koningskos")* will not only ensure that we eat like kings, but in our gratitude will always honour the King who provides us with our daily bread.

On behalf of the Police Officers' Women's Club a sincere word of thanks to:

1. Promedia for their invaluable assistance and support with the printing.
2. All our donors and advertisers who sponsored a large amount of the printing costs.
3. The contributors who put their selected recipes at our disposal.

May this valuable collection enrich your knowledge and make your cooking a pleasure.

Pretoria

Mollie de Witt
CHAIRWOMAN
1985

The kitchen prayer

Lord, of all pots and pans and things
since I've not time to be
A Saint by doing lovely things
or watching late with tea or
dreaming in the dawn light
or storming heaven's gates.
Make me a Saint by getting meals
and washing up the plates
Although I must have Martha's hands
I have a Mary mind
And when I black the boots and shoes
the sandals, Lord, I find
I think of how they trod the Earth
what time I scrub the floor
Accept this meditation, Lord —
I haven't time for more
Warm all the kitchen with thy love
and light it with thy peace —
Forgive me all my worrying
and make my grumbling cease
Thou who didst love to give men food
in room or by the sea
Accept this service that I do
I do it unto thee.

Klara Munkres

Dedicated to Joey Pienaar, former chairwoman of the club and all her capable assistants who made the printing of this book possible. Joey Pienaar has won first prizes for her baking at the Pretoria Show since 1982.

Beverages

Greek punch

1	bot	champagne (750 ml)
2	bot	white wine (2 x 750 ml)
250	ml	brandy (1 c)
4	ℓ	soda water
1		lemon thinly sliced
2		bananas (sliced finely)
1		tin pineapple chunks (410 g — with the syrup)
1		tin granadilla pulp (100 g)

Method:
Mix champagne, wine and brandy with fruit and refrigerate. Add cold soda water to mixture just before serving.
Joey Pienaar

Fruit drink
(For ± 20 people)

2	c	sugar
1	c	strawberries, crushed
1	c	bananas, sliced
juice of 6 oranges		
2	c	water
2	c	granadilla pulp
1		grated pineapple
2.5	ℓ	soda water

Method:
Prepare the syrup by boiling the sugar and water for 10 min. Strain and mix in all other ingredients except the soda water. Cool and add the soda water just before serving.
Joey Pienaar

Heredity is something we believe in, when our children are gifted.

Traditional gingerbeer
(Delicious)

2½	lb	sugar (5 c)
6	ℓ	water (32 c)
¼	lb	whole ginger pieces (bruised) (125 g)
½	c	raisins (crushed)
½		cake yeast
1	pkt	cream of tartar (3 t)
1	t	tartaric acid

Method:
Boil the first three ingredients for 1 hour. Cool and add the raisins and yeast. Cover with a cloth and leave until raisins float on the surface (12-24 hrs or longer). Add the last three ingredients. Stir thoroughly and leave until it ferments (± 3 hrs). Add 1 bottle (30 ml) lemon essence. Strain and bottle. Do not fill bottles — leave 5 cm in the neck. Place a raisin in each bottle and cork tightly. Cork tops can be tightened with a string. Leave to ferment slightly. Place in refrigerator before serving.
Joey Pienaar

Milkshake

1	c	milk
3	Tsp	ice-cream
2	Tsp	fruit syrup

Method:
Beat all ingredients until light and frothy. Serve cold.
Joey Pienaar

---

*What really flatters a man is that you think him worth flattering —
George Bernard Shaw.*

Tomato Drink
(A cold drink as well as a cold soup)

Cut a large amount of ripe tomatoes into small pieces. Stew the tomato pulp slowly until the tomatoes are soft and juicy. Rub the pulp through a fine sieve and flavour with salt, pepper and Worcestershire sauce to taste. Cool the tomato juice in the refrigerator and serve very cold. It is a delicious starter instead of soup on a hot day.
Joey Pienaar

Banana ice-cream drink
(If you have a liquidiser, you can make this drink in seconds — 2 glasses)

1		scoop ice-cream
1		banana, peeled
500	ml	milk (2 c)

Method:
Mix all ingredients in liquidizer. Turn for 10 counts and serve the delicious drink in glasses.
Joey Pienaar

Easy gingerbeer

9	bot	water (750 ml x 9)
4	c	sugar
4	t	Jamaica Ginger
4	t	dry yeast

Method:
Combine ingredients and dissolve yeast in a little water. Mix with other ingredients and stir well. Bottle with cork tops tied down. Leave overnight and place in refrigerator.
Joey Pienaar

The willing horse does all the work.

Punch
(For large reception — 200 guests)

825	g	tin pineapples
825	g	tin guavas
825	g	tin peaches
825	g	tin pears
12x250	ml	sugar (12 c)
18x250	ml	water (18 c)
750	ml	granadilla squash
1		large carton granadilla juice (5 ℓ)
750	ml	lemon squash
2x750	ml	orange squash
3x750	ml	grape juice
9	ℓ	ginger-ale
9	ℓ	lemonade
9	ℓ	soda water

Method:
Liquidise fruit the previous night and place in refrigerator. Boil water and sugar for 10 min. Allow to cool well, then add fruit. Mix fruit squash and add to fruit. Add grape- and granadilla juice, ginger-ale, lemonade and soda water just before serving.
P.S. If an alcohol-based punch is required, mix fruit with 1 bottle gin the previous night and place in refrigerator. Just before serving, add 5 bottles semi-sweet dry wine to the mixture.
Joey Pienaar

I know an undesirable character when I see one; I've been one for years — Christopher Fry.

Easy punch recipe
(Quick and delicious)

1		bottle Passion Fruit Squash
1		tin crushed pineapple pieces (410 g)
1		tin granadilla pulp (100 g)
1	ℓ	lemonade
1	ℓ	soda water
		lots of ice

Method:
Mix ingredients in a punch bowl. Can be served immediately.
Joey Pienaar

Punch (alcoholic)

½		bottle gin (375 ml)
1		bottle Lieberstein wine (750 ml)
1		bottle orange squash (Oros) (750 ml)
½		bottle lime juice (375 ml)
6	ℓ	lemonade
6		granadillas or 1 tin granadilla pulp (100 g)
825	g	canned pears (cut in pieces)
825	g	canned peaches (cut in pieces)
825	g	pineapple (cut in pieces)

Method:
Soak fruit overnight in gin and wine. Add the rest of the ingredients. Add lemonade before serving. Canned fruit can also be liquidised.
Joey Pienaar

One joy dispels a hundred cares — Anonymous.

Punch
(Delicious)

2	c	black Rooibos tea
1		bottle granadilla squash (375 g)
1		tin crushed pineapple (825 g)
2x1 ℓ		cartons guava juice (Liqui-fruit)
2x1 ℓ		cartons peach juice (Liqui-fruit)
2x1 ℓ		cartons granadilla juice (Liqui-fruit)
2	c	sugar
4	c	water

Method:
Boil water and sugar. Allow to cool. Mix ingredients well. Keep in refrigerator.

Add just before serving:

2	ℓ	ginger-ale
2	ℓ	soda water
		ice blocks
1		bottle semi-sweet dry wine (can be omitted)

Joey Pienaar

Cream liqueur
(Makes 750 ml)

1		tin sweetened condensed milk (397 g)
250	ml	fresh cream (1 c)
125	ml	whisky (½ c)
125	ml	brandy (½ c)
2		egg yolks
10	g	dark chocolate, melted
2.5	ml	vanilla essence (1 Tsp)

Method:
Mix all ingredients in a liquidiser. Whisk ± 15 min. Keep cool and serve.

Joey Pienaar

Men are the reason for women disliking one another — An old French proverb.

Van der Hum liqueur

1	ℓ	brandy
5		cloves
1		stick cinnamon
3	ml	grated nutmeg

Method:
Mix the ingredients. Cork tightly and seal with wax. Leave for 45 days. Strain and mix as follows:

For every 2	c	flavoured brandy
1		glass gin
1	c	syrup

Syrup:

1½	c	sugar
¾	c	water

Boil until syrup becomes thready.
Joey Pienaar

Liqueur
(Makes 4 ℓ)

Boil 4½ bottles water (750 ml x 4½)
Add 8 c sugar. Boil for 20 min. Allow to cool.
Mix green cake colouring with syrup. Add 500 ml (2 c) "witblits".
Joey Pienaar

Sailors have a port in every storm.

16

Coffee liqueur
(Makes 1.7 ℓ)

500	ml	water (2 c)
500	g	white sugar (625 ml) (2½ c)
250	ml	strong black coffee (ground coffee) (1 c)
375	ml	vodka (1½ c)
375	ml	cane spirit (1½ c)
200	ml	dessert wine (¾ c)
25	ml	vanilla essence (2 Tsp)

Method:
Boil water and sugar to a syrup, blend with the coffee. Allow to cool. Mix in vodka, cane spirit, dessert wine and vanilla. Allow to cool. Pour into bottles and seal. Leave 3-4 weeks before use.
Mollie de Witt

Lemon drink

250	ml	lemon juice (1 c)
500	ml	sugar syrup (2 c)

Method:
Mix ingredients. Refrigerate. Mix with iced water for use.

Syrup:

1	kg	sugar
1	ℓ	boiling water

Boil the sugar and water for 5 min until sugar has dissolved.
Joey Pienaar

War is like love: it always finds a way — Bertolt Brecht.

Blessed are the peacemakers: For they are the children of GOD.
— Matthew 5:9.

18

Dips

Quick dip

250	ml	cream (1 c)
250	ml	yoghurt (1 c)
34	g	white onion soup

Method:
Mix all ingredients. The cream can be omitted. The dip will be just as delicious and less fattening.
Dimples Wandrag

Avocado dip

2		ripe finely mashed avocados
12,5	ml	lemon juice (1 Tsp)
5	ml	salt (1 t)
80	ml	mayonnaise ($\frac{1}{3}$ c)
$\frac{1}{4}$	t	Aromat
12,5	ml	grated onion (1 Tsp)
		a pinch of cayenne pepper

Method:
Mix all ingredients and refrigerate. Sprinkle a little parsley over the top.
Mollie de Witt

Onion dip

250	g	cottage cheese (250 ml)
125	ml	yoghurt ($\frac{1}{2}$ c)
40	g	onion soup powder
		chopped parsley to taste

Method:
Mix all ingredients.
Joey Pienaar

Plain cooking cannot be entrusted to plain cooks — Countess Morphy.

Mustard sauce
(Mild)

2	Tsp	mustard
2	Tsp	cream
2	Tsp	sugar
2	Tsp	vinegar
2	Tsp	apricot jam
2	Tsp	butter
½	c	milk
		a pinch salt and pepper

Method:
Boil milk, butter, sugar, salt and pepper. Stir in vinegar, mustard, jam and cream and boil for 5 min. Stir continuously.

Use as a dip for Vienna sausages, small smoked cocktail sausages and delicious with hot dogs.
Joey Pienaar

Ham dip

85	g	ham spread
150	g	cottage cheese (150 ml)
5	ml	grated onion (1 t)
10	ml	tomato sauce (2 t)
		or
5	ml	tomato paste (1 t)
3		drops tabasco sauce
12,5	ml	chopped parsley (1 Tsp)
25	ml	chopped olives (2 Tsp)
50	g	ham, chopped
		salt and pepper to taste
¼	t	Aromat

Method:
Mix all ingredients well.
Joey Pienaar

The greatest revelation is stillness — Lao-Tse.

Mustard sauce
(Medium hot)

50	ml	sugar (4 Tsp)
50	ml	vinegar (4 Tsp) (white)
10	ml	mustard (2 t)
1		egg, beaten

Method:
Mix all ingredients and beat over boiling water till thick.
Mollie de Witt

Horse-radish sauce
(A sharp sauce)

250	ml	sour cream (1 c)
12,5	ml	lemon juice (1 Tsp)
12,5	ml	sugar (1 Tsp)
50	ml	drained horse-radish (4 Tsp)
		or
		grated fresh horse-radish
1		green onion, finely chopped
		a pinch of cayenne pepper

Method:
Mix all ingredients thoroughly. Cover container and leave in re-frigerator for a few hours to allow the flavours to blend. Stir before serving.

Variation

250	ml	sour cream (1 c)
50	ml	grated fresh horse-radish or tinned horse-radish (4 Tsp)
2	ml	salt
5	ml	sugar (1 t)

Method:
Place ingredients in a blender, blend and cool.
Joey Pienaar

Love gives you the right to be free — Whitney Houston.

Avocado dip

3		avocado pears (2 c)
125	ml	mayonnaise (½c)
50	ml	lemon juice (4 Tsp)
2	ml	tabasco sauce
10	ml	salt (2 t)
1	ml	black pepper
2		garlic cloves
10	ml	onion juice (2 t)
2	ml	paprika
1	ml	cayenne pepper
5	ml	sugar (1 t)
25	ml	chopped spring onion (2 Tsp)
½	t	Aromat

Method:
Place all the ingredients in a liquidiser, except the spring onion. Liquidise until thick and creamy. Garnish with spring onion.
Joey Pienaar

Onion dip

190	ml	cream
3	Tsp	mayonnaise
1x250	g	cottage cheese (chunky)
1	t	onion juice
		a pinch of cayenne pepper
¼	t	Aromat

Method:
Mix ingredients and place in refrigerator for approximately ½ hour. Garnish with parsley.
Mollie de Witt

He who smiles rather than rages is always the stronger —
Japanese wisdom.

Cucumber-yoghurt sauce

1		medium cucumber
2		Spring onions, finely chopped
125	ml	plain yoghurt (½ c)
1	ml	salt
¼	t	Aromat

Method:
Peel the cucumber and chop. Mix with other ingredients.
Ina Steyn

Dip

250	ml	cream (1 c) mixed with ½ t mustard
⅓	c	mayonnaise
2	Tsp	grated onion
250	ml	cottage cheese (1 c)
2	Tsp	Worcestershire sauce
1	t	anchovy paste

Method:
Mix all ingredients thoroughly.
Ina Steyn

Tomato dip

250	ml	mayonnaise (1 c)
75	ml	tomato sauce (6 Tsp)
75	ml	chutney (6 Tsp)
¼	t	Aromat

Method:
Mix ingredients thoroughly.
Joey Pienaar

Freedom from desire leads to inward peace — Lao-Tse.

Sweet and sour dip

439	g	baked beans in tomato sauce (1 can)
1	ml	cayenne pepper
2	ml	ground cinnamon
1	ml	ground cloves
1	ml	black pepper
		a pinch of aniseed
1		garlic clove
100	ml	water (8 Tsp)
250	ml	smooth plum jam (1 c)
37,5	ml	soya sauce (3 Tsp)
37,5	ml	vinegar (3 Tsp)

Method:
Mince the beans or rub through a sieve or use an electric mixer. Beat the bean puree and spices. Crush the garlic clove till fine and mix with the water, jam and vinegar. Stir and boil for 5 min. Mix in bean puree and boil another 10 min. Use as a dip for a meat fondue, or as a sauce for duck, barbecued chicken liver, pork or meatballs.

Remark
The dip will keep well in the refrigerator and freezes well. Spices and herbs can be added or omitted according to taste.
Mollie de Witt

When you smile, the whole world smiles with you.

Chicken dip

100	g	cream or cottage cheese (100 ml)
12.5	ml	mayonnaise (1 Tsp)
75	g	cooked chicken, minced (150 ml)
12.5	ml	finely chopped celery or parsley (1 Tsp)
10	ml	finely chopped green pepper (2 t)
25	ml	finely chopped olives (2 Tsp)
40	g	cooked pineapple, finely chopped (50 ml) (4 Tsp)
25	ml	milk (2 Tsp)
		salt and cayenne pepper to taste
¼	t	Aromat

Method:
Mix the cheese and mayonnaise. Add the rest of the ingredients and sufficient milk to form a batter.
Joey Pienaar

Cheddar dip

250	g	cottage or cream cheese (250 ml)
50	ml	milk (4 Tsp)
250	g	Cheddar cheese, coarsely grated (625 ml)
1		garlic clove
		a pinch of cayenne pepper
2	ml	celery salt
5	ml	prepared mustard (1 t)
125	ml	chopped, pickled gherkin (½ c)
2	ml	Aromat

Method:
Use an electric beater and beat the cottage cheese with 50 ml milk until smooth. Add the rest of the ingredients, except the gherkin. Mix till smooth. Add the gherkin and mix lightly.
Joey Pienaar

When money talks, nobody criticizes its accent.

Cream cheese dip

10	ml	grated onion (2 t)
3	ml	flavoured salt eg. celery salt
350	g	cream or cottage cheese (350 ml)
		milk, if needed
12,5	ml	finely chopped green pepper or parsley
12,5	ml	paprika (1 Tsp)

Method:
Beat the onion, salt and cottage cheese together. Add milk if mixture is too firm. Cool for a few hours to allow flavours to blend. Add the green pepper or parsley. Pour into container and decorate with paprika. Serve with savoury biscuits or cooled carrot strips.

Variations
If desired, any of the following can be added:
1 - 2 tins sardines, finely chopped
1 tin asparagus, finely chopped
85 g ham paste
5 gherkins, finely chopped
2 grated, medium radishes
or
25 ml horse-radish (2 Tsp)
1 tin tomato paste and few drops tabasco sauce.
Mollie de Witt

More diets begin in clothing stores than in doctors' surgeries.

Blaauwkrantz dip

120	g	"Blaauwkrantz" cheese, crumbled (250 ml)
100	g	cream or cottage cheese (100 ml)
25	ml	milk (2 Tsp)
40	ml	salad cream or mayonnaise (8 t)

Method:
Beat all ingredients together — an electric beater can be used.
Joey Pienaar

Delicious dip

250	g	cream cheese
125	g	liver paste
½	c	grated cheese
125	ml	milk (½ c)
5	ml	Worcestershire sauce (1 t)
12,5	ml	lemon juice (1 Tsp)
1,5	ml	Aromat (¼ t)

Method:
Mix ingredients until creamy.
Joey Pienaar

The longer you nurse a grudge, the longer it takes to heal.

Entrées

Decoration for starters

Press rim of dish into slightly whisked egg white, then into coloured sugar crystals or jelly. Allow to set. If it is a savoury starter, use chopped parsely instead of jelly..
Joey Pienaar

Crayfish mayonnaise

6		crayfish tails
2		grated onions
		juice of 1 lemon
¼	t	tabasco sauce
		salt and pepper
3-4		hard-boiled eggs (chopped)
2	c	seafood mayonnaise
1	Tsp	Worcestershire sauce
		a pinch of paprika

Method:
Boil a considerable quantity of salt water. Place crayfish in the boiling water. Boil for 10 min. Mix the rest of the ingredients thoroughly. Place the fish in cold water to cool. Cut along both sides where the stomach wall and shell link. Remove the stomach lining. Start at the tail and gently remove the flesh ensuring that it does not break. Remove the large intestine which stretches from the stomach to the tail. Cut into blocks and add to remaining mixture. Garnish with paprika. Serve.
Joey Pienaar

Most people are too lazy to open the door when opportunity knocks.

Tuna and banana starter
(Cold — 6 helpings)

1		tin (± 450 g) tuna, flaked
50	ml	mayonnaise (4 Tsp)
		pickled onions and gherkins (finely chopped), to taste
		lettuce
3		bananas, sliced (sprinkled with lemon juice)
50	ml	white onion soup (powdered) (4 Tsp)

Method:
Mix all ingredients. Rinse lettuce and place on the base of the starter dish (or shell). Place mixture on lettuce and garnish with parsley.
Joey Pienaar

Fish salad starter

250	ml	cooked, cold rice (1 c)
250	ml	flaked fish such as smoked snoek or angelfish (1 c)
1		hard-boiled egg, chopped
25	ml	chopped parsley (2 Tsp)
12,5	ml	lemon juice (1 Tsp)
5	ml	grated onion (1 t)
¼	t	Aromat
		mayonnaise
		lettuce

Method:
Place all ingredients, except mayonnaise and lettuce, in a mixing bowl. Stir in mayonnaise till ingredients bind. Serve on lettuce or mould into shapes and turn out on lettuce.
Joey Pienaar

I like me cause God don't make junk — Anonymous child.

Kipper Kedgeree
(Serve warm)

1		pkt seafood rice
1		kg cooked kippers — flaked and boned
25	ml	lemon juice (2 Tsp)
20	g	chopped parsley (30 ml) (6 t)
4		hard-boiled eggs — roughly chopped

Method:
Cook rice according to instruction. Mix with remaining ingredients. Season to taste. Bake for 20 min at 180 °C and serve in shells or small plates.
Joey Pienaar

Garlic shrimps
(Enough for 12)

250	ml	olive oil (1 c)
4		large garlic cloves (peeled and crushed)
3	ml	salt
1		dried chilli
900	g	shrimps (shelled and intestines removed)
		chopped parsley

Method:
Place oil, garlic, salt and chilli in an earthenware ovendish. Bake in a hot oven at 220 °C for 10-15 min. Do not overheat the oil because the garlic will burn. Add shrimps and fry for 5-7 min till pink and hot. Remove chilli. Serve as a starter on toothpicks or in small earthenware bowls. Garnish with parsley.
Joey Pienaar

Flattery is the art of telling someone exactly what he thinks of himself.

How about a delicious cold punch for your next party? (See p 15)

This page was sponsored by Park Tours – tel (016 - 311720/1)

The filling in these scrumptious sausage rolls is exquisitely unique – also delicious in meat pies. (See p 43)

Snails in garlic butter

1		tin snails (24 snails)

Garlic butter

125	g	butter
1	Tsp	parsley
1	t	crushed garlic
⅛	t	Aromat
⅛	t	pepper
		a pinch of coriander
		a pinch of nutmeg
		a pinch of thyme
⅛	t	tabasco sauce
1	Tsp	brandy

Method:
Mix the ingredients for the garlic butter and refrigerate. Rinse and dry snails. Place a lump of garlic butter in the shells. Place the snails in the shells and fill each hole with garlic butter. Heat till garlic butter starts melting. Serve with brown bread.
Joey Pienaar

Fish salad

1½	kg	white fish, cooked and flaked
4		chopped onions, fried in
2	Tsp	oil
60	ml	condensed milk (¼ c)
		juice of 1 lemon
		salt and pepper
½	t	Aromat
375	ml	mayonnaise

Method:
Mix all ingredients. Serve on lettuce and garnish with paprika.
Joey Pienaar

Charity begins at home.

33

Mock crayfish
(6 - 8 helpings)

1,5	kg	hake
1	ℓ	water
25	ml	vinegar (2 Tsp)
5	ml	salt (1 t)
		a pinch of pepper

Sauce:

250	ml	mayonnaise (1 c)
125	ml	tomato sauce (½ c)
5	ml	Worcestershire sauce (1 t)
5	ml	brandy (1 t)
		grated onion
		few drops tabasco sauce
		a pinch of salt
¼	t	Aromat

Garnishing:
lettuce leaves
chopped parsley
lemon slices

Method:
Boil fish in large saucepan with water, vinegar, salt and pepper until tender. Drain, skin and bone. Flake. Leave to cool. Mix ingredients for sauce and cool. Add fish and mix lightly. Serve on lettuce, garnish with parsley and lemon slices.
Joey Pienaar

The folly of one man is the fortune of another.

Liver paté
(Delicious)

4		large onions
1		garlic clove
½	t	sugar
250	g	bacon
3	pkts	chicken livers
1		small liver sausage
		few drops of lemon juice
		salt and pepper
		mushrooms (± 300 g)
		a handful of freshly cut parsley

Optional
4	Tsp	brandy
½	c	cream
2	Tsp	melted butter

Method:
Fry onion, garlic and sugar in butter. Add cut bacon and cook. Add chicken livers, lemon juice, salt and pepper and simmer till cooked. Liquidise. Add liver sausage. Add brandy, cream and melted butter.

HINT: Makes a large amount. Freezes well.

Vossie Kruger

You need a very clever woman to manage a fool.

Tasty Tuna starter
(Serve warm)

1		tin tuna — flaked
		(keep oil)
2		hard-boiled eggs
½	c	mayonnaise
1		grated onion
4		grated gherkins
		(medium sized)
		salt and pepper
1		large pkt "Barbecue" potato chips (150 g)
		lettuce and parsley

Method:
Mix all ingredients well, except chips. Place in a greased oven-proof dish. Crush chips and sprinkle on top. Bake until chips are golden brown. Serve hot on lettuce in shells and garnish with parsley.
Joey Pienaar

Mushrooms with garlic butter
(Delicious and original)

15		large mushrooms
75	g	butter (⅓ c)
15	ml	cooking oil (3 t)
2		garlic cloves, chopped
100	ml	chopped parsley (8 Tsp)
15	ml	lemon juice (3 t)
5	ml	salt (1 t)
2	ml	freshly ground black pepper

A flower is the poetry of reproduction.

Method:
Remove the mushroom stems gently and wipe the heads with a paper towel till clean. Place in a saucepan with concave sides up. Heat the butter and cooking oil and add remaining ingredients. Pour mixture over mushrooms. Bake for 12-15 min in oven at 160 °C (325 °F). Serve with homemade whole wheat bread or as a side dish.
Joey Pienaar

Avocado pear and shrimp shells
(Cold)

2		avocados
150	ml	white wine (½ c + 2 Tsp)
2		gherkins, sliced
		mayonnaise
		lettuce
220	g	shrimps (2 tins)
100	g	cream cheese (100 ml)
		tomato sauce
		walnuts (shelled)
		lemon juice

Method:
Dice the avocados and baste with lemon juice. Sprinkle with salt and pepper. Marinade the shrimps in white wine for ± 2 hrs. Soften the cream cheese with the mayonnaise and tint slightly with tomato sauce. Line the shells with lettuce leaves. Fill with avocado, gherkins, cream cheese and shrimps. Place a large serving of mayonnaise on top. Decorate with halved walnuts.
Mollie de Witt

Not without design does God write the music of our lives — John Ruskin.

Gambas al ajillo
(*Prawn starter*)

2	Tsp	olive-oil per person
5		average large prawns per person
1-2		garlic cloves per person (chopped)
½	t	lemon juice per person
1		small slice red pepper per person
		a pinch of salt
		a touch of black pepper

Method:
Each portion is cooked separately in ovenproof bowls. Heat olive-oil in bowls. As soon as a piece of bread browns when placed in the oil, the oil is ready for use. Fry the prawns in the oil for 3-4 min. Add the garlic, lemon juice, red pepper, salt and pepper and fry one minute. Serve hot.
Joey Pienaar

Seafood sauce

300	ml	mayonnaise (1 c + 4 Tsp)
37,5	ml	thick cream (3 Tsp)
		juice of ½ lemon
2	ml	pepper (½ t)
37,5	ml	tomato sauce (3 Tsp)
12,5	ml	brandy (1 Tsp)
2	ml	salt (½ t)
¼	t	Aromat

Method:
Mix mayonnaise, lemon juice, salt and pepper. Add the tomato sauce and stir continuously. Add the cream and stir in the brandy. Add more salt and pepper if needed. Refrigerate for at least one hour before serving. Pour over seafood dishes.
Joey Pienaar

---

*One laugh of a child will make the Holiest day more sacred still —
R.G. Ingersoll.*

Mushrooms with tuna — sour cream filling
(Cold)

25	ml	lemon juice (2 Tsp)
10		large mushrooms
1		slice white bread (remove crusts)
1		tin tuna
1		small onion
10	ml	chopped parsley (2 t)
1		garlic clove
125	ml	sour cream (½ c)
		salt and pepper
125	ml	salad oil (½ c)

Method:
Mix lemon juice and oil. Marinade mushrooms overnight.
Liquidise remaining ingredients. Remove mushrooms and fill with
tuna mixture. Serve cold as a starter.
Ina Steyn

A single rose can be my garden: a single friend my world.

Let no-one who loves be called altogether unhappy; even love unreturned has its rainbow.

Savouries and Snacks

Easy Pizza
(6 helpings)

Pie-crust:
500	ml	self-raising flour (2 c)
150	ml	boiling water (½ c + 2 Tsp)
125	ml	cooking oil (½ c)
		a pinch of salt

Method:
Place ingredients in a sealed plastic bag. Shake the bag until a soft dough forms. Spread the dough evenly in a swiss roll pan. Place a damp cloth over it and leave until required.

Filling:
4		medium soft tomatoes, peeled and chopped
1		large onion, chopped
10	ml	tomato sauce (2 t)
125	g	bacon sliced
150	g	grated cheddar cheese (375 ml) (1½ c)
10	ml	Aromat (2 t)

Method:
Braise the tomatoes and onion until soft. Leave to cool. Baste the raw dough with tomato sauce. Spread the braised tomatoes over dough. Place the bacon on top. Sprinkle with Aromat and then the cheese. Preheat oven to 180 °C (350 °F) and bake pizza for 30 min on the middle rack. Serve hot.

Joey Pienaar

Beauty ends where the artist begins.

Meat pie pastry
(Does not shrink. Use for all savoury pastries)

Rub 625 g margarine into 6 c flour, ½ t cream of tartar and 1½ t salt.
Mix with:

3		egg yolks and
60	ml	vinegar (¼ c) whisked in
¾	c	ice water

Place into plastic bag and refrigerate for at least 6 hrs. Best results are obtained with cold pastry. Roll out and use the following meat filling.

Meat filling for sausage rolls

Cook together:

1	kg	minced meat
½	t	salt
¼	c	chutney

Method:

When meat is done, add ½ t Aromat, ¼ t cloves, ½ t mustard, ½ pkt Knorr "Meat Ball Maker, ¼ c oatmeal, 1 slice soaked brown bread. Mix well with the meat and leave to simmer for 1 min. Mould in glass bowls and leave to set in refrigerator. Cut into strips and place on rolled dough. Fold dough and roll. Cut into desired size. Brush with whisked egg. Bake, unfrozen, at 180 °C (350 °F) till nicely browned. Can be frozen. Allow to thaw before baking.
Joey Pienaar

Peace will come through being.

Savouries

Dough:
Use meat pie pastry recipe. Roll out thinly and cut 60 mm rounds.
Place in muffin pans.

Filling:
37,5	ml	flour (3 Tps)
2	Tsp	margarine
750	ml	milk (3 c)
		salt
4		eggs
1		tin Vienna sausages (sliced) (375 g)
12,5	ml	grated onion (1 Tsp)
750	ml	coarsely grated cheese (3 c)
		a pinch of cayenne pepper
2	ml	mustard powder

Method:
Using first 4 ingredients, make a white sauce. Beat eggs and add
to sauce. Add other ingredients and blend thoroughly. Place
spoonfuls in muffin-pans. Bake at 180 °C (350 °F) until light
brown.
Joey Pienaar

Asparagus tart

Prepare as for cheese and ham tart on page 46, but use 500 ml
(2 c) cooked asparagus, diced, instead of ham. Reduce the cheese
to 125 ml (½ c). Add chopped, fried bacon.
Joey Pienaar

---

*Hint: Grass stains: soak garment in methylated spirits for short
periods. Wash.*

44

Savoury balls

Grate 1 small polony in:
2	c	flour
2	t	baking powder
1	t	salt

Method:
Beat 1 egg, 1 c milk and 2 Tsp oil. Mix with dry ingredients. Place teaspoonfuls of batter in hot oil. Fry until golden brown. Remove from oil and place on paper towel. Sprinkle with lemon pepper, Aromat and garlic salt.
Brenda Vlotman

Quick Asparagus tart

250	g	bacon, diced
2		onions, chopped
1		tin asparagus salad cuts (410 g)
100	g	cheddar cheese, grated (250 ml)
2		eggs
250	ml	milk (1 c)
3	ml	salt
1	ml	cayenne pepper
		pastry as for meat pies on p. 43.

Method:
Fry bacon and onion. Spread on pastry. Place the asparagus pieces and grated cheese on top of bacon and onion. Whisk egg, milk, salt and cayenne pepper. Pour over bacon-cheese mixture. Bake in a medium oven at 180 °C (350 °F) for 45 minutes.
Joey Pienaar

Beauty more than bitterness breaks the heart.

Cheese and ham tart

12,5	ml	butter (1 Tsp)
25	ml	flour (2 Tsp)
4	ml	salt
		a pinch of cayenne pepper
5	ml	dry mustard (1 t)
250	ml	milk (1 c)
250	g	cooked ham, minced
		or
4		rashers bacon, diced and slightly fried
100	g	cheddar cheese, coarsely grated (250 ml)
2		hard-boiled eggs, chopped
10	ml	finely chopped parsley (2 t)
1		egg, whisked
		Pie-crust as for meat pies on p 43.

Method:

Mix the butter, flour, salt, cayenne pepper and mustard over a low heat. Stir in the milk and mix well. Stir and boil for 2 min. Add remaining ingredients. Pour the mixture into a rectangular pan or baking dish lined with the pastry and bake for 15 min in a hot oven (200 °C (400 °F)). Reduce the temperature to 190 °C (375 °F) and bake for another 30 min.

Cheese and bacon tart

50	g	butter or margarine (50 ml) (4 Tsp)
25	g	flour (50 ml) (4 Tsp)
2	ml	salt
2	ml	mixed herbs
5	ml	dry mustard (1 t)
		a pinch of cayenne pepper
500	ml	milk (2 c)
250	g	bacon, diced and slightly fried

Where thou art; that is home.

1		chopped onion (sauté in bacon fat)
200	g	mushrooms (sauté in bacon fat)
100	g	cheddar cheese, grated (250 ml) (1 c)
10	ml	chopped parsley (2 t)
3		eggs, separated
		Pie-crust as for meat pie

Method:
Stir the butter, flour, salt, mixed herbs, mustard and cayenne pepper over a low heat. Add the milk and stir until smooth. Stir and boil for 2 min. Add the rest of the ingredients, except egg whites. Fold in stiffly beaten egg whites. Pour into a pie dish lined with pastry and bake for 45 min in a medium oven (180 °C (350 °F)). Before the tart is placed in the oven, grated cheese can be sprinkled on top.
Mollie de Witt

Minced meat fritters

Whisk:

250	ml	milk (1 c)
2		eggs
125	ml	oil (½ c)

Add to above:

250	ml	flour (1 c)
10	ml	baking powder (2 t)
2	ml	salt
2	ml	Fondor

Minced meat

Method:
Dough is very soft. Spray muffin-pans. Pour the dough in first, then the minced meat, then top with more dough. Bake in oven 450 °F (232 °C) until light brown.
Hester Naudé

Honour is a steep island without a shore.

Vienna sausage tart

Pie-crust:

2	c	self-raising flour
1		egg
⅓	c	oil
		milk

Method:
Break egg in a cup with oil and fill with milk. Sift flour and mix with egg mixture. Spread in pie dish.

Filling:

1		large tin vienna sausages (375 g)
1		large tin mushrooms (285 g)
½	c	chopped onion
2		tomatoes
1	c	grated cheese
2	Tsp	oil

Method:
Place sliced vienna sausages on top of pastry. Fry mushrooms and onion in oil. Pour over sausages. Place sliced tomato over the top. Sprinkle with cheese. Bake for 10-15 min in a warm oven.
Annamarié Strydom

All doors open to courtesy.

Asparagus tart

Pie-crust:

2	c	flour
½	t	salt
½-⅔	c	butter
⅓	c	ice water
1	Tsp	lemon juice

Method:
Sift flour and salt together. Rub butter in. Add lemon juice. Add just enough ice water to make a stiff dough. Place in refrigerator for 1 hr. Grate the dough roughly into a rectangular pie dish and flatten.

Filling:

2	Tsp	butter
4	Tsp	flour
1	t	salt
		a pinch of cayenne pepper
2	t	mustard powder
2	c	milk
1	pkt	bacon (slightly fried) (125 g)
2	c	cheddar cheese, grated
6		hard-boiled eggs (chopped)
1		tin asparagus pieces (410 g)
1		whisked egg

Method:
Make a white sauce using the first 6 ingredients. Add remaining ingredients. Pour into pie crust and bake in a hot oven at 200 °C (400 °F) for 15 min. Reduce heat to 190 °C (375 °F) and bake for another 15 min.
Mollie de Witt

The burden of life becomes light when love carries it.

Lollies' asparagus tart
(Delicious)

Pie-crust:
250	ml	flour (1 c)
500	g	cheddar cheese, grated
125	g	butter
		cayenne pepper

Method:
Mix and flatten ¾ of the plain crust in pie dish.

Filling:
460	g	sliced asparagus
170	g	grated cheese
100	ml	fried bread crumbs (8 Tsp)

White sauce:
25	ml	flour (2 Tsp)
25	ml	butter (2 Tsp)
375	ml	liquid (asparagus water and milk) (1½ c)

Method:
Make the white sauce and pour half into pie-crust. Place asparagus on top of white sauce and cover with the rest of the white sauce. Sprinkle breadcrumbs on top and bake for ± 20 min at 180 °C (350 °F).
Joey Pienaar

Snoek tart

250	g	smoked snoek or haddock poached in water with
15	ml	lemon juice (3 t)
30	g	margarine or butter (37,5 ml)
1		large onion (chopped)

Peace cannot be kept by force. It can be achieved only by understanding.

100	g	mushrooms, sliced
2		eggs
5	ml	dry mustard (1 t)
125	ml	cream (½ c)
125	ml	cream cheese (½ c)
50	g	cheddar cheese, grated (125 ml)
15	ml	lemon juice (3 t)
20	ml	chopped parsley (4 t)
		salt and pepper
		pastry as for meat pie on p 43 or the plain pastry below.

Method:

Flake the fish and bone. Fry the mushrooms and onion in the butter and add to fish. Pour over pastry. Beat the rest of the ingredients and add salt and pepper if needed. Pour over the fish and bake for 45 min in a medium oven (180 °C (350 °F)).

Plain pastry

500	ml	flour (2 c) (150 g)
5	ml	salt (1 t)
2	ml	cayenne pepper
150	g	margarine (162,5 ml)

Method:

Mix the dry ingredients, grate the margarine over the mixture and cut with a flexible knife blade or rub in until the mixture resembles rough mealie-meal. Flatten firmly with a spoon until 5 mm thick, in a pie dish.

Joey Pienaar

The only thing the stupid ever catch is a cold.

Quick Pizza

500	ml	self-raising flour (2 c)
125	ml	cooking oil (½ c)
150	ml	boiling water (½ c + 2 Tsp)
½	t	salt

Method:
Mix and flatten dough into pizza pan. Fill with minced meat or fish (tuna). Top with mushrooms, tomato puree and cheese to taste. Bake for 20 min in a medium oven (180 °C (350 °F)).
Henda Gous

Crustless savoury tart

3		eggs
375	ml	milk (1½ c)
1		onion, chopped
1		tomato, sliced
½		green pepper, chopped (optional)
10	ml	butter (2 t)
100	g	cheddar cheese, grated (250 ml) (1 c)
1		tin corned beef (300 g)
200	g	Vienna sausages (fresh or tinned)
2		hard-boiled eggs
10	ml	chopped parsley
		salt and pepper to taste
5	ml	dry mustard (1 t)
25	ml	flour (2 Tsp)
60	g	bacon
5	ml	Aromat (1 t)

Method:
Beat eggs and milk. Sauté the onion, tomato and green pepper in the butter. Mix all ingredients. Pour mixture into a greased pyrex dish and bake at 180 °C (350 °F) for 30-45 min.
Joey Pienaar

One spark of hope can light a bonfire of joy.

Pizza

170	g	flour (280 ml) (1 c + 6 t)
5	ml	baking powder (1 t)
100	ml	milk (8 Tsp)
90	g	margarine
1	ml	salt

Method:

Preheat oven to 200 °C (400 °F). Sift the flour, salt and baking powder. Rub margarine into dry ingredients. Add the milk and knead into dough. Seperate the dough into 4 parts. Roll out each part approximately 3 mm thick. Grease 4 pizza pans. Bake for 10 min. Prepare the filling then spread over dough. Sprinkle grated cheese over the top. Bake for 10 min at 180 °C (350 °F).

Filling:

450	g	mushrooms (sliced)
1		onion (chopped)
1		green pepper (chopped)
3		ripe tomatoes
4		rashers bacon
250	ml	grated cheese (1 c)
		black pepper

Ina Steyn

One step backwards in the wrong road is also one step ahead.

Mustard butter
(A spread for ± 20 doz hot-dog bread rolls generously spread)

225	g	mustard powder (450 ml) (1 ¾ c)
225	g	maizena (450 ml) (1 ¾ c)
1	Tsp	salt
5	c	sugar
6		eggs
2	bot	vinegar (2x750 ml)
750	ml	water (3 c)
3	pkts	margarine (3x500 g)

Method:
Boil the vinegar, ½ bot water (375 ml) and sugar. Mix the rest of
the water, mustard, maizena and salt. Whisk egg whites until firm.
Beat egg yolks until smooth. Add boiling vinegar, water and sugar
to mustard-mixture, egg yolks and egg whites. Return to heat and
stir until cooked. Allow to cool to blood temperature. Add margarine to mustard mixture and mix well. Mustard butter can be suc-
cessfully frozen for 3 months.
Zelda Bothma

Cheese puffs
(Very easy, quick and delicious — for 12 puffs)

1	c	grated cheese (cheddar)
½	t	salt
1	Tsp	melted margarine
¼	t	pepper
1	c	flour
1		egg, beaten with 200 ml milk
4	t	baking powder
½	t	dry mustard

Method:
Preheat oven to 230 °C (450 °F). Sift dry ingredients. Mix rest of

---

This day is a new day that you can practically turn into anything.

ingredients and add to dry ingredients. Mix to a soft dough. Spoon into a shallow muffin-pan (fill ⅔). Bake for 12-15 min. Serve hot or cold with cheese, jam or honey.
Joey Pienaar

Pizza omelette

6		eggs
125	ml	water (½ c)
		salt and pepper
50	ml	butter (4 Tsp)
5	ml	mixed herbs (1 t)
10	ml	tomato puree (2 t)
250	ml	chopped ham (1 c)
2		tomatoes, peeled and sliced
6		slices cheddar cheese

Method:
Beat the eggs, add the water and season to taste. Melt the butter in a large pan. Add eggs when butter sizzles. Pull the coagulated egg away from the edges to allow raw egg to filter in. Sprinkle the spices over the top as soon as the base has coagulated, but the top is still moist. Mix tomato puree and ham. Spread over the omelette. Arrange tomato and cheese slices over the ham and allow to melt in the oven.
Hester Naudé

Not knowing some things is a great part of wisdom.

Applause is the only appreciated interruption.

Soups

Gourmet vegetable soup

(Soup freezes well)

1	kg	beef shin
1	pkt	minestrone soup powder (69 g)
6	ℓ	water
3		carrots, peeled and grated
1		large onion, finely chopped
3		large potatoes, peeled and grated
½	c	oatmeal
500	ml	macaroni pieces (2 c)
		salt and pepper to taste
¼	t	curry powder
1		tin tomato puree (410 g)
30	ml	finely chopped parsley (2½ Tsp) optional

Method:

Cook meat in water until tender. Add carrots, onion and potato and boil until tender. Remove fat, if any, from the surface. Add macaroni and soup powder. Heat to boiling point and simmer for 25 minutes. Season with salt, pepper and curry powder. Add tomato puree and oatmeal and cook another 10 min. Add parsley just before serving. Makes 10-12 generous helpings.

Joey Pienaar

A knife that cuts both ways often proves to be a dagger.

Vegetable-pea soup

4		carrots
4		potatoes
1	pkt	chicken noodle soup (69 g)
4		tomatoes
2		onions
½	c	split peas
1		soup bone
		salt and pepper
4	Tsp	pea flour
¼	c	tomato sauce
4	Tsp	Worcestershire sauce

Method:

Soak the peas overnight. Simmer the peas, onion and soup bone together. Grate carrots and potatoes and add to the mixture. Peel and slice the tomato and add to mixture. Boil until tender. Mash the vegetables. Add sufficient boiling water to make a reasonably thick soup. Mix soup according to directions on the packet and add this to the mixture. Mix the pea-flour with a little water to form a paste. Stir into soup. Add the other seasoning. Boil for 5 min and serve. Freezes well.
Joey Pienaar

The devil shies away from happy people.

Croutons

2-3   slices stale bread (crusts removed)
oil for frying

Method:
Cut bread into squares and fry in enough oil to cover the bread. Oil must be hot. Turn over the squares and fry evenly. Remove, drain, sprinkle with salt and serve with soup.

Carrot soup
(Serve cold)

500	g	carrots
2	Tsp	chopped onion
30	g	butter
1		tin chicken soup (400 g)
125	ml	milk ($\frac{1}{2}$ c)
$\frac{1}{2}$	t	sugar
		salt, pepper and Aromat
60	ml	cream ($\frac{1}{4}$ c)
		chopped parsley or spring onion

Method:
Scrape the carrots and slice thinly. Melt the butter and stir into carrots and onion. Cover saucepan and simmer over low heat until vegetables are tender. Place in a liquidiser and add chicken soup, milk and seasoning. Mix at maximum speed for 1 min. Place in a dish and leave to cool. Stir in cream and cool in refrigerator. Serve in soup bowls sprinkled with a little parsley or spring onion.
Joey Pienaar

History of free men is written by choice.

Bean soup

500	g	sugar beans
2,5	ℓ	water
1		soup bone
125	g	bacon, cut into squares
15	ml	salt (3 t)
2	ml	pepper
2		medium onions, sliced
5	ml	chopped parsley (1 t)

Method:
Rinse the beans and soak overnight. Drain and add the soup bone and 2,5 ℓ water. Simmer beans and meat until almost tender. Add the other ingredients, except the parsley and boil for a further hour. Add parsley. Serve with brown bread and butter.
Mollie de Witt

Quick asparagus soup (hot)

1		tin Chicken Noodle soup (400 g)
1		tin Cream of Asparagus soup (400 g)
2	c	croutons
1	Tsp	chopped parsley
½	t	garlic salt
¼	c	cream
		asparagus pieces

Method:
Boil the tinned soup according to directions, drain asparagus and add. Place a few croutons in each bowl and pour the hot soup over. Mix the cream and parsley, and place a small helping in each bowl.
Joey Pienaar

A man's home is his wife's castle.

Quick cheese soup (hot)

3	c	boiling meat extract
1		egg
2	Tsp	grated cheese

Method:

Whisk egg, add cheese and mix well. Add to meat extract and beat continuously with a fork. Simmer for 5 min and pour into 6 bowls. Sprinkle with 1 t chopped parsley and 1 t parmesan cheese and serve with hot cheese straws.

Ina Steyn

A weed is no more than a flower in disguise.

Fish

63

Fish-cakes

400	g	cooked fish, finely flaked (2 c)
		salt and pepper
2		medium cooked potatoes, mashed (250 ml) (1 c)
12,5	ml	chopped parsley (1 Tsp)
25	ml	melted butter (2 Tsp)
1		egg, whisked
12,5	ml	milk (1 Tsp)

Method:
Sprinkle fish with salt and pepper, add the potato, parsley, butter and egg. Shape into flat, round cakes. Roll in fine breadcrumbs, then in egg, mixed with 12,5 ml milk, then again in breadcrumbs. Fry both sides in deep oil till brown. Serve hot with lemon slices.
Joey Pienaar

Batter for fish

250	ml	flour (1 c)
2	ml	salt
3	ml	baking powder
250	ml	water, or water and milk (1 c)

Method:
Sift dry ingredients and add enough liquid to make a thin batter.

Method to fry fish:
Dry the fish and sprinkle with salt and pepper. Dip into the batter and fry in hot oil. Turn the fish once only. Takes approximately 2 min on either side of fish. Drain the fried fish on absorbent paper. Serve hot.
Joey Pienaar

The sea has fish for every man.

Yogurt bread (p 225) and white bread (p 229) as seen here are simply delicious with Gourmet vegetable soup. (See p 58)

Seat yourself in this divine setting of roast leg of mutton and roast potatoes (p 178), lemon sweetpotatoes (p 167), ovenbacked rice, chicken pie with mushrooms (p 154) and stewed green beans with salted rib of mutton (p 168)

Snoek roll/Tuna roll

4	Tsp	butter
½	c	flour
		salt
2	c	milk
4		egg yolks
1	t	sugar
4		egg whites

Method:
Line a swiss roll pan with grease-proof paper, grease and sprinkle with flour. Melt the butter. Stir in the flour and salt. Add the milk slowly. Boil for 4 min, stirring continuously. Remove from stove. Stir in beaten egg yolks and sugar, then the beaten egg whites. Spread the dough evenly in the greased pan (± 30 x 25 cm) and bake the roll for 40-45 min till light brown (160 °C — 325 °F). Leave to cool. Turn out on wax paper. Remove paper lining. Spread the snoek filling over the roll. Serve hot or cold with sour cream (optional).

Filling:

500	g	smoked snoek or tuna
1	Tsp	cheese spread
1	Tsp	salanaise
3	Tsp	chutney
¾		of a small bottle Jennypost Seafood mayonnaise (± 1 c)

Annamarié Strydom

Not beauty but fine qualities keep a husband.

Baked tuna

2		tins tuna (200 g each)
1		tin mushroom soup (405 g)
2	c	frozen peas
1		large pkt potato chips (150 g) (plain)
¾	c	milk
		salt and pepper to taste

Method:
Flake the tuna finely. Grease an ovenproof baking dish. Place layers of chips, tuna and peas into dish. Mix the mushroom soup, milk, salt and pepper. Beat well. Pour mixture over the layers of chips, tuna and peas. Bake in oven at 180 °C (350 °F) for 25 min. Serve with rice and salad.
Petro Erasmus

Fish salad
(Delicious as a starter on lettuce or as a side dish)

250	g	stockfish (hake)
4		boiled eggs (more eggs can be used)
±2	Tsp	grated onion
±½	c	grated or diced cheese
		mayonnaise
		salt and pepper to taste

Method:
Boil fish and flake. Chop boiled eggs. Add remaining ingredients and mix well. Serve cold.
Francis Schoeman

All is fish that comes to net.

Soufflé roll
(Something special)

For the roll:

50	ml	butter (4 Tsp)
125	ml	cake flour (½ c)
500	ml	milk (2 c)
5	ml	sugar (1 t)
4		eggs
		salt

Method:
Melt butter, add flour and salt. Remove from heat and add a little milk to make a smooth paste. Replace on heat and add rest of milk gradually. Stir until thick. Remove from heat. Beat egg whites until stiff. Add lightly beaten egg yolks to mixture, then sugar. Add egg whites. Line a swiss roll pan with grease-proof paper and grease both sides well. Pour mixture into pan and bake for 45 min at 180 °C (350 °F). Leave to cool slightly and turn out on a damp dish cloth. Remove paper gently. Spread the filling over the roll. Fold and roll slowly. Allow to cool.

Filling:

1		tin salmon (drained) (± 200 g)
1		avocado (mashed)
15	ml	lemon juice (3 t)
30	ml	mayonnaise (6 t)
15	ml	finely chopped gherkins (3 t)
		a few drops tabasco sauce
		salt and pepper to taste

Method:
Mix all ingredients together. Serve cold.
Joey Pienaar

Too many cooks spoil the broth.

Braised snoek
(4-6 portions)

500	g	smoked snoek, flaked and boned
2		onions, sliced
25	ml	oil (2 Tsp)
25	ml	butter (2 Tsp)
2		potatoes, peeled and diced
2		large, ripe tomatoes, peeled and chopped
2		red chilli, finely chopped or ground or 5 ml chilli powder (1 t)
		freshly ground black pepper
500	ml	cooked rice (2 c)
62,5	ml	sultanas (5 Tsp) optional
		lemon juice (1 t)
		chopped parsley

Method:
Fry onion until light brown in oil and butter. Add the potatoes, tomatoes and chilli and stir. Fry until potato starts to brown. Flavour with pepper. Add fish, rice and sultanas, cover and simmer until potato is cooked. Stir in lemon juice and sprinkle with parsley. Serve immediately. Braised snoek is traditionally served with grape jam or fruit pickles and homemade brown bread.
Joey Pienaar

Every cloud has a silver lining.

Stuffed trout
(Enough for 4)

4		whole trout (cleaned)
50	g	melted butter (± 4 Tsp)
300	ml	white wine (1 c + 4 Tsp)
15	ml	maizena (3 t)

Filling:

125	g	fresh breadcrumbs (500 ml) (2 c)
12,5	ml	chopped parsley (1 Tsp)
2	ml	grated lemon rind
2	ml	dried thyme
25	ml	chopped celery (2 Tsp)
2		medium sized tomatoes (peeled and chopped)
2	ml	salt
25	g	soft butter (30 ml) (6 t)
		pepper to taste

Method:
Mix filling ingredients. Gut the cleaned trout and divide filling between the 4 trout. Stitch the back with a thick needle and cotton. Line an ovenproof dish with aluminium foil, grease well with butter and place the fish in it. Pour the melted butter over the fish and add the wine. Fold foil over and bake in a preheated oven at 180 °C (350 °F) for about 45 min. Remove from oven and place trout gently on serving dish and pour the sauce in the ovendish into a saucepan. Mix the maizena with a little water and add to the sauce in the saucepan stirring continuously. Stir until thick and transparent. Pour over fish just before serving. Garnish with parsley, lemon slices and tomato.

Joey Pienaar

The deafest man can hear praise.

Grandma's pickled fish

1.7	kg	yellowtail fish, cleaned, boned and sliced
		oil
6		lemon leaves
6		large onions, cut in rings
750	ml	brown vinegar (3 c)
250	ml	water (1 c)
175	ml	sugar (approximately ¾ c)
12.5	ml	turmeric (1 Tsp)
37.5	ml	curry powder (3 Tsp)
25	ml	flour (2 Tsp)
8	ml	salt (1 ½ t)
12.5	ml	freshly ground black peppercorns (1 Tsp)
250	ml	sultanas (1 c) optional

Method:

Fry fish in hot oil for about 1½ min on each side until just done. Spice well and leave aside. Simmer onions for 10-12 min in vinegar and water, with lemon leaves, sugar, turmeric, curry, salt and peppercorns until cooked but still firm. Mix flour with a little of the hot sauce and stir back into the sauce. Simmer until the sauce is well done, and thick. Fill an airtight container with layers of fish, onion and sultanas. Pour the sauce over this and refrigerate. The fish will be ready for use within 3 days. Freezes well for up to 6 months.

Joey Pienaar

Shrimps with peri-peri sauce
(Delicious)

4	Tsp	peri-peri oil
125	ml	cooking oil (½ c)
1	Tsp	tomato sauce

One man's meat is another man's poison.

1	Tsp	Worcestershire sauce
1	Tsp	tabasco sauce
		juice of 1 lemon
.5	ml	barbecue spice (1 t)
5	ml	garlic flakes (1 t)
2,5	ml	Aromat (½ t)
		salt to taste
		shrimps

Method:
Make a sauce using all the ingredients. Place shrimps in sauce and leave in refrigerator for 4 hours. Cook till ready and serve with rice.
Joey Pienaar

Tuna salad

1	tin tuna (200 g) flaked
1	tin sauerkraut (400 g) drained
1	tin pineapple chunks (410 g) drained

Method:
Add ingredients and mix with mayonnaise. It's a delicious light meal on a hot summer's day when served with whole wheat bread.
Lena Colyn

Curried fish

Mix flour and curry — 2 t or 3 t if you like hot curry. Place a layer of sliced onion in a thick based saucepan. Roll fish in flour, curry and salt and place in saucepan with skin at the bottom. Repeat until all the fish is in the saucepan. Pour vinegar over fish and cook slowly until done.
Dimples Wandrag

He makes no friend who never made a foe.

Oven baked fish
(6 helpings)

1	kg	frozen hake fillets
1		large onion, chopped
4		garlic cloves, crushed
4		eggs
50	ml	cooking oil (4 Tsp)
50	ml	vinegar (4 Tsp)
50	ml	finely chopped parsley (4 Tsp)
2	ml	dried thyme
		a pinch of cayenne pepper
150	g	grated cheddar cheese (375 ml) (1½ c)
		salt and pepper to taste

Method:
Allow fillets to thaw slightly before placing in a greased casserole or roasting-pan (if preferred the skin can be removed. The skin of frozen fish removes easily). Sprinkle onion and garlic over fish. Beat the eggs, cooking oil, vinegar, parsley, thyme and cayenne pepper until blended. Add cheese and mix. Pour the egg mixture evenly over the fish. Flavour with salt and pepper. Preheat oven to 200 °C (400 °F) and bake for 45 min on the centre shelf.
Joey Pienaar

Islands in the stream: that is what we are — Dolly Parton.

Meat

Meat dish for the Gourmet

5		pieces of beef (need not be super)
		onion
		oil
2	Tsp	Worcestershire sauce
6		cloves
		flour
		salt and pepper
2	Tsp	tomato sauce
2½	c	boiling water

Method:

Pound flour, salt and pepper into meat with a mallet. Brown the meat in a little oil, remove from the pan and brown the onion. Place alternate layers of meat and onion in a greased ovenproof dish. Pour the remaining oil from the frying pan leaving about 2 spoonfuls. Sprinkle 2 spoons of flour over the oil. Add the boiling water, Worcestershire sauce, tomato sauce, and cloves. Allow to boil and pour over the meat. Cover and allow to simmer for 3 hrs in oven (150 °C — 300 °F).

Joey Pienaar

Meat is much but manners are more

Meat dish with mushroom soup

1½	kg	topside
2	Tsp	oil
½	c	flour
1		tin mushroom soup (410 g)
		salt and pepper

Method:
Pound the flour, salt and pepper into the meat with a mallet. Fry meat in oil until brown. Place in a casserole and pour the mushroom soup over. Seal in foil and bake at 350 °F (180 °C) until tender.
Joey Pienaar

Liver in caul (mouse)

1	t	Aromat
1		sheep's liver, minced
1		slice white bread, soaked in milk
75	g	currants
		salt, pepper and grated nutmeg
1		egg
1		finely chopped onion
2	Tsp	vinegar
350	g	caul (membranous fat covering sheep's stomach)

Method:
Mix all ingredients and place on the spreaded caul in a frying pan. Fold and pin with skewers. Pour a little water in the pan and bake for ± 1 hr in a moderate oven (180 °C) until nicely browned. Baste occasionally. Can also be barbecued over an open fire.
Joey Pienaar

A friend in power is a friend lost.

Stroganoff with a difference
(Delicious)

Step 1:
1   kg   rump or fillet steak
         salt and pepper

Cut into thin slices and sprinkle with vinegar and mustard powder
½ hr before needed. Flavour with salt and pepper and fry quickly
in oil and butter. Remove from pan and thicken sauce with flour.
Pour over meat and leave aside.

Step 2:
2   large onions
3   garlic cloves or garlic flakes

         Slice onion and fry with garlic in butter until golden
         brown.

Step 3:
1   tin tomato puree (65 g)
250 ml sour cream (1 c)
4   Tsp brandy
         Fondor

Stir the tomato paste and sour cream in carefully, as well as the
brandy. Add Fondor to taste.

Step 4:
300 g   fresh mushrooms
1   tin mushroom soup (410 g)

Fry the mushrooms lightly in butter and add with the mushroom
soup to the sauce. Mix sauce and meat and warm. Serve with rice
and green peas. (Sour cream can be substituted by 500 ml Ultramel cream. The mushroom soup is then omitted.)
Lena Colyn

True power and politeness are above vanity.

Curried beef

Cut pounded rump into portions.
Add salt and pepper and leave overnight in sauce. (8-10 hours).

Sauce:
Beat 1 egg and add:

2	Tsp	tomato sauce
2	Tsp	Worcestershire sauce
2	Tsp	vinegar
2	t	curry powder
1	Tsp	cooking oil
2	Tsp	chutney
1		onion, grated
3		cloves garlic, chopped

Method:
Barbecue the meat until done and baste with the marinade occasionally. Heat remaining marinade and serve with meat.
Dimples Wandrag

Stroganoff
(Easy to prepare)

454	g	rump steak, diced

Roll the meat in flour, fry in butter in a saucepan until brown.

Add:

1	tin chopped mushrooms (285 g)
1	medium sized onion (chopped)
1	garlic clove (chopped)

Cook for 5 minutes.
Joey Pienaar

I believe the children are our future — George Benson.

Sauce for ox tongue
(Enough for 2 tongues)

½	c	sugar
½	t	salt
2	t	dry mustard
2	Tsp	flour

Mix sauce with 1 c of boiling water

Add:

1	c	Salanaise
¼	c	white vinegar
2	Tsp	oil

Method:
Slice cooked tongue and pour sauce over it. Sprinkle bread-crumbs over and bake in slow oven until the sauce thickens.
Annemarié Strydom

Wiener schnitzel

6		veal cutlets or fillets
2		eggs, lightly beaten
50	ml	bacon fat or lard (4 Tsp)
250	ml	thick sour cream (1 c)
		salt and pepper
		juice of 1 lemon
		flour

Method:
Spice meat with salt and pepper. Dip first in egg then in flour, fry until brown. Simmer in covered casserole for about 30 min. Stir often. Add sour cream. Serve over meat and garnish with lemon slices.
Joey Pienaar

Do not pray for easy lives.

Pork chops with pineapple

10		small chops
1		large onion, chopped finely
		salt and pepper to taste
250	ml	water (1 c)
1		large tin pineapple chunks
15	ml	mustard powder (3 t)
250	ml	tomato sauce (1 c)
125	ml	flour (½ c)

Method:
Fry meat until brown on both sides. Arrange meat and pineapple in layers in heavy based saucepan with lid. Make a sauce with the pineapple juice, mustard, tomato sauce, water, onion and 125 ml flour and pour over meat and pineapple. Preheat oven to 180 °C (350 °F) and bake for 1½ hrs.

Joey Pienaar

Lollie's chasseur sauce
(Fantastic)

1	pkt	cream of mushroom soup (69 g)
170	g	tin Ideal milk
1½	c	water
250	g	fresh mushrooms
3	Tsp	sherry

Method:
Heat a little butter and fry mushrooms for 5 min. Add remaining ingredients and boil for another 10 min. This sauce is delicious. Serve with chops, beef, sausages or hamburgers . . . especially over barbecued beef.

Joey Pienaar

Praise is always pleasing.

Delicious mutton chops
(Enough for 4)

4		mutton chops
1	ml	garlic salt
1		tin creamed mushrooms (285 g)
250	ml	chopped green pepper (1 c)
250	ml	chopped onion (1 c)
2		medium sized tomatoes (sliced)
10	ml	paprika (2 t)
2	ml	dried rosemary
5	ml	salt (1 t)
1	ml	pepper
60	ml	red wine (¼ c)
125	ml	beef extract (½ c)

Method:
Wipe meat with a damp cloth and sprinkle with garlic salt. Place in an ovenproof dish and place mushrooms, green peppers, chopped onion and sliced tomatoes over meat. Mix rest of ingredients well and pour over top. Cover and bake in a preheated oven at 160 °C (325 °F) for about 40 min (depends on how well cooked you prefer your meat). Remove lid after the first 25 min. Serve hot with rice and peas.
Mollie de Witt

Corned meat

Use any portion of meat such as leg of pork or cheaper beef cuts such as brisket. If the portion is large, double the brine to cover meat completely. (Place glass dish on top.) The ingredients in the recipe are sufficient for 2 kg meat.

2	ℓ	water
500	g	course salt

Trust in the Lord and don't despair; He is a friend so true.

200	g	white vinegar (250 ml) (1 c)
1	pkt	saltpetre or potassium nitrate (50 g)
		(obtainable from pharmacies)
5	ml	bicarbonate of soda (1 t)

Method:

Boil all ingredients. Leave to cool. Once cold, add meat and leave for 4 days. Ensure that meat is completely covered by the brine. Remove meat after 4 days and boil in fresh water until cooked. Cool in the water it was boiled in. Remove, cut and serve with salad.

Joey Pienaar

Mustard tongue

Sauce:

125	ml	sugar ($\frac{1}{2}$ c)
5	ml	salt (1 t)
2	ml	dry mustard
25	ml	flour (2 Tsp)

Mix with 250 ml water (1 c)

Add:

250	ml	mayonnaise (1 c)
125	ml	white vinegar ($\frac{1}{2}$ c)
250	ml	oil (1 c)
		juice of 1 lemon

Method:

Cook tongue, slice and arrange in layers in casserole alternately with sauce. Sprinkle with bread or rusk crumbs. If required, raisins can be added. Grill in oven until nicely browned.

Joey Pienaar

The tongue is more venomous than a serpent's sting.

Brawn
(Makes 3 bowls, each 33 x 23 x 5 cm)

2		large cowheels
2,5	kg	shin or shank
3,5	ℓ	boiling water
50	ml	salt (4 Tsp)
12,5	ml	dried thyme
2,5	ml	ground cloves (½ t)
		pepper to taste

Method:
Scrape the shin well with a sharp knife. Boil the cowheels and shin in 500 ml water until very tender. Add extra boiling water if necessary. Remove the meat from the saucepan and bone. Cut the meat very finely, do not mince. Place back in saucepan with gravy. Add the remaining 3 ℓ of water, as well as the salt, thyme, cloves and pepper. Allow the mixture to cook well. Dish into containers and leave to cool. Place the brawn in refrigerator to set.
Joey Pienaar

Stuffed fillet of beef in puff-pastry

1	kg	fillet of beef
1		chopped green pepper
250	ml	chopped mushrooms (1 c)
250	ml	bread crumbs (1 c)
		salt and pepper
1		onion, grated
250	ml	liver sausage (1 c)
125	ml	dry sherry (½ c)
1		egg, beaten
		puff pastry

It is easier to be critical than correct.

82

Method:

Sprinkle fillet with salt and pepper. Make a slit for the filling. Fry the onion, green pepper, liver sausage and mushrooms for 5 min. Add sherry and breadcrumbs to make a firm filling. Cool and fill the fillet. Place filled fillet on rolled pastry and fold in edges. Brush with beaten egg. Bake for 1 hour at 190 °C (375 °F).

Joey Pienaar

Grilled monkey gland steak in beer

1	kg	rump steak (cut into 10 x 5 cm squares and rolled in flour, salt and pepper)
1		large onion, finely sliced
30	ml	chutney (6 t)
1		tin mushrooms (285 g)
1		tin beer
4		rashers bacon, finely sliced

Method:

Fry onion and bacon in butter and remove from stove. Fry meat rapidly until brown. Add bacon, onion, chutney and beer and simmer for about 1 hr. Add mushrooms and simmer another 5 min. Serve with rice. (Delicious if prepared the previous day. Reheat and again add a little beer.)

Joey Pienaar

A couple is unhappy not merely from limited means.

Roast Suckling-pig

Clean the piglet well and wipe in- and outside with a damp cloth. Rub with pepper and salt. Stuff the pig. Make sure that it is not overstuffed. Stitch or use skewers to seal. Press the front paws to the back and the hind paws to the front and pin with skewers. Rub the outside with butter. Place the piglet in a kneeling position, place an apple in the mouth and wrap in foil. Place in a casserole and bake for ± 3½ hrs in a low to moderate oven (160 ° — 180 °C) (325 °F — 350 °F) until nearly tender. Remove the foil for the last 30 min. Allow the piglet to brown. Baste occasionally.

Filling:

500	ml	minced meat (2 c)
25	ml	minced ham (2 Tsp)
1½	t	coriander
1		thick slice of bread soaked in milk
2	ml	ground cloves (½ t)
		salt and pepper
1	Tsp	vinegar
2	Tsp	grated onion
1		egg, beaten
2	t	Aromat

Method:
Mix all the ingredients and stuff piglet.
Joey Pienaar

Courage imperils life; fear protects it.

Small sosaties
(Threaded on toothpicks)
(Delicious for finger lunches)

3	lbs	mutton (1 ½ kg) (reasonably fat)
1	c	dried apricots
3		large onions
1	Tsp	curry
1	c	vinegar
		salt and pepper to taste
2	Tsp	oil
6		lemon leaves
1	Tsp	sugar
½	c	water

Method:
Dice the meat. Soak the apricots overnight in water and boil the next day until soft and mash slightly. Fry the sliced onion, add the apricots and all other ingredients except the meat and cook well. Leave to cool and pour over the meat threaded on toothpicks (firm type) about 4 pieces to each toothpick. Leave for 24 hrs. The sosaties can be stacked but just ensure that every layer is covered with the cooled sauce. Fry gently in sauce in moderate oven at 350 °F (180 °C). Just before serving, place under grill for a few minutes. Keep hot. Use the same recipe for large sosaties. Barbecue.

Joey Pienaar

Power pollutes whatever it touches.

Cottage Pie
(8 servings)

500	g	minced beef
500	g	minced pork, lean
500	ml	soft breadcrumbs (2 c)
250	ml	milk (1 c)
1		egg
1		medium onion, chopped
1		garlic clove, chopped
10	ml	salt (2 t)
		a pinch of pepper and 1 t Aromat
25	ml	Worcestershire sauce (2 Tsp)
50	ml	chutney (4 Tsp)
4		medium potatoes

Method:
Mix all the ingredients, except the chutney and potatoes. Spread lightly into a greased casserole. Bake for 1½ hours in cool oven (160 °C — 325 °F). Boil the potatoes in the meantime. Mash and add salt, a piece of butter or margarine and a little milk as for ordinary mashed potatoes. Spread the chutney over meat and dish the mashed potatoes on top of the meat. Roughen the surface with a fork. Bake in a hot oven until the potato edges are brown.
Joey Pienaar

Roasted pork chops

Sprinkle salt, pepper, a little mixed herbs and 1 t Aromat over the chops. Roll each chop in flour and layer in a roasting pan or casserole. Sprinkle white wine or lemon juice over chops and cover with foil. Roast in a hot oven. Remove the foil about 20 min before serving and brown. Serve with stewed dried peaches.
Mollie de Witt

A woman's place is in the home.

Grilled hamburgers

500	g	minced meat
5	ml	salt (1 t)
		a pinch of pepper
1	Tsp	chutney
6		hamburger rolls
		butter or margarine
		Tomusto Mustard sauce
1		large onion, sliced
1		large tomato, sliced

Method:

Mix the meat, salt, pepper and chutney. Form meatballs and flatten to about 10 mm (Or use a large instant coffee bottle cover. Grease with a little oil and press meat firmly on a bread board until you have a firm, compact, flat fricadel.) Fry under an oven element or in a frying pan with a little fat. Halve the rolls and spread each half with butter and mustard sauce. Pour boiling water over the onion slices to lessen the sharp taste. Leave for 5 min, drain, leave to dry slightly and sprinkle with salt. Arrange a tomato slice, a few onion slices and a fricadel on one half. Cover with the other half of the bread roll.

Joey Pienaar

T-bone steak

(Something special)

Roll the meat in dry onion soup powder. Add salt and pepper if required. Wrap each T-bone in foil. Place in oven for at least 1½ hrs at 150 °C (300 °F).

Ina Steyn

We have confused power with greatness.

Beef slices with garlic butter

Garlic butter:

60	g	butter or margarine (75 ml) (6 Tsp)
2		garlic cloves, finely chopped or grated
30	ml	finely chopped parsley (6 t)
15	ml	lemon juice (3 t)
2	ml	salt
1	ml	pepper

Beef slices

1 T-bone, fillet or rump steak, 2,5 cm thick, per person.
Salt and pepper (preferably freshly ground) to taste.

Method:

Cream butter. Add garlic, parsley, lemon juice, salt and pepper and mix thoroughly. Place mixture on a piece of foil and shape into a roll of 3 cm in diameter. Fold foil and keep in refrigerator or freezer until needed. Slit the fat rind of the meat about 2,5 cm. Heat a cast-iron or thick-base pan until hot. Place one beef portion in pan and brown quickly on both sides. Reduce heat and grill 3-5 min for rare and 5-7 min for medium, turn frequently. Keep hot until all the meat is done. Flavour meat with salt and pepper and serve immediately with a slice of garlic butter on each helping.
Mollie de Witt

It's a long, long way to the land of milk and honey — Ella Marie.

Stewed mutton

1	kg	mutton rib
2		small onions
1	t	mustard
500	g	green peas
		salt and pepper
1	Tsp	flour
¼	c	vinegar
½	t	parsley
1	t	Aromat

Method:

Cut the meat into small portions. Slice the onion and fry with meat in the fat. Sprinkle with flour. Add salt and pepper and cover the meat with water and vinegar. Stew for about 2 hrs. (In pressure cooker, much quicker.) Shell the peas and add to meat a ½ hr before serving. (N.B. Tinned peas can also be used, but the water must be removed and the peas just heated.) Serve the meat on a hot dish. Arrange mashed potatoes around the meat and sprinkle with parsley. Arrange small cooked carrots around the potato ring.

Joey Pienaar

Home is where the heart is.

Pickled leg of pork with pineapple crust

Order 2,25 kg pickled leg of pork, the upper portion, from your butcher.

Method:
Weigh the meat. Wrap in foil, shiny side on the inside and bake at 180 °C (350 °F). Allow a ½ hr for every 500 g and another ½ hr for browning. Remove foil. Remove the rind and as much fat according to taste. Make a paste with 125 ml brown sugar and freshly grated pineapple. (Squeeze excess juice from grated pineapple to ensure that the paste is not too thin in which case it will drain from the meat. Mix juice with gravy in casserole and thicken to a sauce.) Spread the paste generously over the meat and place under the oven grill to brown. Place the meat reasonably far from the grill to prevent it from burning. Serve hot or cold.
Joey Pienaar

Liver in gravy
(6 helpings)

750	g	liver
25	ml	oil (2 Tsp)
25	ml	flour (2 Tsp)
7	ml	salt (1½ t)
1	ml	pepper
300	ml	creamy milk (1 c + 4 Tsp)
1		sprig parsley, chopped finely

And gather honey all the day from every opening flower
— I. Watts.

Method:

Dip the liver in boiling water, remove the membrane and cut in slices of 15 mm. Brown both sides in hot oil. If the oil is too hot, the liver will dry out and become tasteless. Remove the liver. Place the flour, salt and pepper in the frying pan, add the milk and stir well until mixture is smooth. Place liver in the gravy, cover the pan and simmer for 15 min.

Joey Pienaar

Liver with sour sauce

1		mutton chitterling (vetderm)
2		sheep's kidneys
1		sheep's heart
500	g	mutton flank or left over mutton pieces when cutting up the sheep (or stewing meat)
1		sheep's liver, the membrane removed
10	ml	salt (2 t)
3	ml	pepper
25	ml	vinegar (2 Tsp)
25	ml	flour (2 Tsp)
25	ml	cold water (2 Tsp)

Method:

Clean the chitterling, wash the kidneys and heart, cut into pieces and place in a saucepan. Add salt and pepper, cover with water and simmer until nearly tender. Cut liver in small cubes, add vinegar and simmer with the rest of the meat for another 15 min. Mix the flour with the cold water and add to thicken sauce. Serve on rice or with fresh new potatoes.

Joey Pienaar

A man's feet should be planted in his country, but his eyes should survey the world — George Santana.

Liver in sour sauce
(4 helpings)

500	g	liver
25	ml	oil, butter or margarine (2 Tsp)
50	ml	flour (4 Tsp)
5	ml	salt (1 t)
1	ml	pepper
50	ml	vinegar (4 Tsp)
12,5	ml	sugar (1 Tsp)
375	ml	water (1½ c)
5	ml	Aromat (1 t)

Method:
Dip the liver in boiling water, remove the membrane and cut into small pieces about 20 x 20 x 10 mm. Brown both sides. Sprinkle flour over and stir. Add the rest of the ingredients and simmer for 15 min.

Liver patties
(6 helpings)

60	g	soft breadcrumbs (250 ml)
150	ml	milk (½ c + 2 Tsp)
500	g	minced sheep or ox liver
5	ml	salt (1 t)
2	ml	pepper
5	ml	Aromat (1 t)
1		medium onion, roughly grated
12,5	ml	vinegar (1 Tsp)
60	g	currants (100 ml) optional (8 Tsp)
2	ml	grated nutmeg
2		sprigs parsley, chopped
12,5	ml	flour (1 Tsp)

The laughter of a child is like the pealing of little bells.

Method:
Mix all the ingredients except the parsley. Fry spoonfuls in oil, butter or fat. Brown both sides of patties. Garnish with parsley and serve.
Joey Pienaar

Chicken liver with curry
(4 helpings)

8		chicken livers, rinsed and diced
		a pinch of pepper
5	ml	salt (1 t)
1		egg, beaten
50	ml	dry breadcrumbs (100 ml)
		butter, margarine or oil for frying
1		small onion, finely chopped
25	ml	flour (2 Tsp)
5	ml	curry powder (1 t)
250	ml	water or meat extract (1 c)

Method:
Sprinkle salt and pepper over liver pieces and roll in breadcrumbs. Dip in egg and roll in breadcrumbs again. Fry the liver in hot oil or fat until done. Remove the liver and slightly brown the onions. Add the flour and curry. Stir and fry a short while. Add the water. Stir and boil till the sauce is smooth and cooked. Pour the sauce over the liver.

HINT: This dish can be made without the curry.
Joey Pienaar

He who is really kind can never be unhappy — Confucius.

Offal
(Delicious)

Soak the cleanly scraped offal in cold salt water for 30 min.
Treat the head as follows:
Remove the skin over nasal bone and fold back. Chop through the nasal bone just below the eyes to the underlying jawbone and remove. This is not used. Examine the nasal cavity for worms which may be present and are easily seen. Wash thoroughly. Chop open the top part of the head, remove the brains and tie in a piece of tripe with string or cotton. Split the toe slit to the first joint and remove the glands between the toes. Cut trotters at the first joint. Rinse in cold, salt water.

Cooking:

1		tripe
1		head
4		trotters
10	ml	salt (2 t)
2	ml	pepper
6		cloves
500	g	neck
4		medium onions, sliced
50	ml	vinegar (4 Tsp)
3	ml	grated nutmeg
6		medium potatoes, peeled and cut in half
½	pkt	thick vegetable soup

Method:
Keep the paunch intact as it burns more easily if cut open. Place it with the head, trotters, salt, pepper and cloves in a heavy base saucepan, cover with water and boil slowly for 2-3 hrs. (Much quicker with a pressure cooker (± 1 hr)). Add the neck and cook until tender. Stir occasionally to prevent burning. Bone, cut the paunch into pieces, add the onion, vegetable soup, vinegar and cloves. Place the potatoes on top of the meat and boil slowly until potatoes are soft. If a pressure cooker is used, the paunch can be slit at the start.
Joey Pienaar

A covetous person will always dress an egg and give the offal to the poor.

Curried tripe (offal)

4		medium onions, sliced
12,5	ml	fat or oil (1 Tsp)
25	ml	curry powder (2 Tsp)
12,5	ml	sugar (1 Tsp)
50	ml	vinegar (4 Tsp)
1	Tsp	apricot jam
1		cooked offal (head, tripe and trotters)
10	ml	Aromat (2 t)

Method:
Sauté the onion in fat or oil and add the curry, sugar and vinegar. Stir the curry sauce into the offal and boil slowly for 30 min. Serve hot on rice with chutney topping.

Variation:
Brawn: Garnish the sides and bottom of a mould with slices of hardboiled eggs and pickles. Spoon the cooled offal into it. Allow to set.
Joey Pienaar

The human heart is amazing. It can break a hundred times and still heal.

Braised kidneys
(4-6 helpings)

8		sheep or 2 ox kidneys
50	ml	flour (4 Tsp)
50	ml	butter, oil or margarine (4 Tsp)
1		medium onion, chopped finely
3		medium tomatoes, cut open
10	ml	salt (2 t)
1	ml	pepper
		toast or mashed potatoes
2		sprigs parsley
5	ml	Aromat (1 t)

Method:
Wash the kidneys in cold water and cut lengthwise. Remove the membranes and cut out the tubes and lightish coloured parts with kitchen scissors. Roll in flour. Sauté together with onion in the fat or oil until the onion is light brown. Add the tomatoes, salt and pepper and cook slowly for about 10 min.
Ina Steyn

In love what a woman takes for disguise, is often simply a clear vision — Balzak.

Liver pie
(4 helpings)

500	g	liver, sliced
5	ml	salt (1 t)
1	ml	pepper
1		medium onion, chopped finely
2		rashers bacon
250	ml	water or meat extract (1 c)
4		potatoes
25	ml	butter or margarine (2 Tsp)
50	ml	milk (4 Tsp)
5	ml	Aromat (1 t)

Method:
Pack thin layers of liver slices on the bottom of a greased casserole dish and flavour with salt and pepper. Sprinkle with onion and arrange the bacon on top. Pour liquid over and bake for 45 min in a cool oven (160 °C — 325 °F). Boil the potatoes in the meantime and mash with half of the butter and milk and place on top of the cooked liver. Dot with the rest of the butter and brown slightly.

Mollie de Witt

What is good for the liver is bad for the spleen.

Dumplings

2	c	flour
4	t	baking powder
1	c	milk
1	t	salt

Method:
Sift the flour, baking powder and salt. Add all the milk at once and stir carefully until all the dry ingredients are mixed. Place spoonfuls of dough on top of simmering meat. When meat is done, cook for 10 min without the lid. Cover and cook for another 10 min. Serve immediately.
(The ingredients will make 8-10 large dumplings.)
Cheese dumplings: Add ½ c grated cheese to mixture.
Joey Pienaar

Samp ("stampmielies")
(4-6 helpings)

250	ml	samp, washed (1 c)
1,25	ℓ	water
5	ml	salt (1 t)
12,5	ml	butter (1 Tsp)

Method:
Soak the samp overnight in the water. Heat the samp in the water and cook slowly for 2-3 hours. Stir occasionally to prevent burning. Add the salt when it begins to soften and add the butter just before serving. Serve with offal, meat and vegetables.
Joey Pienaar

Do you need proof of God? Does one light a torch to see the sun?
— Oriental wisdom.

Pearl wheat with raisins (stamp koring)

250	ml	pearl wheat (1 c)
1	ℓ	boiling water
25	ml	sugar (2 Tsp)
1		cinnamon stick
1	t	salt
125	ml	seedless raisins (½ c)
12,5	ml	butter (1 Tsp)

Method:
Wash the pearl wheat. Add the cinnamon stick and salt to the boiling water. Add the pearl wheat slowly and boil rapidly until almost cooked. Pour the water off and steam the pearl wheat with raisins over boiling water. Add the butter and sugar, stir and serve.

Boiled rice
(6 helpings)

1	c	rice
2	c	boiling water
1	t	salt

Method:
Slowly stir the rice into salted boiling water. The water must continue to boil, cover and cook slowly. It takes about 20-30 min.

HINT: Instead of cooking on the stove, the rice can be cooked in the oven. Use a container with a lid, with the same quantity as above. The advantage is that the rice can never burn. You can use every grain of rice — temperature 180 °C (350 °F).

He who is content is wealthy — Lao-Tse.

Pearl wheat
(6-8 helpings)

200	g	pearl wheat, rinsed (250 ml) (1 c)
750	ml	water (3 c)
5	ml	salt (1 t)

Method:
Place all ingredients in a saucepan. Reduce the heat as the water starts boiling and place the lid at a slight angle. Leave to cook slowly for 40 min. Stir occasionally to prevent burning. Add more water if needed.
Joey Pienaar

Better by far you should forget and smile, than you should remember and be sad — C. Rosetti.

Minced meat dishes

Sausage ("Wors")
(For 25 people)

½	c	oats
50	ml	coriander (4 Tsp)
2	ml	grated nutmeg
1	ml	ground cloves
2	ml	ground thyme (optional)
2	ml	ground pimento (all spice)
5	ml	pepper (1 t)
25	ml	salt (2 Tsp)
1,5	kg	beef
1,5	kg	pork
125	ml	vinegar (½ c)
50	ml	Worcestershire sauce (4 Tsp)
70	g	sausage casings
¼	c	ice water
500	g	speck

Method:
Roast the coriander and grind. Add the rest of the seasoning. Cut the meat into suitable pieces after removing tendons and membranes. Place the beef and pork alternately in layers in an enamel dish and sprinkle a little of the seasoning over each layer. Mix thoroughly and leave for 1 hour. Cut the speck into squares about 5-8 mm thick. Roughly mince the meat. After each layer of minced meat, sprinkle a handful of speck squares and a little vinegar and Worcestershire sauce as well as the oats over the meat mixture. Sprinkle with ice water. Mix the speck, vinegar and Worcestershire sauce lightly into the mixture with a knife or fork. The minced meat must be handled carefully. If the meat is kneaded, the sausage texture will be too firm. Stuff the meat into the casings. Do not fill tightly.
Joey Pienaar

Waste not; want not.

Sausage

(For dried boerewors)

3	kg	beef
500	g	sheep's tail-fat
25	g	salt
3	ml	pepper
2	ml	grated nutmeg
50	ml	ground, roasted coriander (4 Tsp)
3	ml	ground cloves (optional)
25	ml	vinegar (2 Tsp)

Method:

Sprinkle the salt, spices and vinegar over the meat pieces and fat. Mince and stuff in the usual way but not as firmly as normal sausage. Hang to dry. Flatten the sausage slightly when flash-dry for a neater appearance and to prevent cavities.

HINT: Sausage is dried when the climate is dry and cold.

Joey Pienaar

No-effort rice dish

500	g	minced meat
1		onion, sliced
1	tin	Minestrone soup or vegetable soup (410 g)
25	g	margarine (30 ml) (6 t)
180	g	uncooked rice

Method:

Set oven at 180 °C (350 °F) and grease a deep casserole dish. Brown mince in margarine and stir frequently to prevent lumps forming. Place in dish, sprinkle with onion, then the rice and finally the soup. Fill the soup tin with water and pour over. Cover and bake for 1 hour or until rice has absorbed all the liquid.

Joey Pienaar

The wise man is always silent; the fool is noisy.

Boerewors
(Small quantities)

3	kg	beef (boned)
2	kg	pork with fat
250	g	speck cut into 5 mm squares
55	g	salt (50 ml) (4 Tsp)
25	ml	pepper (2 Tsp)
40	g	coriander, roasted and ground (100 ml) (8 Tsp)
125	ml	vinegar (½ c)
100	g	sausage casings
¼	c	iced water
1	c	oats

(In large quantities)

36	kg	beef, boned
18	kg	pork
500	g	salt (450 ml) (1¾ c)
50	g	pepper (100 ml) (8 Tsp)
500	g	coriander, roasted and ground
25	ml	cloves (2 Tsp)
1		nutmeg, grated
2	kg	speck, cut in 5 mm squares
1	ℓ	vinegar
1	kg	sausage casings
3	c	iced water
6	c	oats

Method:
Remove tendons and cut meat into suitable pieces to mince. Mix ·the salt, spices and oats. Place the beef and pork alternately in layers in a dish and sprinkle mixed seasoning over each layer. Leave for one hour. Mince the meat. Sprinkle a few tablespoons of cut speck and a little vinegar over each layer of minced meat, as well as iced water. Mix lightly with a large fork and handle as little as possible. Stuff the casings, but not too firmly.
Joey Pienaar

Nature is God's gift to the world.

Spaghetti bolognaise
(Delicious) (Makes 6 helpings)

50	ml	cooking oil (4 Tsp)
2		large onions, sliced
2		garlic cloves, crushed
750	g	minced beef
4		medium tomatoes, peeled and chopped
1	tin	tomato puree (115 g)
10	ml	sugar (2 t)
7	ml	salt (1½ t)
1	ml	chilli sauce or a pinch of cayenne pepper
1	pkt	spaghetti (500 g)
150	g	grated cheese (375 ml) (1½ c)
25	ml	finely chopped parsley (2 Tsp)
5	ml	Aromat (1 t)

Method:
Heat oil in a saucepan with a thick base and fry onion and garlic until onion is tender. Add minced meat, stir with a fork and fry until pinkish colour disappears. Add tomatoes, tomato puree, sugar, salt and chilli sauce, cover and stew for a ½ hour over low heat. Meanwhile, cook the spaghetti in salt water, according to the directions, until tender, drain and keep hot. Just before serving, add half the cheese to the minced meat. Mix with the spaghetti, place in a serving dish and sprinkle the rest of the cheese and parsley over the top.
Joey Pienaar

You can always count on me; that's what friends are for —
Dionne Warwick and friends.

Curry and rice
(Delicious)

5	kg	minced meat
2	kg	pkt mixed frozen vegetables
2	c	raisins, seedless
¼	t	cloves
½	t	coriander
1	c	vinegar
1¼	c	apricot jam
6	Tsp	mild curry powder
½	c	oil
1	t	mustard
1		small tin tomato puree (115 g)
		salt and pepper to taste

Method:
Fry onion. Add minced meat. Simmer for 15 min. Add vegetables. Stir in flavouring and simmer for 30 min. Add tomato puree and raisins and cook well. For 5 kg meat use 2 kg rice.
Joey Pienaar

Curry and rice

500	g	meat, diced
1	dsp	curry powder
4		potatoes, diced
1		onion
1	dsp	sugar
½	c	vinegar

Beauty is the promise of happiness.

2		tomatoes, peeled and sliced
1	t	turmeric
1	t	salt (heaped)
1	Tsp	maizena (heaped)
¼	t	pepper
1	dsp	apricot jam

Method:
Fry the onion and the meat, salt and pepper until slightly browned. Add the water and cook until tender. Add the diced potato and tomato and simmer (do not stir). Add the curry, turmeric, sugar, vinegar, maizena, jam and sufficient water and leave to simmer. Stir slightly when serving.
Mollie de Witt

Rice (Steamed)
(Sufficient for 6 people)

1	c	rice
1	t	salt
2	c	water
		a dab of butter

Method:
Wash the rice, place on stove in cold water.
Boil precisely 7 min and remove. Rinse rice through a sieve, under cold water until the starch is removed. Place the rice in a saucepan with a ¼ c water, salt, butter and t lemon juice. Steam the rice over boiling water until separated and soft.
Mollie de Witt

Beauty is its own excuse for being.

Spiced minced meat

1	kg	minced meat
2		onions, chopped finely
2		garlic cloves, chopped finely
½	t	ground ginger
⅛	t	ground cloves
⅛	c	vinegar
2		peeled tomatoes, chopped finely
2-3		large potatoes, boiled
1	t	coriander
1	t	salt
1	t	Aromat

Method:
Fry onion in a little butter. Add the meat. Fry until golden brown. Add the tomatoes then the garlic. Cook until tender. Add the vinegar and the spices. Allow to simmer. Just before serving add the boiled potatoes and leave a few minutes to cook until most of the gravy has been absorbed. Stir. Can be served with rice or vetkoek.
Joey Pienaar

The art of ending is greater than that of beginning.

Bobotie
(6 helpings)

2		thick slices of brown bread
500	ml	milk (2 c)
2		large onions, chopped
15	ml	apricot jam (3 t)
5	ml	ginger (1 t)
2		eggs
		paprika
1	kg	minced meat
		oil for frying
15	ml	curry powder (3 t)
75	g	seedless raisins
1	pkt	oxtail soup powder (69 g)
2	ml	dry mustard
		salt to taste
5	ml	Aromat (1 t)

Method:
Soak bread in half the milk. Fry onion in a little oil until tender and golden brown. Add the curry powder, ginger, apricot jam and raisins and stir. Add meat and stir, fry thoroughly. Add soup powder and bread. Whisk egg, remaining milk, mustard and salt. Add ½ the mixture to the meat. Pour into a casserole dish. Pour the rest of the mixture over the top. Bake for about 45 min at 180 °C (350 °F). Sprinkle with paprika and serve.
Joey Pienaar

Faith is to believe what you do not see.

Bobotie with a difference
(Delicious)

		Group A: The spices
15	ml	curry (1 Tsp)
30	ml	ginger (2 Tsp)
30	ml	brown sugar (2 Tsp)
15	ml	turmeric (1 Tsp)
10	ml	salt (2 t)
5	ml	pepper (1 t)

		Group B:
100	g	raisins (seedless)
30	ml	apricot jam (2 Tsp)
30	ml	vinegar (2 Tsp)
60	ml	chutney (4 Tsp)
30	ml	Worcestershire sauce (2 Tsp)
30	ml	tomato puree (2 Tsp)
30	ml	Knorr Meatball Maker (2 Tsp)
1	kg	topside mince

Method:
Use a saucepan with a thick base, heat well. Add the ingredients of group A in saucepan and heat well. Add a piece of butter and braise 5 medium coarsely chopped onions. Remove from heat and add group B ingredients. Add the meat and 2 slices of bread soaked in water. Simmer over low heat for about 20 min. Place in a greased casserole and pour 2 eggs beaten in 375 ml milk (1½ c) over the top. Bake for about ¾ hr at 180 °C (350 °F).
Joey Pienaar

While it is still before; afterwards has no power.

Bobotie
(Delicious)

1	kg	minced meat
2	c	water
		Cook. Remove water and leave aside.

Add to meat:

1	c	seedless raisins
2		large onions, finely chopped and slightly fried
¼	c	margarine
2	t	Aromat
2		level Tsp curry (Mild)
1	Tsp	vinegar
1	t	salt
2		slices bread soaked in the meat extract
4		bananas (sliced)
½	c	milk
1	c	soaked dried apricots
2	Tsp	Apricot jam (smooth)
2		eggs, beaten

Method:
Grease dish. Place ½ the meat mixture in dish. Spread a layer of apricot jam over, then a layer of soaked dried apricots and a layer of bananas. Repeat layers. Pour 2 eggs whisked in a ½ c milk over the top. Bake at 180 °C (350 °F) for ± 30 min until firm and nicely browned. Serve with chutney, coconut and chopped pineapple.

Mollie de Witt

Honey is every flower takes a bee to get it.

Minced meat and noodle dish
(Delicious)

200	g	spinach noodles (home-made)
		salt water to cook noodles
50	ml	butter (4 Tsp)
50	ml	flour (4 Tsp)
375	ml	milk (1½ c)
3	ml	salt
5	ml	Aromat (1 t)
1	ml	black pepper
5	ml	prepared mustard (1 t)
100	g	cheddar cheese, grated (250 ml) (1 c)
1		large onion, chopped
12,5	ml	oil (1 Tsp)
600	g	minced meat
25	ml	tomato puree (2 Tsp)
		paprika (to sprinkle over)

Method:
Step 1:
Boil spinach noodles until cooked. Remove from heat and drain. Place aside. Prepare a white sauce by melting butter in a saucepan and stirring in flour. Stir over heat for 1 min. Add milk gradually and stir over a low heat until sauce is smooth and thick. Flavour with salt, pepper, mustard and half the cheese. Stir until mixed. Sauté onion in oil for 2 min, add meat and tomato puree and stir over heat until meat starts browning. Sprinkle with Aromat. Remove from heat.

Step 2:
Place meat in a greased casserole. Place the spinach noodles on top. Pour white sauce over and sprinkle the remaining cheese on top. Sprinkle with a little paprika and bake in a preheated oven at 180 °C (350 °F) until cheese has melted and is slightly browned. Serve immediately.
Joey Pienaar

Running beer gathers no foam.

Sabanang meat

500	g	minced mutton
1		large onion
		garlic clove
1	Tsp	butter
500	g	mashed potato
		a little curry powder
		a little milk to mix the curry powder
		cloves
		a few bay leaves

Method:

Sauté the finely chopped onion and garlic in the butter. Add the meat and fry for 10 min whilst stirring. Mix the meat and potatoes. Add curry powder and milk and mix. Place in a shallow casserole and flavour with cloves, dabs of butter and bay leaves. Bake for about ½ hr in a moderate oven (180 °C — 350 °F).

HINT: Delicious with stewed sweet potatoes, green beans and dumplings with cinnamon sugar.

Joey Pienaar

Never blow your own trumpet.

Lasagne with cheese sauce

1		large chopped onion
1		green pepper
		a pinch of oregano
½	c	red wine
¼	lb	green or white ribbon noodles (125 g)
2	c	cheese sauce
1		rasher bacon, finely chopped
2		tomatoes (skinned and chopped)
1		garlic clove (chopped)
3	Tsp	cooking oil
		salt and pepper to taste
1	Tsp	tomato puree

Method:

Fry onion, green pepper and garlic in oil until transparent. Add meat and bacon and fry until brown and crumbly. Add salt, pepper, oregano, tomato puree and tomatoes. Leave to simmer until tomatoes are cooked. Add wine and simmer for 10 min. Meanwhile, boil the noodles rapidly in boiling salt water and 1 tsp oil until tender. Rinse well in cold water and pour more boiling water over. Drain well.

Cheese sauce:

2	Tsp	butter
2	Tsp	flour (heaped)
2	c	milk
1	t	dry mustard
		salt and pepper
1	c	grated cheddar cheese
1	t	Aromat

Method:

Melt butter and stir in flour. Add milk gradually and stir continuously until sauce is thick. Flavour with salt, pepper and mustard. Remove from stove and add grated cheese. Grease a casserole and arrange a layer of noodles on the base. Top with a layer

---

Homekeeping hearts are the happiest.

114

of meat and then a layer of cheese sauce. Repeat, ending with a layer of cheese sauce. Sprinkle with Aromat. Sprinkle with the grated cheese and bake for 20-30 min in a moderate oven (180 °C — 350 °F)
Joey Pienaar

Liver cakes
(Makes 24 cakes)

1		thick slice stale white bread
350	ml	cold water
400	g	sheep's liver
1		large onion
2		eggs
1		large potato, peeled
25	ml	cooking oil (2 Tsp)
7	ml	salt (1½ t)
		a pinch of pepper
		a pinch of ground nutmeg
50	g	flour (100 ml) (8 Tsp)
		cooking oil for shallow frying

Method:
Dip the bread into the cold water and immediately squeeze the water out. Mince the liver, bread, onion and potato. Add eggs, oil, salt, pepper and nutmeg and mix well. Finally add flour and mix. Place tablespoonfuls in hot, shallow oil and fry on both sides over medium heat until nicely browned. Drain on absorbent paper towels. Serve hot.
Mollie de Witt

Public relations begins with you.

Bobotie
(Enough for 6-8 people)

75	g	dried apricots (125 ml) (½ c)
50	g	seedless raisins (85 ml) (⅓ c)
75	g	dried apple rings (187,5 ml)
		water for soaking
500	g	minced meat
1		thick slice of bread
500	ml	milk (2 c)
3		eggs
1		large onion (chopped)
25	ml	butter (2 Tsp)
15	ml	curry powder (3 t)
30	ml	sugar (6 t)
30	ml	vinegar (6 t)
10	ml	salt (2 t)
2	ml	black pepper
3		bay leaves
		shelled almonds

Method:

Step 1:
Soak apricots, raisins and apple rings in water until soft. (As an alternative, they can be soaked in lemon juice.) Soak bread in 100 ml milk. Mix meat and bread well and leave aside. Sauté onion in butter until tender. Add curry powder and stir another min over heat. Add sugar, vinegar, salt and pepper and mix. Drain fruit and keep the water. Chop fruit and add to mixture in the pan. Use 100 ml of the water drained from dried fruit and add to mixture. Simmer for about 5 minutes or until mixture thickens slightly. Beat remaining milk (500 ml) and eggs well.

Step 2:
Remove from heat and mix the fruit and mince. Pour into an oven-proof dish. Press the almonds and bay leaves half way into the mixture and pour the milk and egg over. Bake in a preheated oven at 180 °C (350 °F) for about 45-50 minutes or until custard mixture on top is set and golden brown. Serve.

Ina Steyn

Have you hugged your child today? — S.A. Child Welfare.

One-dish-evening meal

Mix:
1	c	self-raising flour
½	c	Smash or Maggie mashed potatoes
½	c	water
½	c	cooking oil
½	t	baking powder
		salt

Mix
500	g	minced meat
1	pkt	spring vegetable soup (69 g)
1	c	boiling water
½	c	bread crumbs

Method:
Spread the dough mixture in a casserole and add meat mixture on top. Place grated cheese, tomato or bacon on top. Bake about ¾ hr at 180 °C (350 °F).
Sue Kühn

Never trust a man who hides his past — Xhosa saying.

"Waterblommetjie" Bobotie
(4-6 helpings)

1	kg	minced meat
1		onion, cut in thin rings
125	ml	seedless raisins (½ c)
25	ml	apricot jam (2 Tsp)
20	ml	butter or margarine (4 t)
1		slice white bread
3		eggs
250	ml	milk (1 c)
125	ml	dried apricots (½ c)
10	ml	curry powder (2 t)
5	ml	turmeric (1 t)
2		lemon leaves or bay leaves
10	ml	salt (2 t)
400	g	"Waterblommetjies" (Aponogeton) (fresh or tinned)
1		large apple

Method:

Warm the milk slightly and soak the apricots in the milk. Remove stalks from fresh "waterblommetjies" and wash thoroughly to remove grit. Place in a saucepan and heat quickly to boiling point. Remove from the heat. Pour ½ the milk in which apricots were

A bird in the hand is better than two in the bush.

soaked over the bread. Mash the bread and cut the apricots. Add all the ingredients except the butter, eggs, remaining milk, leaves and "waterblommetjies" and brown in the pan in butter. Beat the eggs and the rest of the milk. Mix the "waterblommetjies" with the meat mixture.

To serve guests: Serve individually in small bowls.

For the family: Pour the mixture into a casserole.

Pour the egg mixture over the meat and garnish with the lemon leaves for flavour. Bake in an oven at 180 °C (350 °F) — ± 50 min for a large dish and 30 min for a smaller dish. Serve hot with rice.

Joey Pienaar

There's many a slip between the cup and the lip.

Many a good tune is played on an old fiddle.

Venison

Stuffed leg of Venison

1		medium leg of venison 2-2,5 kg
250	g	speck
250	ml	vinegar (1 c)
25	ml	salt (2 Tsp)
5	ml	pepper (1 t)
2	ml	ground ginger
12,5	ml	sugar (1 Tsp)
75	g	seedless raisins (125 ml) (½ c)
2		garlic cloves, chopped (optional)
1		large onion, sliced
12,5	ml	apricot jam (1 Tsp)
6		cloves
25	ml	flour (2 Tsp)

Method:
Remove the shin bone and wipe the meat with a damp cloth. Cut speck into 10 mm strips and leave in the vinegar, salt, pepper, ginger and sugar mixture for 1 hr. Make slits in the meat with a sharp knife. Stretch the holes by inserting index finger. Push a raisin, a small piece of garlic and a strip of speck into each hole. Arrange the onion slices on the leg and pour the vinegar mixture over the top. Leave for 3 days and turn twice daily. Spread the apricot jam over the leg and place in a thick based saucepan. Add the vinegar in which it was soaked, supplemented with 250-375 ml water, and the cloves and cook slowly until meat is tender. Turn a few times then allow to brown after all the liquid has evaporated. Remove the meat, add more water and thicken the sauce with the flour.

Variations:
Use wine instead of vinegar. Pour 125 ml sour cream over the leg while it is browning. Delicious.
Joey Pienaar

I came; I saw; I conquered — Julius Caesar.

Kudu (or any other venison stroganoff)
(Delicious)

1	kg	kudu fillet cut into cubes
1		medium onion chopped
1		chopped garlic clove
125	g	margarine
300	g	fresh mushrooms, rinsed
		or 1 tin whole mushrooms, drained (285 g)
125	ml	flour (½ c)
5	ml	salt (1 t)
1	ml	pepper
1		cube beef extract dissolved in 1 c boiling water
15	ml	sherry (3 t)
250	ml	sour cream (1 c)
5	ml	Worcestershire sauce (1 t)
1		small tin tomato puree (115 g)
1	t	Aromat

Method:
Fry the onion and garlic in a thick based saucepan with a little of the margarine until tender. Keep aside. Add more margarine if needed and fry the mushrooms in the same saucepan until done. Place aside. Mix the flour, salt, pepper and the cubes of meat until well covered. Add rest of the margarine to the saucepan. Fry fillet cubes until well browned. The cubes must be nicely browned on the outside but juicy inside. Add the fried onion and garlic, meat extract and sherry. Allow to boil. Place the lid on the saucepan and allow to simmer for about 25 minutes. Remove the saucepan from the heat and stir in the sour cream, Worcestershire sauce, mushrooms, tomato puree and Aromat. Return to stove and warm over low heat. Serve hot.
Joey Pienaar

A good heart these days is hard to find — Biesie.

Dried sausage (Venison)

22	kg	venison
3	kg	sheep's tail-fat
200	ml	salt (¾ c)
50	ml	pepper (4 Tsp)
500	ml	ground, roasted coriander (2 c)
1	c	vinegar (250 ml)
12,5	ml	grated nutmeg (1 Tsp)

Method:

Remove all membranes and tendons from the meat. Cut the meat into suitable pieces to mince. Cut the sheep's tail-fat into cubes. Sprinkle salt, vinegar and spices over the meat before mincing. Leave for 30 minutes. Mince the meat and tail-fat coarsely to ensure a crumbly texture. Handle the meat as little as possible. Use a fork to mix. Stuff the meat into sausage casings but less firm than for normal sausage. Flatten the sausage slightly when flash-dry, to ensure neatness in form and to prevent cavities in the sausage.

Joey Pienaar

Venison

2-3	kg	venison
250	g	bacon, sliced
2		onions
½		green pepper
2		tomatoes
		salt and pepper
½	c	chutney
½	t	mixed herbs

Power is pleasure, and pleasure sweetens pain.

1		tin cream of mushroom soup (410 g)
		soya sauce
		Worcestershire sauce
1	c	sultanas
2	c	red wine
125	ml	sour cream (½ c)
½	pkt	Knorr Meat Ball Maker

Method:

Stew venison for 4 hours (in a pressure cooker it takes 1 hr) in water, chutney and bacon until tender. Fry the onion, green pepper and tomatoes in oil, add soya, Worcestershire sauce, salt, pepper, mixed herbs, cream of mushroom soup and sultanas. Add boned meat, sour cream and Meat Ball Maker to the onion mixture and pour the red wine over the top. Cover with foil and bake in oven for 2 hours.

Joey Pienaar

Venison sausage (for frying)

(Delicious)

1½	c	ice water
18	kg	venison (preferably topside)
12	kg	pork (fat)
500	ml	salt (2 c)
250	ml	roasted, ground coriander (1 c)
125	ml	white pepper (½ c)
50	ml	herb cloves (4 Tsp)
25	ml	grated nutmeg (2 Tsp)
750	ml	vinegar (3 c)
1	kg	oats (1 pkt)

Method:

Cut the meat into cubes. Sprinkle thoroughly with mixed herbs, oats, ice water and vinegar and mince coarsely. Mix lightly but thoroughly. Stuff sausage casings but not too firmly.

Joey Pienaar

A mother is the greatest gift that one could ever have — Ella Marie.

Venison fricadel

3	kg	minced venison
8		eggs
½		loaf brown bread, soaked in water (do not remove all the water — it helps to give the meat a loose texture)
1	c	chopped onion
4	Tsp	finely grated carrots
6	t	salt
1	t	pepper
1	Tsp	Aromat

Method:
Mix ingredients thoroughly with a fork. Shape into balls and bake in oven or fry in a saucepan. Freezes well if uncooked.
Joey Pienaar

The good of praising oneself is that you can lay it on thick.

Barbecues

Pot-bread

		Yeast:
½		cake compressed yeast
1	t	sugar
1	t	salt
1	c	lukewarm water
900	g	flour (7½ c)
1-2	c	hot water
1	t	salt

Method:
Place the first 4 ingredients in a covered dish, place lid on and leave to rise for ½ hr. Sift the flour and salt together. Make a well in the dough and add the yeast. Add the hot water and mix until the dough is easy to handle. Grease hands with oil, margarine or butter and knead the dough. Grease the hands twice more until the dough is firm and elastic. Cover the dough well and leave overnight to rise. Knead the dough the following morning and shape into small round balls. Melt a little fat or butter in a heavy-based saucepan or pan and fry the dough. The bread can also be baked in the oven 220 °C (400 °F) or outside on a grill.
Joey Pienaar

Poverty with joy isn't poverty at all.

What could be nicer than delicious offal with baby potatoes (p 94) which can be served with samp (p 98) and stewed fruit (p 387)

This page was sponsored by T.F.M. — tel (011 - 7867015)

Try a barbecue with a difference – sosaties (p 85), venison sausage (p 125), a tangy cheese (p 134) and quick wholewheat bread (p 232). Round the feast off with preserved orange halves (p 379)

Tomato sauce for pap

1	pkt	tomato soup (69 g)
2	c	meat- or sausage gravy
		stewed onion
½	t	mixed herbs

Method:
Add tomato soup to the gravy and boil for 5 min. Add onion, stir in mixed herbs and serve hot with pap.
Ina Steyn

Curried chops

1½	kg	mutton chops
2	Tsp	curry powder
20		lemon leaves
		salt to taste
4		large onions
1½	c	vinegar

Method:
Sprinkle the salt and the curry powder on both sides of each chop. The curry must cover the meat with a slight yellow layer. Peel the onions and cut into slices. Bruise the lemon leaves on a wooden surface. Place a layer of onion slices and lemon leaves at the bottom of a shallow dish. Then place a layer of meat and another layer of onions and lemon leaves. Continue procedure and end with a layer onion and lemon leaves. Pour the vinegar over and cover. Place in refrigerator for 3 days. Turn the meat once daily to ensure that the top layer of meat ends on the lowest level.
After 3 days, the meat can be fried in a pan or barbecued.
Joey Pienaar

Poverty makes you sad as well as wise.

Potatoes in their jackets

12		small potatoes
250	g	butter
1	pkt	onion soup powder (69 g)

Method:
Slit the potatoes. Sprinkle with soup powder. Melt butter, pour over potatoes and powder. Use an ovenproof dish and bake in a medium oven. Delicious served with a barbecue.
Ina Steyn

Greek leg of mutton (boned)
(Delicious for barbecue)

Bone the leg of mutton and slay out. Pound with a mallet till meat has the same thickness.

Mix marinade:

250	ml	olive oil (1 c) (olive oil is important)
250	ml	lemon juice (1 c)
2	t	flaked garlic
		or
2		garlic cloves, crushed
10	ml	flavoured salt (Aromat or Fondor) (2 t)
		salt and pepper to taste
2,5	ml	paprika (½ t) (sprinkle over meat before barbecue-ing)

Method:
Marinade meat for 3 days. Turn daily. Place in a grid to maintain it's shape. Barbecue on each side for ± 15 minutes or until done. Cut into slices.
Joey Pienaar

Poverty of the soul is irreparable.

Garlic beans

½	kg	fresh green beans
1		clove of garlic
30	ml	salad oil (6 t)
30	ml	vinegar (6 t)
		salt to taste

Method:
Split the green beans lengthwise. Boil 15-20 min (beans must still be firm). Drain and allow to cool. Mix the oil, vinegar and finely chopped garlic. Pour over the beans. Serve cold as a salad.
Dimples Wandrag

Garlic bread

1		French bread or
6		bread rolls
1		garlic clove
		butter flavoured with Aromat
		grated cheese

Method:
Cut the garlic lengthwise and rub the split sides over the entire bread or rolls. Cut the bread or rolls in 2,5 cm (1 inch) slices, but do not cut through. Leave a crust of about 1 cm (¼ inch). Spread generously with butter between each slice and add the grated cheese. Wrap the bread or rolls in foil. Place in a lukewarm oven or between coals and allow to warm.
Mollie de Witt

Garlic makes a man wink, drink and stink.

Sosaties
(36 sosaties)

1		garlic clove
1		fat leg of mutton, about 1,5-2 kg
5		crushed orange or lemon or bay leaves
10	ml	salt (2 t)
3	ml	ginger (optional)
3	ml	pepper
25	ml	ground coriander (optional) (2 Tsp)
125	ml	milk (½ c)
150	g	dried apricots (250 ml) (1 c)
10	ml	Aromat (2 t)

Method:
Rub an earthenware dish with the garlic. Dice the meat, large enough to thread onto skewers. Mix with the rest of the ingredients and place in the earthenware dish. Leave overnight then pour the sosatie sauce over.

Sosatie sauce:

4		large onions, sliced
250	ml	water (1 c)
1		small green pepper, seeded and finely chopped
25	ml	sugar (2 Tsp)
25	ml	curry powder (2 Tsp)
3	ml	salt
5	ml	turmeric (1 t)
25	ml	apricot jam (2 Tsp)
500	ml	vinegar (2 c)

Method:
Mix all the ingredients, except the vinegar, and boil for 5 minutes. Add the vinegar and allow to cool. Mix the sauce and the meat and leave in refrigerator for 1 or 2 days. Thread the meat alterna-

---

Act well your part; there all the honor lies.

ting lean and fat pieces with the apricot and onion on skewers. Grill slowly on coals until brown and done. Thicken the sauce with a little flour and serve with the sosaties.

HINT: The sosaties can be grilled in the oven or fried in a pan.
Joey Pienaar

Salted rib of mutton

1		fat mutton rib, 1,5-2 kg
100	g	salt (75 ml) (6 Tsp)
2	ml	pepper
2	ml	Saltpetre (obtainable from pharmacies)
5	ml	of a mixture of 2 of the following: coriander, thyme, cloves, ginger, pimento, sage, mace (1 t)
125	ml	vinegar (½ c)

Dressing
Bone meat or chop through rib bones so that it can be easily separated into portions. Make criss-cross cuts on the meat side with a sharp knife. Mix the rest of the ingredients except the vinegar and rub well into ribs. Place the rib in a dish and sprinkle with the vinegar. Leave for 2 days and turn twice daily. Hang out to dry and store till required.

Cooking
Rinse the rib and place in cold water. Use lots of water to remove excess salt. Boil slowly until meat is tender but not soft. Air-dry and barbecue until brown.

HINT: The salted rib can be smoked after salting. Formerly this was done by hanging it in a chimney.
Joey Pienaar

Happy is he whose armour is honest thought.

Delicious dessert with barbecue for one person
(Increase ingredients per guest)

1	banana, peeled
2	marshmallows
2	squares chocolate (taken from 1 large slab)

Method:
Wrap above-mentioned in foil. Place over slow coals. Serve in the foil.

Joey Pienaar

Cheese bread

500	g	self-raising flour
500	ml	buttermilk (2 c)
5	ml	salt (1 t)
375	ml	grated cheese (1½ c)
1	t	dried parsley
5	ml	mustard powder (1 t)
5	ml	Aromat (1 t)
½	pkt	thick white onion soup powder (59 g)

Method:
Mix all ingredients with 1 c cheese. Pour into a greased breadpan. Sprinkle the rest of the cheese on top (½ c). Bake at 200 °C (400 °F) for 45 min. Serve as soon as possible (still lukewarm). It is delicious especially at a barbecue.

Mollie de Witt

Practise what you preach.

Sosaties
(Delicious — 100 sosaties)

12	kg	diced mutton, beef or pork (20x20x20 mm)
1,5	kg	dried apricots for threading
50	ml	salt (4 Tsp)
12,5	ml	pepper (1 Tsp)

Method:
Thread 6 pieces of meat and 1-2 apricots on a skewer. Pack layers of sosaties in an enamel dish and sprinkle with salt, pepper and cooled sauce. Leave for 24-48 hours in the refrigerator. Turn once to ensure that the top layer eventually forms the bottom layer.

Sauce:

2	kg	onions
½	c	oil
125	ml	maizena (½ c)
2	ℓ	vinegar
500	ml	sugar (2 c)
250	ml	mild curry powder (1 c)
500	ml	chutney (2 c)
500	ml	sour or fresh milk (2 c)
100		wooden kebab skewers, 200 mm in length

Method:
Slice and sauté the onions in hot oil. Blend the maizena with 250 ml (1 c) vinegar and add all the other ingredients, except the chutney, milk and rest of vinegar to the onions. Stir and boil for 3 minutes. Add the chutney, milk and rest of vinegar and bring to the boil. Leave to cool and pour over the sosaties.

Joey Pienaar

Better to weep at joy than at weeping.

Mealie-pap Tart
(Something special at a barbecue)

1¼	ℓ	boiling water
1	t	salt
		Enough mealie meal to make a stiff porridge. The texture must however still be pliable.
½	c	sunflower oil
500	g	mushrooms, sliced and slightly fried
250	g	crisp fried bacon
		parsley
250	g	Cheddar cheese
50	ml	evaporated milk (4 Tsp)

Method:
Place the following layers in a greased dish: Porridge, mushrooms, bacon, oil, cheese and 15 ml evaporated milk. Repeat until all ingredients are used, ending with a mushroom and cheese layer followed by the rest of the milk. Sprinkle with parsley. Bake for 1½ hours at 350 °F (180 °C).
Joey Pienaar

Steamed green mealie bread
(4 helpings)

5		young mealies (500 ml mealie kernels) (2 c)
2	ml	salt
5	ml	sugar (1 t)
5	ml	baking powder (1 t)

Method:
Remove kernels from the cobs and mince. Add the other ingredients and pour into a greased tin or mould (⅔ full) with an airtight lid and steam for 2 hours. Turn out gently, cut into slices and serve with butter.
Joey Pienaar

A minute to smile; an hour to weep.

136

Marinaded Steak
(6-8 helpings)

2	kg	steak or any portions of meat suitable for barbecue
5		garlic cloves, bruised
		seasoning

Marinade:

$^2/_5$	c	salad oil
$^2/_5$	c	wine vinegar
2	Tsp	Worcestershire sauce
1	t	soya sauce

Method:
Make holes in the meat with the tip of a knife and place a garlic clove in the insertion. Add sufficient seasoning. Pour the marinade over the meat and leave overnight in refrigerator. Turn the meat occasionally. Barbecue the meat for 15 minutes on each side, sprinkle with salt and baste with the marinde occasionally. Heat the remaining marinade and serve with the meat.
Joey Pienaar

Choose your wife rather by ear than by eye.

Sauce for Grilled Chicken

*(3 broilers ± 1 kg each or 3 kg chicken
thighs or legs)*

100	ml	vinegar (8 Tsp)
100	ml	oil (8 Tsp)
12,5	ml	Worcestershire sauce (1 Tsp)
12,5	ml	finely chopped onion (1 Tsp)
		garlic clove, crushed
5	ml	paprika (1 t)
12,5	ml	apricot jam (1 Tsp)
25	ml	tomato sauce (2 Tsp)
5	ml	dry mustard (1 t)

Method:

Mix all the ingredients 24 hrs before preparation. Cut open the
chickens and rub with butter. Roast in a preheated oven for half
an hour. Remove, place in sauce for 1 hr. Place on grid and barbecue over coals. Baste with the marinade before meat is turned.
Joey Pienaar

Griddle cake

Griddle cake is served as a delicious side dish at barbecues. Knead
flour, baking powder, water and salt (5 ml baking powder for
every 250 ml flour). Whole-wheat flour with yeast tastes even better.

500	ml	lukewarm water (2 c)
12,5	ml	brown sugar (1 Tsp)
5	ml	dry yeast (1 t)
		Mix the above and leave for 10 min.
1	kg	whole-wheat flour (6 c)
5	ml	salt (1 t)
12,5	ml	oil (1 Tsp)

Only love should rule between man and wife.

Method:

Mix ingredients well. It must form a reasonably firm dough. Pour about 12,5 ml oil into a plastic bag and shake to spread the oil. Place the dough into the bag and leave to rise to double its size for about 30-60 minutes. Carefully flatten the dough to ± 2,5 cm, on a breadboard sprinkled with flour. Cut into squares. Grill on an oil-greased grid over medium coals until well done. Turn frequently. Serve with fresh farm butter and apricot jam.

Joey Pienaar

Green mealie bread

6		green mealies
25	ml	sugar (2 Tsp)
5	ml	salt (1 t)
2		eggs, beaten
10	ml	baking powder (2 t)
10	ml	butter (2 t)
		milk
25	ml	cake flour (2 Tsp)

Method:

Choose young fresh mealies. Place mealies in boiling water and bring to the boil again. Remove and allow to cool. Cut kernels from the cob, mince and measure. There must be 1 ℓ. Add the rest of the ingredients and enough milk to make a smooth mixture, about 150 ml. Pour into a small greased breadpan, dot with butter and bake for 1½ hrs in a moderate oven (190 °C — 375 °F)

Joey Pienaar

A woman is as old as she looks;
A man is old when he stops looking.

Grilled chicken marinade
(Enough for 10 chickens)

Cut into quarters or portions.
Fry 750 ml chopped onion in 500 ml oil.
Mix separately:

25	ml	mustard powder (5 t)
62,5	ml	salt (¼ c)
5	ml	pepper (1 t)
250	ml	sugar (1 c)
750	ml	tomato sauce (3 c)
375	ml	lemon juice (1½ c)
125	ml	Worcestershire sauce (½ c)
750	ml	water (3 c)

Method:
Add the mixture to the fried onions in the saucepan. Bring to boiling point and simmer for 10-15 min. Leave to cool. Layer the chicken in the sauce and marinade overnight. Remove from the marinade and bake the pieces in the oven until almost tender. Grill over coals until tender.
Mollie de Witt

Mealie meal porridge (stiff)
(6 helpings)

500	ml	water (2 c)
3	ml	salt
10	ml	butter or fat (2 t)
225	g	mealie meal (375 ml) (1½c)

Method:
Boil the water, salt and butter and add the mealie meal. Do not stir. Place the lid on the saucepan and boil slowly for 10-15 min.

A stitch in time saves nine.

Stir with cutting movements to mix the dry mealie meal with the water. Replace the lid and allow to cook over low heat. It takes about 1 hr. Serve with barbecue or with milk and sugar for breakfast. To prevent burning, a double boiler can be used or the saucepan can be put in a cool oven (100-120 °C) after the mealie meal and water have been thoroughly mixed.

Joey Pienaar

Animelles

A traditional barbecue delicacy is lamb testicles. Place the meat immediately in brine for about 30 minutes. Remove thread and cut. Wash in clean water. Place in boiling water and boil until the lamb's testicles are "dry". Add butter, salt and freshly ground black pepper and stir-fry in a saucepan until brown and crisp. The dish can be served cold. The taste is similar to that of offal.

Brine

500	ml	boiled water (2 c)
10		peppercorns
100	ml	salt (8 Tsp)
50	ml	brown sugar (4 Tsp)

Method:
Pour boiling water over rest of ingredients and stir until all the salt has dissolved and allow to cool.

Joey Pienaar

A fool and his money are soon parted;
how did they ever get together in the first place?

Pumpkin fritters
(6 helpings)

500	ml	cooked, mashed pumpkin (boerpampoen) (2 c)
60	g	flour (125 ml) (½ c)
5	ml	baking powder (1 t)
		a pinch of salt
2		eggs, beaten
		cinnamon

Method:
Mix the pumpkin, flour, baking powder and salt and blend with the egg to make a reasonably soft batter. Fry spoonfuls in hot oil or fat till brown. Drain on absorbent paper and sprinkle with cinnamon.
Joey Pienaar

Cooked onion salad (reddish tint)
(Slaphakskeentjies)

1,5	kg	small onions
250	ml	bleached sultanas (1 c)
150	ml	sugar (½ c + 2 Tsp)
250	ml	white vinegar (1 c)
250	ml	water (1 c)
1	tin	tomato puree (115 g)
50	ml	cooking oil (4 Tsp)
3	ml	salt
1	ml	cayenne pepper

Method:
Peel the onions. Place in a stainless steel saucepan. Add the sultanas, salt, sugar, vinegar, water, tomato puree, cooking oil and cayenne pepper. Replace the lid, or cover with a plate if pressure cooker is used, and boil the mixture over a low heat for one hour. Remove the lid and cook further until the sauce is reasonably thick. Bottle the hot onions in sterilized bottles and seal.
Joey Pienaar

Don't take life too seriously;
You'll never get out of it alive.

Instant mealie bread

1	pkt	self-raising flour (500 g)
5	ml	salt (1 t)
1	tin	creamed sweetcorn (410 g)
2		eggs
60	ml	milk (¼ c)
25	ml	cooking oil (2 Tsp)

Method:
Preheat oven to 190 °C (375 °F). Grease a small breadpan. Sift the flour and salt. Add sweetcorn. Whisk the eggs, milk and cooking oil and add. Mix with a knife. Pour dough into breadpan, level the top, and bake about 45 minutes or until cooked. Slice and spread with butter. This bread is delicious with a barbecue.
Joey Pienaar

Crumbly mealie meal porridge ("Putupap")
(6 helpings)

375	ml	water (1½ c)
5	ml	salt (1 t)
300	g	mealie meal (500 ml) (2 c)

Method:
Boil the water and salt in a saucepan. Add the mealie meal slowly so that it forms a centre pile with the boiling water around it. Do not stir. Replace the lid and simmer for 10-15 min. Beat well with a large fork. Replace lid and cook over a very low heat. It takes about 1 hour.
Joey Pienaar

To wear too much rouge and not enough clothes is always a sign of despair in a woman.

Quick whole-wheat bread
(Delicious with a barbecue; served hot with butter)
(makes 1 loaf)

500	ml	natural yoghurt (2 c)
450	g	(900 ml) whole-wheat flour
10	ml	sugar (2 t)
7	ml	(1½t) bicarbonate of soda
5	ml	salt (1 t)
1	t	lemon juice

Method:
Preheat oven to 180 °C (350 °F). Grease a 11x25x7,5 cm bread-pan. Mix all ingredients well. Shape into a loaf, place in breadpan and bake for 45 min on the centre shelf of the oven. Turn breadpan in oven and bake for a further 15 min. Turn bread out on a cooling rack, wrap in a cloth and leave to cool.
Joey Pienaar

Sweetcorn fritters

1		egg
4	Tsp	milk
¾	c	flour (190 ml)
1	c	sweetcorn (tinned)
¼	t	salt
2	t	baking powder (10 ml)

Method:
Beat the egg and mix with the milk. Stir in the flour until smooth. Add the sweetcorn and salt and mix well. Add the baking powder just before frying. Place spoonfuls in hot fat or oil in a frying pan and fry fritters on both sides until golden brown.
Mollie de Witt

Men become old but they never become good.

144

Bread for a barbecue

500	ml	buttermilk (2 c)
1	pkt	thick vegetable soup (69 g)
500	g	self-raising flour
1	Tsp	oil
		salt
		grated cheese
		paprika
		parsley

Method:
Mix the dry ingredients with buttermilk and oil. Place in a bread-pan. Sprinkle with paprika, parsley and cheese. Bake at 180 °C (350 °F) for ± 1 hr.
Zena Conradie

Green bean salad
(Delicious for a barbecue) (makes 4-6 helpings)

1		large onion, chopped
25	g	butter or margarine (30 ml) (6 Tsp)
1		green pepper, seeded and sliced
2		large green tomatoes, sliced
200	g	cooked, sliced green beans (350 ml)
		(or 1x410 g tin, drained)
25	ml	soft brown sugar (2 Tsp)
5	ml	salt (1 t)
		a pinch of pepper
5	ml	Aromat (1 t)

Method:
Sauté onion in butter in a medium saucepan. Add green pepper and tomatoes and braise over low heat for 10 min. Add the rest of the ingredients, mix lightly and braise another 5 min.
Joey Pienaar

A rolling stone gathers no moss.

Stuffed chitterling

(Something special)

Few barbecue dishes taste as delicious as stuffed chitterling.
* The intestine (about 80 cm long) must be washed well, turned inside out and left in coarse salt for at least 10 minutes.
* Wash it thoroughly afterwards to remove any sliminess.
* Rinse off thoroughly and turn it inside out so that the fatty part is on the inside.
* Tie the one end to make stuffing easier.
* Fill the intestine with seasoned (salt and pepper) shredded tender beef.
* Grill the intestine like sausage over reasonably hot coals until the fat is crisp and crackling. Turn frequently.
* Instead of beef, fill the intestine with minced liver.

Joey Pienaar

Mealie tart

2		thick slices white bread
250	ml	milk (1 c)
2		eggs
1	tin	creamed sweetcorn (420 g)
		salt and pepper
12,5	ml	melted butter (1 Tsp)
25	ml	sugar (2 Tsp)

Method:

Soak bread in the milk and mash. Beat eggs and add to milk and bread. Mix thoroughly with the sweetcorn. Add the rest of the ingredients. Spread in a greased, ovenproof dish and bake at 180 °C (350 °F) until nicely browned.

Joey Pienaar

Single men may be either tall or short; married men are always short.

Chicken dishes (Poultry)

Paella
(Delicious)

This dish is absolutely delicious for entertaining a large number of guests. 1 large chicken cut into portions and fried till brown, or 1-2 drumsticks per person can be used.

Add:

125	g	ham, cubed
2		onions, chopped
4		peppercorns
1	t	salt
25	g	sliced salami
2		green peppers, chopped
1	t	coriander
2	t	oregano
2	t	vinegar

Method:
Cook above ingredients over low heat until chicken is done. Boil 2 c Tastic rice to serve with chicken.

Mix:

6	Tsp	tomato puree
2	t	turmeric
1	kg	cooked shrimps

Mix everything and cook for a while.

Add:

500	g	frozen peas
2	c	crayfish pieces
2	tins	smoked clams
2	tins	smoked oysters (105 g)

Method:
Mix everything lightly with a fork. Leave a while so that the flavours can blend. The dish can be made in the morning. Serve with a green or mixed salad.
Mrs Yvonne Coetzee

A penny saved is a penny taxed.

Chutney chicken
(Delicious)

1		large chicken
1	pkt	brown onion soup (69 g)
½	c	mayonnaise
½	c	chutney
½	t	salt

Method:
Cut chicken into portions, or use thighs or drumsticks and place in a casserole. Blend mayonnaise, soup powder and chutney in a separate dish. Pour over the raw chicken and add the salt. Cover and bake 1½-2 hours at 180 °C (350 °F) (for first hour) and thereafter at 140 °C (300 °F) uncovered. Another delicious method is: To roll the chicken pieces in cream of tomato soup powder. Sprinkle with Aromat and ½ t salt and bake as above until done.
Joey Pienaar

Kentucky chicken

Cut chicken into pieces. Mix the following dry ingredients well: Flour, salt, pepper, Fondor, ground cloves, mixed herbs, barbecue spice and a little garlic salt.

Method:
Roll portions of the chicken in the mixture and fry in a pan ¼ filled with oil until well browned. Place in a casserole and bake at low heat for 1 hour. Can be served hot or cold.
Ina Steyn

Don't count your chickens before they are hatched.

Spanish chicken

(Delicious with rice and tossed salad) (makes 6-8 helpings)

4		medium potatoes, peeled and thinly sliced
1		medium onion, peeled and sliced
3-4		medium carrots, peeled and sliced or diced
1		chicken, cleaned and cut into portions
1	pkt	(65 g) thick vegetable soup powder
500	ml	water
50	ml	mayonnaise
50	ml	chutney
50	ml	tomato sauce
15	ml	chopped parsley
2		bay leaves
		Aromat and salt to taste

Method:

Preheat oven to 160 °C (325 °F). Place the potatoes at the bottom of a large casserole. Add onion, carrots and finally the chicken portions. Mix the soup powder and water. Mix the mayonnaise, chutney, tomato sauce and parsley. Add to soup mixture and pour over the meat. Insert the bay leaves and sprinkle with seasoning. Cover and bake for 2 hours. Baste the chicken occasionally with the gravy. Serve hot.

Joey Pienaar

Children do make a difference to the home;
but it can easily be repaired.

150

Chicken pie with sour cream pie crust

1		chicken
5	ml	ground nutmeg
8		whole cloves
8		peppercorns
500	ml	chicken stock
125	ml	vinegar or lemon juice
12,5	ml	Worcestershire sauce
3		whisked eggs
5	ml	Aromat and salt to taste

Method:

Cook chicken until tender, bone and cut finely. Add chicken stock, ground nutmeg, cloves, peppercorns, vinegar or lemon juice and Worcestershire sauce, and enough salt. Boil for 5 minutes, remove from stove, stir in eggs and spoon into pie dish. Sprinkle with Aromat. Leave to cool. Cover with pie crust and bake until light brown.

Pie crust
(Make the previous day and keep in refrigerator)

230	g	margarine
240	g	flour
		salt
250	ml	sour cream
5	ml	baking powder

Method:

Grate margarine into the sour cream. Add flour, baking powder and a pinch of salt. Mix well.
Joey Pienaar

After a good dinner one can forgive anybody,
even one's own relations.

Chicken á la King
(6-8 helpings)

1		large chicken
1		chicken stock cube
2		onions, chopped finely
50	g	butter or margarine (60 ml) (¼ c)
1	tin	(285 g) creamed mushrooms
25	ml	finely chopped parsley (2 Tsp)
1	pkt	(59 g) cream of mushroom soup

Method:
Cook the chicken with the stock cube and enough water to ensure that 400 ml gravy remains after the chicken is done. Bone the chicken and cut the meat into pieces. Fry onion in the butter until tender. Add mushrooms and parsley. Mix the soup powder with 250 ml of the chicken gravy and stir into the onion mixture. Add remaining gravy after the mixture is thick in texture, stir and allow to boil. Add the chicken, turn heat down and simmer for 10 min. Stir occasionally.
Mollie de Witt

Chutney chicken

1		chicken cut into portions
250	ml	oil (1 c)

Sauce:

1		chopped onion
250	ml	tomato sauce (1 c)
25	ml	Worcestershire sauce (2 Tsp)
225	g	flour (475 ml) (1¾ c)
		salt and pepper
250	ml	chutney (1 c)

Be kind to those you meet on your way up;
you may meet them again on your way down.

| 38 | ml | vinegar (3 Tsp) |
| 140 | ml | water (⅓ c) |

Method:
Place the chicken, flour, salt and pepper in a plastic bag and shake well. Heat the oil in a deep frying pan. Fry chicken until brown and tender. Remove from the pan. Pour oil out but leave about 25 ml oil in pan. Add the chopped onion to the oil and fry until brown. Add all the ingredients including the chicken pieces. Replace the lid and simmer until the gravy thickens.
Joey Pienaar

Spanish chicken paella

1		chicken, cooked and boned
4		large tomatoes
1	pkt	cream of mushroom soup
250	g	shell noodles
2		large onions
250	g	bacon
500	ml	chicken stock
10	ml	turmeric (2 t)
1	tin	peas (385 g)

Method:
Fry chopped onion. Add sliced bacon. Add diced tomatoes and braise. Add chicken. Mix soup with stock and flavour with turmeric. Add to meat mixture. Boil noodles in salted water until tender and add with peas to the meat. Simmer for 10 minutes. Serve with green salad. Freezes well.
Joey Pienaar

Grandchildren are God's gift to an old man.

Chicken pie
(Delicious)

Pie crust:
3		egg yolks
6	c	flour
1½	t	salt
750	g	margarine (1½ lb)
1	t	cream of tartar
¼	c	white vinegar
¾	c	ice water

Method:
Mix dry ingredients. Grate and rub in margarine. Add beaten egg yolks, vinegar and ice water. Mix thoroughly until the flour forms a firm dough. Place dough in a plastic bag and place in refrigerator for at least 8 hours. Divide into 3 parts and place in freezer. As needed, take out the night before and place in refrigerator to defrost. Roll out and use.

Filling:
1		chicken (large)
12		peppercorns
3		cloves
2		onions
2	Tsp	sago
1		wineglass white wine
		juice of a lemon
½	c	shell noodles
1		hard-boiled egg
1	t	Aromat
½	pkt	mushroom soup
1		small tin sliced mushrooms (285 g)
½	t	salt

To err is human
to forgive is divine.

Method:
Stew the chicken with the herbs and onions until tender, then bone the meat. Soak the sago beforehand until soft and then stir into the meat, with the shell noodles and boil slowly. Once the sago and noodles are cooked, add the white wine, lemon juice, mushrooms and mushroom soup. Stir until thick and creamy. Pour the meat into a pie dish and slice the hard boiled egg on top. Cover with the rolled dough, brush with the beaten egg and bake in a hot oven at 190 °C or 360 °F for 15-20 minutes.
Mollie de Witt

Economical chicken dish

1		flavoured cooked chicken, boned and cut into small pieces
1	t	salt
1	pkt	bacon, sliced (250 g)
1	c	rice
3		medium onions, grated
2	c	chicken stock (gravy from cooked chicken) or 2 c water and 1 chicken stock cube
125	g	margarine or more

Method:
Cook rice until almost ready then drain. Fry the sliced bacon, onion and rice in the margarine until light brown. Mix with the chicken pieces and spoon into a casserole. Pour the chicken stock over and flavour with Aromat (1 Tsp). Cover and bake in oven until all the liquid has been absorbed.
Ester Liebenberg

Keep your fears for yourself, but share your courage with others — Robert Louis Stevenson.

Curried chicken
(Makes 6 helpings)

1		chicken
		lemon juice
50	g	flour (100 ml)
25	ml	curry powder
25	ml	sugar
5	ml	salt
		pinch pepper
1	pkt	mushroom soup powder (55 g)
400	ml	cold water
125	ml	tomato sauce
50	ml	chutney
50	ml	Worcestershire sauce

Method:
Rinse and dry chicken. Cut into portions and sprinkle with lemon juice. Mix the flour, curry powder, sugar, salt and pepper. Roll chicken portions in the mixture until well coated. Place in a large casserole and leave for half an hour. Mix soup powder, water, tomato sauce, chutney and Worcestershire sauce. Pour mixture over chicken portions. Cover, place in oven, turn temperature to 180 °C (350 °F) and bake for 1 hour or until the meat is tender. Baste occasionally with the gravy in the casserole. Serve with rice.
Joey Pienaar

Winter is on my head, but spring is in my heart — Victor Hugo.

Chicken with fruit

1		chicken cut into portions
1		tin pineapple chunks (410 g)
4		small bananas
1		green pepper, *chopped*
		(or 1 tin peas)
1	Tsp	chutney
2	Tsp	tomato sauce
1	t	curry powder
1		onion, chopped
2	c	white sauce

Method:
Fry the onion and green pepper, add pineapple and bananas, then the chicken, chutney, tomato sauce and curry powder. Add the white sauce and simmer for ½ hour. If you want to freeze the chicken, do not add the fruit. Heat later and add the fruit.
Ester Kleinhans

Marinated chicken

1		chicken cut into portions
2	t	Worcestershire sauce
2	Tsp	sugar
2	t	tomato sauce
½	c	vinegar
½	c	oil
½	Tsp	mustard
2	Tsp	grated onion
1	pkt	Royco Minestrone soup

Method:
Marinate meat in the mixture in refrigerator. Bake in oven until done.
Joey Pienaar

The hoary head is a crown of glory — Proverbs 16:31.

Chicken dish
(Delicious)

1		chicken
1	pkt	mushroom soup powder
125	g	butter or margarine
4		medium tomatoes (peeled and diced)
70	g	flour (125 ml) (½ c)
250	g	grated cheddar cheese
		salt and pepper to taste
100	g	ready cut macaroni or noodles (250 ml) (1 c)
2		medium onions, diced
200	ml	cold water (¾ c)

Method:
Season chicken and cook slowly. Bone and cut meat finely. Supplement chicken gravy with water to 625 ml. Add soup powder. Stir often and boil until thick. Boil macaroni until tender and drain. Melt butter in a large saucepan — add onion and fry until tender. Add tomatoes and boil a while. Mix the flour and water and add to tomato mixture. Add soup and mix. Add chicken, cheese and macaroni. Mix and simmer for a few minutes.
Mollie de Witt

A poor life this if, full of care, we have no time to stop and stare —
William Henry Davies.

Peri-peri chicken

This recipe is delicious and easy to prepare. The chicken can be served cold with salad or hot with rice and vegetables. The advantage of this recipe is that certain ingredients can be added or left out according to the food stock in your cupboard. It can be increased according to circumstances. If too much has been prepared it can be frozen or served cold the next day. It is also delicious in a lunch box or picnic basket.

* 750	ml	tomato sauce or
		cream of tomato soup and
		tomato puree in equal portions (3 c)
400	ml	chutney (essential)
20	ml	Worcestershire sauce (4 t)
10	ml	vinegar (2 t)
1	t	brown sugar
2	Tsp	dried parsley
1	t	peri-peri to taste
		(if the sauce has a strong taste you know
		that it is sufficient)
1	tin	mushrooms (285 g)
1		large onion, chopped
2		tomatoes, chopped
8		chicken thighs

Method:
Mix all the ingredients well except the chicken. Place chicken in a casserole and cover with the sauce. (If time is available, the chicken can be left in the sauce to marinate slightly.) Grill in a medium oven until brown and done. ± 1-1½ hours as required.
N.B. The chicken must be turned regularly in the casserole. The tin of mushrooms, if needed, must be drained and cut into the required size.
* Quantity can be increased or decreased.
Francis Schoeman

My crown is in my heart, not on my head . . . my crown is called content — William Shakespeare.

Delicious chicken dish

10		chicken thighs
1	pkt	oxtail soup powder (69 g)
1	pkt	thick vegetable soup powder (69 g)
125	ml	chutney (½ c)
200	ml	water (¾ c)

Method:
Mix the dry oxtail and vegetable soup powders. Roll each chicken portion in the mixture until well covered. Place the portions in a casserole. Mix the water and chutney. Pour over the thighs. Cover casserole and cook for 45 minutes on the centre shelf of the oven. Remove the lid and bake until the thighs begin to brown. (Remember, no salt must be added as the soup powder already has salt.)
Joey Pienaar

Chicken dish — peri-peri

1		chicken
½	c	oil
½	c	vinegar
1	t	dry mustard
3	t	paprika
1	t	tomato sauce
1	t	cayenne pepper (2 for strong)
3	t	Worcestershire sauce

Method:
Mix all ingredients into a marinade, pour over the chicken. Leave for a few hours and bake in oven till done.
Joey Pienaar

Let us be of good cheer, remembering that the misfortunes hardest to bear are those which never happen — James Russell Lowell.

Your guests will adore this cold sago pudding. It is indeed a dessert fit for a king (p 187)

Moulded carrot and pineapple salad (p 249) is a delicious summer treat

This page was sponsored by Santam Bank tel (012 – 211565)

Kentucky chicken
(With batter)

1		chicken cut into portions
		seasoning to taste
250	ml	flour (1 c)
1	ml	pepper
5	ml	salt (1 t)
250	ml	milk (1 c)
5	ml	baking powder (1 t)
1		egg, slightly beaten
		oil

Method:
Season chicken to taste. Cook in a little water until tender. Drain cooked chicken on absorbent paper and place in refrigerator or freezer. Remove just before preparing. (Remember: The best results are obtained if the meat is chilled beforehand.) Sift the flour, baking powder, salt and pepper in a dish. Add beaten egg and milk and mix thoroughly. Heat enough cooking oil for deep frying in a saucepan normally used for frying chips. Dip each piece of chicken in the batter. Fry a few pieces at a time for about 5 minutes or until golden brown on both sides.
Joey Pienaar

---

*It is one of the most beautiful compensations of this life that no man can sincerely try to help another without helping himself —
Ralph W. Emerson.*

Delicious baked chicken portions
(Makes 6 helpings)

1	pkt	oxtail soup powder (69 g)
1	pkt	thick vegetable soup powder (69 g)
1		large chicken cut into portions or
8		chicken thighs
200	ml	water (¾ c)

Method:
Preheat oven to 180 °C (350 °F). Mix the soup powders. Roll each portion of chicken in the soup mixture until well covered. Place chicken in a casserole. Pour the water over the top. Cover and bake on the centre shelf of the oven for 45 min. Remove the lid and bake till the portions start to brown. Serve hot or cold.
Mollie de Witt

To me the highest thing, after God, is my honour — Ludwig van Beethoven.

Cold curried chicken
(6-8 helpings)

8		chicken thighs
5	ml	salt (1 t)
2		large onions, cut into rings
25	ml	cooking oil (2 Tsp)
15	ml	mild curry powder (3 t)
15	ml	vinegar (3 t)
25	ml	smooth apricot jam (3 t)
250	ml	mayonnaise (1 c)

Method:
Cook chicken thighs in a little salt water until tender. Cool. Fry onion in oil in a large pan until tender — not brown. Add curry powder and vinegar and fry slightly. Add apricot jam and simmer for 5 min. Remove from stove and allow to cool well. Add mayonnaise and mix well. Arrange the chicken thighs in a serving dish and pour the sauce over the top. Cool in refrigerator.
Joey Pienaar

I think, therefore I am — René Discartes.

Better keep yourself clean and bright, you are the window through which you must see the world — George Bernard Shaw.

Vegetables

165

Fried onion rings
(Delicious)

4		large onions
250	ml	flour (1 c)
5	ml	salt (1 t)
250	ml	cold water (1 c)
5	ml	baking powder (1 t)
10	ml	Aromat (2 t)
		cooking oil for deep frying
1		egg

Method:

Slice the onions about 5 mm thick. Cover with boiling water. Leave for 10 min. Separate the onion rings, drain and remove all excess water. Place a little flour in a plastic bag, place the wet onion rings in the bag and shake well until the rings are coated with flour. Mix the flour, baking powder and salt. Whisk the egg and water gradually into the flour and beat until it forms a smooth batter. Dip each ring separately in the batter, remove with a knife and place in hot oil. Fry until golden brown. Place the fried rings on absorbent paper to absorb excess oil. Season the rings immediately with Aromat. Cover with paper and place in slow oven.

Joey Pienaar

No one is ever beaten unless he gives up the fight — W. Beron Wolfe.

Orange sweet potatoes
(Delicious)

Cook sufficient sweet potatoes till tender but not soft. Remove the jackets. Place in a casserole and cover with the following sauce:

Sauce:

		juice of 3 oranges
1	c	golden syrup
2	Tsp	margarine
		a pinch of salt
1	Tsp	flour mixed with a little water

Method:
Boil the juice and syrup, add the other ingredients, stir well and pour over the sweet potatoes. Bake in a hot oven till brown.
Joey Pienaar

Plain herbed rice

Boil 500 ml (2 c) rice in 1 ℓ water.

Add:

1		beef bouillon cube
2	ml	dried mixed herbs
2	ml	sugar
2	ml	salt
		a little oil or butter

Method:
Bring all ingredients to boiling point, cover saucepan and simmer until tender and loose. Just before serving, stir in 25 ml butter.
Mollie de Witt

---

*It is no disgrace to start all over. It is usually an opportunity —
George Mathew Adams.*

Stewed green beans

500	g	green beans (1 lb)
2		large potatoes
1		large onion, sliced
2		pieces mutton rib, cut up and cooked beforehand
		salt and pepper to taste

Method:
Place the sliced beans, sliced potatoes, onion and meat in a saucepan. Add a little boiling water and stew until done.
Mollie de Witt

Curried cabbage

2	kg	sliced cabbage
4	c	sugar
3	Tsp	maizena
6	c	vinegar
1	kg	onions
3 level	Tsp	curry powder (mild)
1	Tsp	salt

Method:
Pour boiling water over the sliced onion. Boil cabbage until almost tender and drain through a sieve. Drain onion when cooled. Place the cabbage and onion in a saucepan and add vinegar, salt and sugar. Stir until sugar has melted and bring to the boil. Mix curry and maizena with a little vinegar. Pour a cup of the boiling vinegar onto the curry mixture and stir. Add to the boiling cabbage and stir well. Boil for ± 15 min over a low heat. Bottle whilst hot in sterilized bottles. Can also be stored in an airtight container in the freezer for a few weeks.
HINT: Curried beans can be prepared in the same way.
Joey Pienaar

It is the greatest of all mistakes to do nothing because you can only do a little. Do what you can — Sydney Smith.

Grecian green beans

500	g	green beans
1		small tin tomato puree (115 g)
		(or slightly less)
375	ml	water (1½ c)
60	ml	olive oil (¼ c)
½		onion chopped finely
1		clove garlic (crushed)
		salt and freshly ground black pepper

Method:
Keep the beans whole or slice lengthwise. Mix tomato puree, water, olive oil, onion and garlic and bring to the boil. Add beans and season with salt and pepper. Simmer over low heat for ± half an hour, until beans are tender and the sauce has thickened.
Joey Pienaar

Green bean bredie
(6 helpings)

500	g	breast of mutton
25	ml	butter or fat (2 Tsp)
2		medium onions, chopped
500	g	green beans
2		medium potatoes
		salt and pepper to taste

Method:
Cut the meat into portions and fry in the butter or fat till brown. Add the chopped onion and fry slightly. Add a little water and stew until nearly tender. String the green beans and slice. Peel and slice the potatoes. Add all the ingredients to the meat and stew until tender. A bredie is always served with rice.
Joey Pienaar

This one thing I do, forgetting those things which are behind . . .
I press towards the mark . . . — Philippians 3:13, 14.

Sweet potato dish
(Delicious)

Boil the sweet potatoes in their jackets until tender (not too soft). When cold, peel and slice. Pour the following sauce over and place in an oven for 15 minutes.

Sauce:
125	ml	brown sugar (½ c)
250	ml	orange juice (1 c)
2	ml	grated lemon rind (¼ t)
2	ml	salt (¼ t)
125	ml	raisins (½ c)
		Boil everything together.

Make a paste from the following:
25	ml	flour (2 Tsp) (maizena)
25	ml	butter or margarine (2 Tsp)
		and add to boiling mixture.

Lastly add the following:
¼	c	nuts
4	Tsp	sherry

The sauce must be firm but not too thick.
Joey Pienaar

Glazed sweet potatoes

Peel sweet potatoes and slice. Add:
1	c	brown sugar
1	Tsp	butter
2	c	water
1	Tsp	golden syrup
3		naartjie peels

Method:
Boil until soft and syrupy.
Ina Steyn

Nothing in life is to be feared. It is only to be understood
— Mari Curie.

170

Curried green beans

2	kg	green beans
5		medium onions
200	g	sugar (250 ml) (1 c)
12,5	ml	salt (1 Tsp)
30	g	curry powder (60 ml) (¼ c)
10	ml	turmeric (2 t)
30	g	cornflower (60 ml) (¼ c)
900	ml	vinegar (7 c)

Method:
Slice the beans, not too finely, and boil in a little water for about 20 minutes until almost tender. Slice the onion, add and boil another 5 min. Mix the dry ingredients with a little vinegar and add to mixture. Add the rest of the vinegar. Simmer for 5 min, bottle whilst hot in sterilized bottles and seal. Curried green beans can be served hot as a vegetable or cold as a salad.
Joey Pienaar

Potato fritters
(4 helpings)

3		medium potatoes
12,5	ml	flour (1 Tsp)
1		egg, whisked
5	ml	salt (1 t)
40	g	cheese, grated (100 ml) (¾ c)

Method:
Scrub, peel and grate the potatoes and mix with the other ingredients. Heat a little oil or fat in a pan and fry spoonfuls of the mixture until brown on both sides.
Joey Pienaar

They are never alone that are accompanied with noble thoughts — Sir Philip Sidney.

Green mealie fritters
(10 fritters)

350	ml	tinned creamed sweetcorn
3	ml	sugar
5	ml	salt (1 t)
5	ml	baking powder (1 t)
1	ml	pepper
30	g	flour (60 ml) (¼ c)
12,5	ml	melted butter (1 Tsp)
2		eggs, beaten

Method:
Mix the sweetcorn and dry ingredients. Add the butter, whisked egg and mix. Place spoonfuls into a pan with a little hot oil or fat and fry until both sides are brown. Drain on absorbent paper and serve immediately.
Joey Pienaar

Potato slices with sour cream and mock caviar

6		medium potatoes
5	ml	salt (1 t)
190	ml	sour cream (¾ c)
125	ml	ground black olives (½ c)

Method:
Scrub the potatoes and boil in salt water until they can easliy be pricked with a fork. Drain. Cut into slices ± 5 mm thick and place onto a serving-dish. Pour the sour cream and then the olives over the slices. Serve immediately. Makes 6 helpings. Delicious with barbecue.
Joey Pienaar

Where there is a will there is a way.

Stuffed, baked potatoes
(For 6 people)

6		medium potatoes
25	ml	butter (2 Tsp)
50	ml	hot milk (4 Tsp)
		salt and pepper
1		egg, whisked
100	g	cheese, grated (250 ml) (1 c)

Method:
Wash and scrub the potatoes and bake until tender. Remove from the oven. Cut a thin slice lengthwise, remove contents of potatoes and mash. Do not break the jackets. Add all the other ingredients, fill the potatoes and pile the mixture slightly in the centre. Sprinkle with a little cheese and bake for about 10 min in a very hot oven (230 °C — 425 °F) until browned on top.
Joey Pienaar

Baked mealie dish
(Delicious)

2	c	mealie kernels, raw or cooked
1	t	maizena
		a pinch of salt
1	c	milk
1	Tsp	sugar
1		egg
1	Tsp	margarine

Method:
Beat the egg and milk and mix with the rest of the ingredients. Pour into a pyrex dish and bake for 20 min at 180 °C (350 °F).
HINT: If you cook green mealies, add a Tsp sugar to the salt in the boiling water. It gives a delicious taste to the mealies.
Joey Pienaar

At twenty will rules; at forty judgement.

Sousboontjies (bean salad)
(6 helpings)

125	g	sugar beans (250 ml) (1 c)
25	ml	sugar (2 Tsp)
50	ml	vinegar (4 Tsp)
5	ml	salt (1 t)
2	ml	pepper
25	ml	butter (2 Tsp)

Method:
Rinse the beans and soak overnight. Drain and boil in fresh water until tender. Then add the rest of the ingredients. The dish must be juicy. Crush a portion of the beans to thicken the sauce. The sauce can be thickened with an egg. Whisk 1 egg, add a little of the hot sauce to the egg, stir into the beans and heat to boiling point. Bean salad is served as a side dish with grilled chicken breasts.
Joey Pienaar

Baked potatoes in their jackets
(1 per person)

Rinse and scrub medium potatoes and rub with oil or fat. Place on oven shelf in a moderately hot oven (190 °C — 375 °F). Bake for 40-50 min or until the potatoes are soft. Place the potatoes in a dish-cloth, squeeze till contents are floury. Cut a cross into each potato to allow the steam to escape, sprinkle salt and pepper into the opening and place a piece of butter on top. Serve with sour cream flavoured with Aromat, salt and pepper. Delicious with steak.
Joey Pienaar

Man's best possession is a sympathetic wife.

Potatoes with bacon and cheese filling

6		large potatoes
		cooking oil
3		rashers bacon
		butter
1		medium onion
500	ml	grated cheddar cheese (2 c)
125	ml	sour cream (½ c)
		or
100	ml	mayonnaise (8 Tsp)
		salt and finely ground black pepper
		cayenne pepper

Method:

Preheat oven to 180 °C (350 °F). Scrub the potatoes and dry with paper towel. Rub the entire potato with oil and place on a flat baking sheet. Place in oven and bake ± an hour until soft. Remove the rind of the bacon and dice. Fry lightly in a little butter. Peel and chop the onion finely. Remove the bacon and fry the onion in the bacon fat until golden brown. When the potatoes are cooked, slice off the top, scoop the inside out and mash without breaking the jackets. Mix the bacon, potato, onion, 400 ml cheddar cheese and cream or mayonnaise. Season with salt and pepper. Place the mixture back into the potato jackets and sprinkle with the remaining cheese. Sprinkle the cayenne pepper lightly over the top. Place the potatoes under the oven grill until the cheese has melted. Serve immediately. Enough for 6 people.

Mollie de Witt

If I bind the future, I bind my will.

Green beans with vinegar sauce

For 4 people use 500 g young green beans. String the beans and slice lengthwise. Boil until tender in a little salt water, drain and pour the vinegar sauce over.

Vinegar sauce:
1		egg
25	ml	sugar (2 Tsp)
2	ml	salt
50	ml	boiling water (in which the beans were cooked) (4 Tsp)
50	ml	vinegar or lemon juice (4 Tsp)

Method:
Beat the egg, sugar and salt, add the boiling water and vinegar or lemon juice. Stir lightly and heat in the top part of a double-boiler. Stir until the sauce thickens. Serve hot or cold.

Joey Pienaar

Curried cabbage

1	kg	cabbage, shredded
350	g	onion, chopped
25	g	flour (50 ml) (4 Tsp)
350	ml	white vinegar (1¾ c)
375	g	sugar (1½ c)
25	ml	mild curry powder (2 level Tsp)
25	ml	golden syrup (2 Tsp)
15	ml	salt (3 t)

Method:
Boil cabbage and onion for 15 minutes in a large saucepan in boiling water until tender and drain well. Mix the flour with a little of the vinegar and add the rest of the vinegar and other ingredients

---

We carry our homes within us.

to the cabbage mixture. Mix, bring to the boil, and boil for 15 minutes. Place in sterilized bottles, seal and leave to cool. Use when required.
Mollie de Witt

Curried beans

2	kg	beans, sliced
1	kg	onions, sliced
2	t	salt (level)

Boil 10 min in steam pot.

1	bot	vinegar (750 ml)
3	c	sugar
2	t	curry (level)
2	Tsp	maizena (heaped)

Method:
Boil vinegar and sugar. Blend maizena and curry with a little cold water. Stir into boiling mixture. Pour over beans. Boil for 5 minutes. Bottle hot.
Annemarié Strydom

Instant salad beans

Use a tin of beans-in-tomato sauce (410 g). Mix with ¼ c vinegar and 2 Tsp brown sugar and simmer for 5 minutes. Serve hot or cold.
Ina Steyn

Whose welfare is assured at home is fortunate.

Spiced vinegar beetroot salad

1	kg	beetroot
		Boil the following for 5 minutes:
1	c	water
2	c	sugar
½	t	ginger
⅛	t	cinnamon
4	c	vinegar
¼	t	pepper
¼	t	salt

Method:
Boil beetroot until tender. Grate or slice. Place in sterilized bottles. Pour the boiling vinegar mixture over and seal. Can be stored for months.
Joey Pienaar

Baked potatoes
(Makes 8 helpings)

800	g	potatoes (8 medium)
250	g	butter or margarine
1	pkt	thick white onion soup powder (69 g)

Method:
Preheat oven to 180 °C (350 °F). Scrub potatoes, do not peel. Slice each potato into 1 cm slices, but do not cut through. Place the potatoes with the sliced side upwards in a shallow casserole (1,5 ℓ volume). Melt margarine over slow heat. Remove from stove and stir in soup powder. Pour mixture over potatoes. Replace lid. Bake 2-2½ hrs and baste occasionally with the sauce in the dish. Place potatoes gently on a hot serving dish and serve hot.
Joey Pienaar

Hollywood money is congealed snow.

Desserts

Cold Christmas pudding

1	Tsp	cocoa
¾	c	chopped nuts
¼	c	seedless raisins
½	c	dates (chopped)
¼	c	ginger preserve (shredded)
¼	c	currants
½	t	salt
1	Tsp	cold water
1	t	vanilla essence
3	Tsp	brandy
2	c	milk
1	t	grated lemon rind
3	Tsp	sugar
1	Tsp	gelatine
¼	c	boiling water
½	t	lemon essence

Method:

Mix the cocoa with a little of the milk, add the rest of the milk and mix thoroughly. Pour in the top of a double boiler and bring to the boil over boiling water. Stir in the nuts, lemon rind, raisins, dates, ginger preserve, currants, sugar and salt. Boil for 5 minutes then remove from stove. Soak the gelatine in the cold water. Dissolve in the boiling water and stir into the fruit mixture. Leave to cool. Stir in the vanilla, lemon essence and brandy. Leave until mixture thickens slightly, stir occasionally. Rinse jelly mould with cold water and spoon the fruit mixture into the mould. Allow to set, then turn out onto a glass dish. Decorate with whipped cream and serve with thin custard or vanilla ice-cream.

Joey Pienaar

Never look a gift horse in the mouth.

Bread pudding with a difference
(6-8 helpings, delicious)

120	g	soft breadcrumbs (500 ml) (2 c)
250	ml	buttermilk (1 c)
		finely grated peel of ½ an orange
250	ml	orange juice (1 c)
40	ml	soft margarine (8 t)
200	g	brown sugar (250 ml) (1 c)
2		eggs, whisked
60	g	flour (125 ml) (½ c)
2	ml	salt
5	ml	bicarbonate of soda (1 t)
2	ml	ground cinnamon
1	ml	mixed spice
75	g	seedless raisins (125 ml) (½ c)
40	g	walnuts (100 ml, chopped) (8 Tsp)

Method:
Mix the breadcrumbs, buttermilk, rind and juice thoroughly and leave aside. Cream margarine and brown sugar, add whisked eggs and mix. Sift flour, bicarb, salt, cinnamon and mixed spice and fold into egg mixture. Add breadcrumbs mixture, raisins and nuts and mix. Pour into a greased, ovenproof dish and bake in a preheated oven at 180 °C (350 °F) for 35-40 minutes, or until golden brown and done. Serve with cream and custard.
Joey Pienaar

Empty barrels make the most noise.

Romany cream dessert

2	pkt	Romany Cream biscuits
		enough sherry to soak the biscuits
2		cartons cream (250 ml each)
		coconut
		nuts
		chocolate (flakes)

Method:
Halve the biscuits lengthwise, but make sure there is chocolate filling on both halves. Line the dish with the biscuits. Pour enough sherry over to soak biscuits. Whip the cream until stiff but not dry. Place a layer of cream in the dish and sprinkle with coconut. Sprinkle with nuts and finely flaked chocolate. Form layers by alternating the cream, nuts and chocolate, end with a layer of chocolate for decoration. Prepare pudding the previous day.
Mrs Jessie le Grange

Ice-cream pudding
(Delicious)

100	g	pecan nuts
125	g	glacé cherries
1	pkt	finger biscuits
¼	c	brandy
1	ℓ	vanilla ice-cream
120	g	chocolate
250	ml	cream (1 c)

Method:
Chop the nuts and cherries. Break the biscuits into small pieces. Grate the chocolate. Whip the cream until stiff. Mix all the ingredients well and pour into a round dish. Place in the freezer until frozen.
Joey Pienaar

A man hoards himself when he has nothing to give.

Pawpaw-wine dessert

A delicious, sweet, ripe pawpaw. (Watermelon and spanspek are delicious on a summer evening.) Cut into halves. Scoop pulp out. Vandyke the edge of the shell with a knife. Fill half of the shell with your favourite wine. Mix pulp with any other fruit, fresh or frozen. Berries — especially strawberries — are delicious. Taste if it is sweet enough, if not sweeten with castor sugar or with a sugar substitute if required. Spoon back gently into the shell without crushing the fruit. Chill thoroughly before serving. (Also delicious with ice-cream.) (This dessert always meets with the approval of my guests.)
Joey Pienaar

Souskluitjies (Cinnamon dumplings)

3	c	milk
3	Tsp	flour
2	Tsp	maizena
1	t	salt
3		eggs
1	t	baking powder

Method:
Boil milk. Mix other ingredients with milk. Boil for 10 minutes. Place spoonfuls in a dish. Place dabs of butter on top and sprinkle with cinnamon.
Henda Gous

Wine wears no breeches.

Pancake without eggs

150	g	flour
2	ml	baking powder
2	ml	bicarbonate of soda
1	ml	salt
440	ml	water (1¾ c)
15	ml	vinegar (3 t)
60	ml	cooking oil (¼ c)

Method:
Sift dry ingredients. Beat water, vinegar and oil slightly and stir into the dry ingredients. Grease a hot pan only once with a little oil — thereafter the dough will not stick to the pan. Fry the pancakes. Makes 5-6 large pancakes. Serve with orange sauce.

Orange sauce:

250	ml	orange juice (1 c)
150	g	white sugar (190 ml) (¾ c)
25	g	butter or margarine (25 ml) (2 Tsp)
100	ml	brandy (8 Tsp)

Method:
Boil orange juice, sugar and margarine together for 5 minutes. Add brandy and pour over the rolled pancakes. Serve hot.
Joey Pienaar

Holidays have no pity.

Sago pudding

4	c	milk
1	c	sago
2	Tsp	butter
¾	c	sugar
4		eggs
1	t	vanilla essence
		apricot jam
		a pinch of salt

Method:
Preheat oven to 180 °C (350 °F). Boil the milk, sugar, salt and sago until the sago is transluscent. Leave to cool slightly. Stir in butter. Add slightly beaten egg yolks and vanilla essence. Pour into a greased ovenproof dish. Spread with apricot jam. Whisk the egg whites until stiff with 6 Tsp sugar. Place on top of the jam and bake until light brown.
Joey Pienaar

Peach dessert
(Delicious)

Use 1 tin peach halves, drain and keep the syrup aside. Place the peach halves in a shallow dish. Place a "Choc-rust" biscuit into each half. Mix the syrup with 2 Tsp Van der Hum liqueur or brandy. Pour slowly over the peach-and-biscuits mixture. Place in a oven for ± half an hour. Serve with ice-cream or whipped cream. Increase the amount of liqueur according to the amount of peaches used.
Ester Kleinhans

East is East, West is West; never the twain shall meet.

Frozen mocha dessert

2	c	evaporated milk — well cooled
2	pkt	dark chocolate instant pudding
1	Tsp	instant coffee made up with
1	Tsp	boiling water
2	c	artificial cream (whipped)
3	Tsp	sweet sherry
⅛	t	salt
2	c	Tennis biscuits roughly broken into pieces

Method:
Add the instant pudding and prepared coffee to the milk and beat to a smooth texture. Stir in the prepared cream, sherry and salt, followed by the Tennis biscuits. Line a small pan of 23 cm x 12,5 cm x 2,5 cm (9" x 5" x 2,5") with aluminium foil, shiny side to the inside. Pour mixture into pan and freeze until firm, preferably overnight. Unmould. Pipe the cream around the edges and on the top and sprinkle chopped nuts over the cream. This dessert must not be frozen for more than 24 hrs.
For decorating: Whipped cream and chopped nuts.
Joey Pienaar

Banana caramel pudding
(Delicious)

1	pkt	Tennis biscuits
		bananas
		apricot jam

Method:
Place the tennis biscuits, sliced bananas and apricot jam in layers in a dish and pour caramel sauce between each layer.

The mill wheel turns forever.

Caramel sauce:

½	c	sugar
½	t	salt
2	t	custard powder
½	Tsp	butter
1¼	c	milk
		vanilla essence

Method:
Melt the butter and sugar in a pan. Add salt. Stir constantly until slightly browned. Add the milk and stir until lumps have dissolved. Mix the custard powder with a little milk, add and allow to cook thoroughly. Add the vanilla essence.
Joey Pienaar

Cold sago pudding
(Delicious and a large quantity)

1	pkt	sago (500 g)
2		tins Ideal milk (large)
3	pkts	red jelly
2	c	sugar
½	t	salt
¼	t	tartaric acid
10	c	cold water

Method:
Soak sago for a few hours in the water then boil sago slowly in water, sugar, salt and tartaric acid over a low heat until transluscent (± 20 min). Mix jelly with 1 c boiling water for each packet. Mix with sago. Leave to cool completely. Beat the Ideal Milk until firm and fold into the cold sago mixture. Place in refrigerator.
Joey Pienaar

If we're not foolish young; we're foolish old.

Caramel dumplings

180	g	flour (375 ml) (1½ c)
12,5	ml	baking powder (1 Tsp)
1	ml	salt
40	g	sugar (50 ml) (4 Tsp)
50	g	butter or margarine (50 ml) (4 Tsp)
190	ml	milk (¾ c)
50	g	chopped walnuts or
		sliced glacé cherries (125 ml) (½ c)

Sauce:

300	g	white sugar (375 ml) (1½ c)
25	g	butter or margarine (25 ml) (2 Tsp)
		a pinch of salt
500	ml	boiling water (2 c)

Method:
Sift flour, baking powder and salt. Add sugar and rub in the butter. Mix with milk and stir in nuts or cherries. Prepare the sauce by caramelizing 100 g sugar. Add rest of ingredients and bring to the boil in a large saucepan. Place spoonfuls of the dough into the boiling syrup. Put the lid on and simmer for 12 minutes over a slow heat. Serve hot with custard, ice-cream or fresh cream. Makes 6 helpings.
Joey Pienaar

Scotch cream pudding
(Makes 6-8 helpings)

20	g	butter or margarine (25 ml)
140	g	unsifted flour (250 ml)
2		eggs, beaten (for batter)
250	ml	milk (1 c)
25	ml	smooth apricot jam or watermelon preserve (2 Tsp)
12,5	ml	vinegar (1 Tsp)

There is a charm about the forbidden

5	ml	bicarbonate of soda (1 heaped t)
500	ml	cream or evaporated milk (2 c)
400	g	sugar (500 ml) (2 c)
2		eggs, beaten (for sauce)

Method:

Preheat oven to 180 °C (350 °F) (gas:mark 4). Rub butter in flour. Add eggs, milk, jam, vinegar and bicarbonate of soda and mix thoroughly. Pour in an ovenproof dish with a 2,5 ℓ capacity. Bake for about 25 minutes until light brown. In the meantime, whisk the cream, sugar and eggs until sugar has melted. Pour over the hot pudding after 25 minutes and bake for a further 20 min until the sauce is thick.

Mollie de Witt

Vinegar pudding

Syrup:

2	c	boiling water
1	c	sugar
3	Tsp	vinegar

1½	c	flour
½	c	sugar
1	c	milk
½	c	butter
1		egg
1	t	bicarbonate of soda
1	Tsp	apricot jam

Method:

Beat butter, sugar and egg. Mix the flour with the milk. Stir in jam. Stir in bicarbonate of soda, mixed with a little milk. Place mixture into boiling syrup. Bake for 1 hour in moderate oven.

Ina Steyn

Fools admire; men of sense approve.

Baked apricot pudding
(Makes 6-8 helpings)

1	tin	apricot halves (410 g)
200	g	sugar (250 ml) (1 c)
50	g	butter or margarine at room temperature (60 ml) (¼ c)
1		egg
140	g	flour (250 ml) (1 c)
12,5	ml	baking powder (1 Tsp)
		a pinch of salt
125	ml	milk (½ c)
5	ml	vanilla essence (1 t)

Method:
Preheat oven to 180 °C (350 °F). Grease a 1,5 ℓ ovenproof dish. Drain the apricots and supplement syrup with water to 375 ml. Add half the sugar and boil rapidly for 5 minutes, stir until sugar has melted. Cream butter and remaining sugar. Add egg and beat well. Sift the flour, baking powder and salt. Add the flour mixture and milk alternately to the butter mixture. Stir in vanilla essence. Pour into dish. Place the apricot halves on top of the batter and pour the hot syrup over the top; bake pudding 30-40 minutes until golden brown. Serve hot.
Ina Steyn

Praise is not pudding.

Baked fruit pudding
(Makes 6-8 helpings)

2		tins quince slices, pie apples (410 g each) or guavas or fruit according to taste
200	g	sugar (250 ml) (1 c)
2		sticks cinnamon
12,5	ml	lemon juice (1 Tsp)
115	g	margarine (125 ml) (½ c)
100	g	castor sugar (125 ml) (½ c)
2		eggs
200	g	flour (375 ml) (1½ c)
10	ml	baking powder (2 t)
2	ml	salt
37,5	ml	milk (3 Tsp)
25	ml	cinnamon (2 Tsp)

Method:
Preheat oven to 180 °C (350 °F). Grease a 2 ℓ ovenproof dish. Drain fruit and supplement the syrup to 500 ml with water. Add the sugar and cinnamon sticks to the syrup and boil for 5 min. Remove cinnamon, add lemon juice and keep syrup hot. Cream the margarine and castor sugar. Add the eggs separately and beat well after each egg has been added. Sift flour, baking powder and salt together. Stir the flour mixture and milk alternately into the egg mixture. Pour half the batter into a dish. Place the fruit on top of the batter and sprinkle with cinnamon. Pour the remaining batter over the top. Pour the syrup over this. Bake the pudding for 40-50 min. Serve with custard, thin cream or ice-cream.

Joey Pienaar

The proof of the pudding is in the eating.

Brown pudding
(Delicious 6-8 helpings)

1		egg
200	g	sugar (250 ml) (1 c)
120	g	flour (250 ml) (1 c)
5	ml	salt (1 t)
12,5	ml	smooth apricot jam (1 Tsp)
12,5	ml	vinegar (1 Tsp)
5	ml	bicarbonate of soda (1 t)
250	ml	milk (1 c)

Sauce:

250	g	margarine
250	ml	Ideal milk (1 c)
125	ml	boiling water (½ c)
200	g	sugar (250 ml) (1 c)

Method:
Beat egg, add sugar and beat thoroughly. Sift the flour and salt and add flour mixture and milk alternately to the egg mixture. Mix the apricot jam, vinegar and bicarbonate of soda well and add the egg mixture. Mix and pour into a greased ovenproof dish. Bake in a preheated oven at 180 °C (350 °F) until golden brown. Stir sauce ingredients in a saucepan over medium heat. Heat to boiling point, remove from heat and pour over the pudding immediately after removing from the oven. Serve with wine sauce.

Wine sauce:

150	g	sugar (187,5 ml) (¾ c)
250	ml	water (1 c)
25	ml	butter (2 Tsp)
3		eggs (whisked)
125	ml	sweet wine (½ c)

Poverty is no perversity.

Method:
Stir the sugar and water in a saucepan over moderate heat until the sugar has dissolved. Bring to the boil, boil for 15 min. Add butter and stir until melted. Add beaten egg and wine and stir well. Stir over moderate heat until hot. Serve with the pudding.
Joey Pienaar

Traditional date pudding

3	c	flour
1	c	sugar
375	g	dates
2	Tsp	apricot jam
2	Tsp	vinegar
¼	t	salt
250	g	butter
2	t	bicarbonate of soda
¼	c	hot milk

Method:
Cream butter and sugar and add the dates. Dissolve the bicarbonate of soda in the hot milk and add the syrup and vinegar. Add to butter mixture. Sift the dry ingredients and add to mixture. Add the apricot jam. Pour the mixture into a greased mould or tie in a damp cloth sprinkled with flour, but leave enough room for the mixture to rise. Leave overnight. Place the cloth or the covered mould in boiling water and steam for 3 hrs. Serve with a wine or caramel sauce.
Ina Steyn

One's cruelty is one's power.

Baked Roly-Poly pudding

1	c	butter
2	c	flour
1	t	baking powder
		smooth apricot jam
		a pinch of salt
2		eggs
¼	c	milk

Method:
Sift the dry ingredients and lightly rub in the butter . Beat the eggs well and add the milk. Add to the dry ingredients and mix well. Roll the dough out thinly and spread the jam over it. Roll like a swiss roll and place in a greased, ovenproof dish. Pour the following sauce over: Boil 3 c water, 1 c sugar and 2 Tsp butter for 5 minutes. Bake in a moderate oven (180 °C — 350 °F) for 1 hr. Serve hot or cold.
Ina Steyn

Corn flake dessert

1	c	sugar
½	c	butter
2	Tsp	custard powder
2	c	corn flakes
5	c	milk
3		eggs, separated
		vanilla essence

Method:
Beat the butter and sugar well and add the corn flakes. Leave aside while making the custard. Mix the custard powder with a little milk and add the essence and beaten egg yolks. Heat the

---

You can lead a horse to the drinking trough, but you can't make him drink.

194

milk and stir in the egg mixture. Allow to boil until the mixture is cooked. Pour the corn flake and the custard mixtures alternately in layers into a greased ovenproof dish. Beat the egg white with 4 Tsp sugar until stiff and spoon over the pudding. Bake in a moderate oven (180 °C — 350 °F) until light brown. Serve with custard.
Mollie de Witt

Milk dumplings
(Makes 4-6 helpings)

40	g	custard powder (75 ml) (6 Tsp)
50	g	sugar (60 ml) (¼ c)
500	ml	milk (2 c)
2		eggs, separated
2	ml	vanilla essence
15	ml	butter or margarine (3 t)
7	ml	ground cinnamon (1½t)

Method:
Mix the custard powder and sugar with a little of the milk to a paste. Heat the rest of the milk in a medium saucepan over moderate heat until boiling point is reached. Thicken with the custard powder mixture. Whisk the egg yolks slightly and stir quickly into custard. Boil until cooked. Remove from stove and add vanilla essence. Whisk egg whites until stiff and fold into custard mixture with a metal spoon. Layer spoonfuls on a serving dish, dot with butter in between each layer and sprinkle with cinnamon. Serve hot.
Joey Pienaar

Never say never; one day you might just.

Baked dumplings
(Delicious and quick and easy)

125	g	margarine
4	Tsp	apricot jam
1	dsp	bicarbonate of soda
1½	c	flour
		salt

Method:
Melt the butter and add the jam. Stir till melted. Add the rest of the ingredients and place spoonfuls into the following sauce.

Sauce:
3	c	boiling water
1	c	sugar
1	t	butter
1	t	vanilla

HINT: Remember that it must be a large pyrex dish with a lid. Bake covered for ± 25 minutes in the oven. (I sometimes add a little vinegar if it is too sweet.)
Ester Coetzee

Praise like gold, owes value to its scarcity.

Baked chocolate pudding

Preheat oven to 180 °C (350 °F)
Sift the following:

1	c	cake flour
1-1½	Tsp	cocoa
3	t	baking powder
¼	t	salt

Whisk the following:

5	Tsp	soft butter
¾	c	sugar
1		egg

Method:

Mix ingredients together in a large mixing bowl and beat until a smooth batter is formed. Add ½ t vanilla or rum essence to the mixture.

Optional: 2-3 Tsp chopped nuts may be added to the mixture.

Syrup:

Mix together in a saucepan:

1	c	brown sugar (¾ cup white sugar may also be used)
1	c	boiling water
2	Tsp	cocoa

Method:

Stir ingredients continually and bring to boiling point. Pour syrup into a well-greased pyrex dish. Add spoonfuls of batter to the hot syrup. Replace lid and bake for 30 min. Delicious with vanilla ice-cream or custard.

Mollie de Witt

Powerlessness may be the disease of the aged.

Montelimar pudding

1		tin unsweetened evaporated milk (place in refrigerator the previous day)
50	g	glacé cherries
50	g	marshmallows
1	pkt	lemon jelly
250	ml	boiling water (1 c)
		juice of ½ lemon
28	g	castor sugar

Method:
Cut the cherries and marshmallows into small pieces. Dissolve jelly in water. Leave to cool into a thick liquid. Whip the evaporated milk until light and frothy. Add jelly and beat well. Stir in cherries, lemon juice, marshmallows and sugar. Pour into a mould and leave to set. Turn out onto a dish and decorate with cherries.
Dalena Dennis

Sweet dumplings

125	g	margarine
2	t	bicarbonate of soda mixed with a little milk
		salt
4	Tsp	apricot jam
2	c	flour

Method:
Melt butter, add apricot jam and allow to melt over heat. Add the rest of the ingredients and pour spoonfuls into the following sauce.

Power pollutes whatever it touches.

Sauce:

3	c	boiling water
1	t	butter
1	c	sugar
1	t	vanilla

Method:
Bake in covered pyrex dish for ± 25 min.
Esther Coetsee

Corn flake pudding

Make 600 ml (2⅓ c) custard without sugar (reasonably thick)

1	c	sugar
2	c	corn flakes (Post Toasties)
½	c	margarine/butter (melted)
3		eggs

Method:
Melt butter. Mix the butter with the sugar and the corn flakes. Whisk the egg yolks well. Add to the butter, sugar and corn flake mixture. Grease a large enough dish with butter. Start with a layer of corn flake mixture then a layer of custard. Layer till all ingredients have been used. Bake at 190 °C (375 °F) for 15 min. Beat the egg whites until stiff. Spread the apricot jam and then the egg whites on top. Bake lightly. Serve with Ideal milk.
Tina van Niekerk

One who digs a hole for others may fall in himself.

Delicious pineapple pudding with a topping

100	g	walnuts, chopped (250 ml) (1 c)
2		eggs
200	g	sugar (250 ml) (1 c)
170	g	flour (300 ml, unsifted) (1 c + 4 Tsp)
10	ml	baking powder (2 t)
		a pinch of salt
150	ml	cold water (½ c + 2 Tsp)

Topping:

1		tin pineapple chunks (820 g)
40	g	butter or margarine (50 ml) (4 Tsp)
100	g	sugar (125 ml) (½ c)
1		egg
80	g	coconut (250 ml) (1 c)
10	ml	vanilla essence (2 t)
50	ml	strawberry jam (4 Tsp)

Method:

Preheat oven to 200 °C (400 °F). Grease a shallow, ovenproof dish ± 2,5 ℓ and dust with flour. Sprinkle nuts on the bottom of the dish. Beat the eggs and sugar. Sift the flour, baking powder and salt and add alternately with water to the egg mixture. Pour batter over the nuts in the dish. Bake for 15 min. Drain the pineapple pieces in the meantime and dice. Stir butter, sugar, eggs, coconut and vanilla essence in a saucepan over a slow heat until mixture starts to simmer: it must not boil. Spread the strawberry jam over the pudding once out of the oven. Place pineapple on top. Sprinkle coconut over the pineapple. Place pudding back into the oven and bake a further 7-10 min until the layer colours. Makes 6-8 helpings. Serve with Ultramel custard to which a ¼ c of brandy has been added.
Joey Pienaar

They are not all saints who use holy water.

Pumpkin fritters
(Makes ± 36 fritters)

750	g	cooked, mashed pumpkin (750 ml) (3 c)
2		eggs
5	ml	salt (1 t)
275	g	self-raising flour (500 ml) (2 c)
15	ml	baking powder (3 t)
500	ml	cooking oil (2 c)

Syrup:

400	g	sugar (500 ml) (2 c)
250	ml	water (1 c)
125	ml	milk (½ c)
25	g	butter or margarine (30 ml) (2 heaped Tsp)
		a pinch of salt
10	ml	maizena (2 t)

Method:
Beat the pumpkin, eggs and salt. Sift the self-raising flour and mix with the pumpkin mixture until a soft batter. Heat cooking oil in a saucepan over medium heat. Spoon dessertspoonfuls of the pumpkin mixture into oil and fry until light brown and cooked. Drain fritters on absorbent paper, place on a serving dish and keep hot. Heat the ingredients for the syrup except the maizena and bring to the boil. Mix the maizena with a little cold water to a paste and stir into syrup. Pour over hot fritters. Makes about 3 dozen fritters.
Joey Pienaar

Home has more variety than café society.

Ouma's delicious pudding

120	g	flour (250 ml) (1 c)
1		egg
100	g	sugar (125 ml) (½ c)
5	ml	baking powder (1 t)
5	ml	bicarbonate of soda (1 t)
		a pinch of salt
25	ml	smooth apricot jam (2 Tsp)
30	ml	vinegar (2 Tsp)
250	ml	milk (1 c)

Sauce:

200	g	sugar (250 ml) (1 c)
125	ml	boiling water (½ c)
250	ml	evaporated milk (1 c)
50	g	butter or margarine (60 ml) (¼ c)
5	ml	vanilla essence (1 t)

Method:

Beat egg and sugar well until light and fluffy. Add flour, baking powder, bicarbonate of soda, jam and vinegar and mix well. Stir milk in until a smooth batter. Pour into a greased, medium baking dish and bake for 45 min at 180 °C (350 °F). Heat the rest of the ingredients and pour over pudding as soon as it is removed from the oven. Serve with cream or hot custard. Six helpings.

Joey Pienaar

It is impossible to write modern history.

Brown caramel pudding

1	Tsp	butter (large Tsp)
		smooth apricot jam (1 small c)
		a pinch of salt
1	t	bicarbonate of soda
100	ml	flour (8 Tsp)
1	t	ground ginger

Method:
Pour bicarbonate of soda over the soft butter (not melted). Add apricot jam to butter, place in the dish intended for baking the pudding in. Add flour and ginger, mix well. Shape the dough lengthwise in the middle of the dish. Pour 1 small cup of sugar and 3 c boiling water over the dough. Place in oven and bake until done. Optional: Add nuts, raisins and cherries to batter.

Red wine sauce

1	c	red wine
½	c	sugar
		rind of ½ lemon
1		stick cinnamon
2	t	maizena mixed with a little water

Method:
Boil the wine, sugar, lemon and cinnamon for 5 min. Mix maizena and water to a paste and stir in until mixture thickens. Boil for 3-5 min and serve.
Badie Bloem

Wedded love is the true source of human offspring.

Caramel pudding
(Delicious)

Sauce:
1	tin	Ideal milk (410 g)
1½	c	sugar
1½	c	milk

Method:
Just bring to the boil in a deep saucepan.

2	Tsp	butter
2	Tsp	apricot jam
8	Tsp	flour
1	c	milk
6	Tsp	sugar
2	t	bicarbonate of soda
2		eggs

Method:
Cream butter and sugar. Add eggs, then jam. Sift the flour and milk alternately into mixture. Finally add the bicarbonate of soda mixed with a little lukewarm milk. Pour mixture into the pan with caramel sauce and bake in a medium oven for ± ¾ hr. (Do not cover. It must be baked in a very deep container.)
Ester Liebenberg

Ginger fruit pudding

Syrup:
500	ml	water (2 c)
200	g	sugar (250 ml) (1 c)
25	g	butter or margarine (30 ml) (2 heaped Tsp)

Weeks may fly by like the speed of light; others may slide by like a funeral procession.

Fruit mixture:

150	g	dried fruit cake mixture (250 ml) (1 c)
75	g	glacé cherries, sliced (125 ml) (½ c)
25	g	butter or margarine (30 ml) (2 heaped Tsp)
25	ml	smooth apricot jam (2 Tsp)

Batter:

140	g	flour (250 ml) (unsifted) (1 c)
50	g	sugar (60 ml) (4 heaped Tsp)
5	ml	ground ginger (1 t)
2	ml	salt
7	ml	bicarbonate of soda (1 heaped t)
125	ml	milk (½ c)
1		egg, beated

Sliced preserved ginger. Stiffly whipped, slightly sweetened cream.

Method:

Preheat oven to 180 °C (350 °F). Grease a deep, ovenproof dish (volume 2 ℓ). Boil syrup: heat water, sugar and butter until boiling point and boil for a minute. Remove from stove and keep aside. Mix dried fruit, cherries, butter and apricot jam in a saucepan and heat over medium heat until the sugar and jam melt. Keep aside. Sift flour, sugar, ginger and salt together. Dissolve the bicarbonate of soda in milk. Add bicarbonate of soda, fruit mixture and egg to the sifted dry ingredients and mix. Pour batter into the dish and pour the syrup over the top. Bake for 25-30 min on the centre shelf of the oven. Decorate with the whole ginger and serve hot or cold with cream. (6 helpings).

Joey Pienaar

If we could count the stars we should not weep.

Baked pudding
(Delicious)

1	c	flour
½	c	sugar
1	c	milk
1		egg
		salt
1½	t	vinegar
1	t	apricot jam
1	t	baking powder
1	t	bicarbonate of soda

Method:
Whisk egg and sugar. Add other ingredients (finally the milk). Mix well and bake in a moderate oven for 1 hr. Pour sauce over the top.

Sauce:

1	c	brown sugar
1	c	milk
½	c	boiling water
200	g	margarine
1	t	vanilla

Method:
Melt. Pour over hot pudding.
Annamarié Strydom

Sago pudding with brandy caramel sauce

70	g	sago (100 ml)
750	ml	milk (3 c)
45	g	butter (50 ml) (2½ Tsp)
200	g	sugar (250 ml) (1 c)
2		eggs, beaten

A friend in need is a friend indeed.

120	g	fresh breadcrumbs (500 ml) (2 c)
50	g	sultanas (85 ml)
100	g	seedless raisins (165 ml)
50	g	dates (85 ml, chopped)
50	g	glacé cherries (85 ml, chopped)
35	g	walnuts (85 ml, roughly chopped)
10	ml	vanilla essence (2 t)
10	ml	bicarbonate of soda (2 t)
		little water to dissolve bicarbonate of soda
50	ml	seville marmalade (4 Tsp)

Method:

Soak sago overnight in milk. Cream butter and sugar until light and creamy, add beaten eggs. Mix well. Add remaining ingredients, mix well and pour into an ovenproof dish. Bake in a preheated oven at 180 °C (350 °F) for about 45-60 minutes. Serve with brandy caramel sauce.

Brandy caramel sauce:

250	ml	sugar (1 c)
125	g	butter or margarine
15	ml	water (3 t)
		a pinch of salt
250	ml	milk (1 c)
2	Tsp	brandy

Method:

Heat sugar and margarine in a saucepan over medium heat and stir constantly until the mixture is light brown: it burns easily. Remove the saucepan from the stove, stir in the milk and boil the sauce until sugar has dissolved. Add 1 t flour, mixed with a little milk, and boil for a few minutes. Add salt and brandy. Stir well.

Mollie de Witt

One cannot weep for the enitre world.

Traditional sweet dumplings
(It never fails)

4	Tsp	flour, heaped
2	Tsp	sugar
1		egg
2	t	baking powder
1	Tsp	butter
		a pinch of salt
		a little milk for mixing

Method:
Mix the dry ingredients and rub in the butter. Break the egg into mixture and with a little milk mix to a reasonably soft batter. Place spoonfuls into 3 cups boiling water in saucepan and cook for 15 minutes. Do not remove the lid from the saucepan. Transfer dumplings to a pyrex dish and add a little more water to the remaining water in the saucepan, as well as a tablespoon of sugar, a dab of butter and cinnamon. Boil for a while. Pour the sauce over the dumplings.
Joey Pienaar

Chocolate sauce
(Delicious with ice-cream)

150	g	dark chocolate
1	tin	condensed milk (225 g) (200 ml)
125	ml	milk (½ c)

Method:
Break the chocolate into squares. Heat with the condensed milk and milk over medium heat until it boils, stirring constantly. Serve hot.
Joey Pienaar

Those who weep recover more quickly.

Marshmallow pudding
(Delicious)

250	ml	flour (1 c)
5	ml	bicarbonate of soda (1 t)
5	ml	apricot jam (1 t)
15	ml	margarine (3 t)
250	ml	milk (1 c)
1		egg
250	ml	sugar (1 c)
5	ml	lemon juice (1 t)

Method:
Cream butter and sugar. Add egg. Add lemon juice, bicarbonate of soda and apricot jam. Stir in the flour and milk alternately. Bake at 180 °C (350 °F) in a pyrex dish for 1 hour.

Syrup:

250	ml	cream (1 c)
125	ml	margarine
250	ml	sugar (1 c)
125	ml	boiling water (½ c)

Method:
Boil all the ingredients together for 2 min and pour over the pudding immediately after removing it from the oven. Bake until caramelized.
Mollie de Witt

A busy person never knows how much he weighs.

Vinegar pudding

2	c	flour
1		egg
½	t	salt
2	Tsp	apricot jam
1	c	milk
½	c	butter
1	t	ground nutmeg
1	c	sugar
2	t	bicarbonate of soda
1	t	ground ginger

Method:

Cream butter and sugar and add the beaten egg. Add the jam. Dissolve the bicarbonate of soda in milk. Sift the dry ingredients and add alternately with milk to the creamed mixture. Mix the syrup with the following ingredients and boil for 5 minutes:

½	c	vinegar
1	c	sugar
1½	c	water
1	t	grated orange peel

Method:

Pour the boiling syrup into an ovenproof dish then pour the batter over. Bake in a moderate oven for 45 minutes.

Joey Pienaar

None knows the weight of another's burden.

Tipsy pudding
(8 helpings)

5	ml	bicarbonate of soda (1 t)
190	ml	boiling water (¾ c)
150	g	dates, chopped (250 ml) (1 c)
25	ml	butter (2 Tsp)
140	g	sugar (175 ml) (½ c + 4 Tsp)
1		beaten egg
200	g	flour (400 ml) (about 1¾ c)
5	ml	baking powder (1 t)
3	ml	salt
50	ml	chopped pecan nuts (4 Tsp)
2	Tsp	chopped cherries

Method:
Dissolve the bicarbonate of soda in the water and pour over dates. Leave to cool. Cream the butter, sugar and egg, sift the dry ingredients and alternately add with the date mixture to the butter, sugar and egg. Add the nuts and cherries and bake for 30-40 minutes in a square baking dish in a moderate oven (190 °C — 375 °F). Leave to cool in the dish and cut into squares. Prepare a sauce with the following ingredients and pour hot over the pudding:

300	g	sugar (375 ml) (1½ c)
190	ml	water (¾ c)
10	ml	butter (2 t)
5	ml	vanilla essence (1 t)
125	ml	brandy (½ c)
		a pinch of salt
12,5	ml	lemon juice (1 Tsp)

Joey Pienaar

Study sickness while you are well.

Delicious sweet dumplings

1	c	flour
2	t	baking powder
2	Tsp	sugar
4	Tsp	milk
½	t	salt
2	Tsp	butter
1		egg

Method:

Sift the dry ingredients and rub the butter in lightly. Beat the egg well while adding the sugar gradually. Add the milk to the egg and mix with the dry ingredients. Boil 3 c water in a saucepan and place spoonfuls of batter into the water. Cover and boil for about 10 minutes. Place the dumplings in an ovenproof dish. Use the liquid to prepare the sauce. If the water is not enough, make up to 2 c. Add ½ c sugar and 1 Tsp cinnamon and boil. Add 2 Tsp butter and pour the hot sauce over the dumplings. Serve hot. N.B.: The sauce can be thickened with 1 Tsp maizena.

Joey Pienaar

Upside down banana pudding
(6 helpings)

50	g	butter (50 ml) (4 Tsp)
60	g	white or brown sugar (75 ml) (6 Tsp)
5		bananas
2		eggs
100	g	sugar (125 ml) (½ c)
5	ml	vanilla essence (1 t)
50	g	soft butter (50 ml) (4 Tsp)
120	g	flour (250 ml) (1 c)

Do good even to the wicked.

10	ml	baking powder (2 t)
		a pinch of salt
20	g	cocoa (50 ml) (4 Tsp)
75	ml	milk (6 Tsp)

Method:
Melt the butter in a baking dish and sprinkle with the 60 g sugar. Slice the bananas and layer on top of the sugar. Beat the eggs, add 100 g sugar and beat until dissolved. Stir the vanilla essence and the soft butter into mixture, add the dry sifted ingredients, and milk alternately. Spoon the batter over the bananas and bake for 40 minutes in a moderate oven (180 °C — 350 °F). Leave for a few minutes, turn out onto a shallow dish and serve hot with cream or custard.
Mollie de Witt

Chocolate sauce for ice-cream
(Delicious)

1	tin	condensed milk (397 g)
2		large Bar One chocolates (53 g each)
8	ml	Milo (1½ t)

Method:
Pour condensed milk into a saucepan. Cut the Bar One chocolates into small pieces and add to the condensed milk. Stir continuously over a low heat until melted. Bring to the boil, remove and stir in Milo. Serve immediately over ice-cream.
* If a thinner sauce is desired, you can add a little cream.
Joey Pienaar

Praises from wicked men are reproaches.

Bread pudding

500	ml	breadcrumbs (2 c)
1	ℓ	hot milk
12,5	ml	margarine (1 Tsp)
2		eggs
60	ml	sugar (¼ c)
5	ml	vanilla essence (1 t)

Method:
Soak bread in milk. Stir in butter and leave to cool. Beat eggs, sugar and essence and add to bread mixture. Bake at 180 °C (350 °F) until brown.

Sauce:

250	ml	sugar (1 c)
125	g	margarine
1		egg
25	ml	boiling water (2 Tsp)
2	ml	vanilla essence (½ t)

Method:
Beat thoroughly. Pour over baked pudding and return pudding to the oven for a few minutes.
Mollie de Witt

There is no peace unto the wicked.

Bread pudding
(6 helpings)

50	g	butter (50 ml) (4 Tsp)
750	ml	hot milk (3 c)
3		eggs, beaten
100	g	sugar (125 ml) (½ c)
		a pinch of salt
		grated peel of 1 lemon
		or
5	ml	vanilla essence (1 t)
5	ml	cinnamon (1 t)
4		slices bread, 10 mm thick and diced

Method:
Melt the butter in the hot milk and mix with the egg, sugar, salt and flavouring. Arrange the bread in a greased ovenproof dish, pour the egg and milk over and bake for 30 min in a moderate oven (180 °C — 350 °F).

Variations:
Bread pudding with meringue
Separate the eggs. Use the yolks and 60 g (75 ml) (6 Tsp) sugar in the mixture and prepare as for bread pudding. Beat the egg whites until stiff and add 40 g (50 ml) (4 Tsp) sugar. Dot the pudding with apricot jam after baking for 25 minutes and then spoon the meringue on top. Reduce the heat to 160 °C (325 °F) and bake for about 15 minutes until the meringue is golden brown.
Joey Pienaar

Wickedness is always easier than virtue.

Baked sago pudding
(6 helpings)

140	g	sago (200 ml) (± ¾ c)
750	ml	milk (3 c)
100	g	sugar (125 ml) (½ c)
		a pinch of salt
2	ml	almond essence
25	ml	butter (2 Tsp)
2		eggs, separated
50	ml	apricot jam (4 Tsp)
40	g	sugar (50 ml) (4 Tsp) for egg white

Method:
Rinse the sago and heat slowly in the milk. Boil over low heat until transluscent. Add the 100 g (125 ml) sugar, salt, essence and butter and stir in the beaten egg yolks. Pour into a greased baking dish and dot with apricot jam. Beat the egg whites until stiff and add 40 g (50 ml) sugar and spoon the meringue on top of the pudding to form small peaks. Bake approximately 20-25 min in a moderate oven (180 °C — 350 °F) until done and the meringue is golden brown. Serve hot or cold.
Joey Pienaar

A lady's heart doesn't agree with a beggar's purse.

Quick fruit pudding
(8 helpings)

500	ml	self-raising flour (2 c)
10	ml	bicarbonate of soda (2 t) (mixed with a little milk)
250	ml	sugar (1 c)
2		eggs, beaten
1	tin	fruit cocktail (410 g)

Method:
Mix all the ingredients well. Pour the mixture into a greased dish and bake 30-40 min in a moderate oven (180 °C — 350 °F).

Sauce:

190	ml	sugar (¾ c)
190	ml	coconut (¾ c)
190	ml	evaporated milk (¾ c)
5	ml	vanilla essence (1 t)
30	ml	butter (2 heaped Tsp)
		pinch of salt

Method:
Mix the ingredients for the sauce and boil for 2 min. Pour the hot sauce over the pudding on removing it from the oven.
Ina Steyn

Begin at the beginning, go on to the end, and STOP.

It is desire that engenders belief.

Rusks and bread

Rusks

First step: 07h00

4	c	lukewarm water
2	Tsp	maizena
2	Tsp	sugar
1	t	salt
1	Tsp	raisins
2		cakes of compressed yeast

Pour into large bottle

Second step: 07h05

Boil together

250	g	margarine
3½	c	sugar for sweet rusks
		or 3 c sugar (less sweet)
2	c	milk

Leave to cool until lukewarm and beat in 3 eggs.

Method:
Third step: 08h00

Remove raisins from bottle and pour both mixtures into a basin. Add 2,5 kg flour and 1 dsp salt to the mixture in the kneading-pan and knead for about 20 min. Rub a little margarine on your hands occasionally while kneading. Cover, but first put a plastic bag which has been cut open over the top of the dough. This prevents a hard layer forming on top of the dough. Leave to rise until twice the original size. Knock back, shape into buns or rolls and place next to each other in a greased pan. Leave the rusks in a warm place to rise until double their size.

Fourth step: approx 16h00

Bake for ± 1 hour at 180 °C (350 °F). Remember to place a sheet of aluminium foil over the rusks after ½ hour in oven and bake until done.

Joey Pienaar

The beauty of the world is of laughter and anguish.

Buttermilk rusks

6		cups flour
2		eggs, whisked
± 500	ml	buttermilk or sour milk
6	Tsp	baking powder (heaped)
1	c	sugar
250	g	margarine
		a pinch of salt

Method:
Rub margarine into the flour, baking powder and sugar with your fingertips. Add eggs. Mix with buttermilk and knead slightly. Shape into balls and place into a greased pan. Bake for 1 hour at approximately 165 °C (325 °F). Break into neat pieces and dry.
Joey Pienaar

All-bran rusks
(Always a success)

2	c	sugar
2	c	buttermilk
4½	c	All-Bran or Raisin Bran (1 large pkt)
3		eggs
1	kg	self-raising flour (2 pkts)
500	g	margarine
1	t	salt

Method:
Soften margarine. Mix buttermilk, sugar and eggs thoroughly. Add to softened margarine. Add dry ingredients and mix. Place in pan. Bake for 45 minutes at 180 °C (350 °F). Once cooled, cut with a sharp knife and dry.
DELICIOUS!
Joey Pienaar

Beauty is only skin deep.

Quick whole-wheat bread

Yeast:
10	ml	dry yeast (2 t)
10	ml	sugar (2 t)
125	ml	lukewarm water (½c)

Method:
Dissolve the yeast in the lukewarm water to which the sugar has been added. Leave until mixture becomes frothy.

Bread dough:
5x250	ml	whole-wheat flour (5 c)
750	ml	flour (3 c)
15	ml	syrup or honey (3 t)
1		beaten egg
15	ml	salt (3 t)
15	ml	melted butter (3 t)
750	ml	lukewarm water (3 c)

Method:
Mix flour well. Beat egg, water, syrup, butter and salt thoroughly. Add flour. Add yeast. Stir with a wooden spoon and pour into pans. Flatten the dough with your hand. Allow to rise for 20 min. Bake at 220 °C (425 °F) for 45 min.
Joey Pienaar

Truth will bear exposure as well as beauty.

Sweet rusks

Yeast:
1	tin	condensed milk
2	c	hot water
4		eggs (thoroughly whisked)
2		cakes compressed yeast
4	c	flour

Method:
Mix everything thoroughly and cover to keep warm. Leave to rise until frothy.

Dough:
2,5	kg	flour
3	c	sugar
1	Tsp	salt
250	g	margarine
4	c	lukewarm water

Method:
Rub margarine into flour mixture. Make a well in the centre of the flour, pour in the yeast and knead with 4 c lukewarm water. Cover to keep warm and allow to rise for 1 hour. Punch down and cover again to keep warm. Leave dough to rise to the top of the bowl. Place buns in greased pans. Let the dough rise to fill the pans and bake for 1¼ hours at 160 °C (325 °F).

Esther Coetsee

Behave in life as if at a banquet.

Delicious slightly coarse bread

Yeast:
15	ml	dry yeast (3 t)
10	ml	sugar (2 t)
125	ml	lukewarm water (½ c)

Method:
Dissolve dry yeast in lukewarm water to which sugar has been added. Leave aside until mixture is quite frothy.

Bread dough:
10x250	ml	flour (10 c)
500	ml	whole-wheat flour (2 c)
15	ml	salt (3 t)
25	ml	butter (2 Tsp)
25	ml	milk powder (2 Tsp)
6x250	ml	lukewarm water (or enough for mixing) (6 c)

Method:
Mix flour, salt and milk powder. Add yeast mixture. Rub your hands with butter and knead thoroughly. Leave to rise overnight. Place in pans and leave to rise until double the size. Bake for 1 hr at 200 °C (400 °F). Rub a little butter over the top of the bread whilst still warm.
Joey Pienaar

Milk bread
(This recipe is suitable for twisted bread and breadrolls)

Yeast:
15	ml	dry yeast (3 t)
15	ml	sugar (3 t)
125	ml	lukewarm water (½ c)

Bread is the staff of life.

224

Cake for a king – the dark fruit cake which won a well-earned first prize at the Pretoria Show (p 258)

This page was sponsored by Oranje Potteries tel (014132 – 391)

To make this chocolate cake (p 266) even nicer, try preparing it with a liqueur-flavoured cream. (Another winner at the Pretoria Show)

Method:
Dissolve yeast in lukewarm water to which sugar has been added. Leave aside until frothy.

Bread dough:
10x250	ml	flour (10 c)
125	ml	milk powder (½ c)
12,5	ml	salt (1 Tsp)
125	g	margarine
75	ml	sugar (6 Tsp)
750	ml	lukewarm water (approximately) (3 c)

Method:
Mix flour, milk powder and salt and rub the margarine into mixture. Dissolve the sugar in lukewarm water and add with the yeast to the flour. Knead thoroughly and leave to rise for 2 hrs. Knock back and leave to rise for another hour. Shape the loaves and allow to rise to double the original size. Brush the whisked egg over the top and bake at 200 °C (400 °F) for 30-40 min.
Mollie de Witt

Yoghurt bread

4	c	Nutty Wheat
2	bot	plain yoghurt
30	ml	brown sugar (2½ Tsp)
10	ml	bicarbonate of soda (2 t)
30	ml	oil (2½ Tsp)
½	t	salt

Method:
Mix all ingredients and place in a pan. Bake in a moderate oven at 180 °C (350 °F) for 35 min. Sprinkle a handful of sunflower seeds over the top before baking. (Optional)
Brenda Vlotman

The bread never falls but on its buttered side.

Oil rusks
(Easy and quick)

5x500	g	self-raising flour
1	ℓ	milk
500	ml	sugar (2 c)
500	ml	cooking oil (2 c)
2		extra large eggs
1 Tsp		salt

(Makes three large pans of rusks)

Method:
Mix milk and sugar thoroughly in a large mixing bowl. Beat the cooking oil, salt and eggs until mixed, add to milk mixture and beat until mixed. Gradually stir in self-raising flour with a wooden spoon. Mix by hand to a reasonably firm dough. Shape into buns and place close together in the well-greased bread pans. Leave to rise for 15 min. Heat oven to 180 °C (350 °F). Bake the rusks for 1 hr on the centre shelf of the oven; cover the rusks in the pan with aluminium foil or brown paper if the crusts brown before baking time expires. Leave rusks to cool. Divide gently with a fork into portions and dry.

Joey Pienaar

Brown rusks
(Easy and delicious)

450	g	(4x250 ml) whole-wheat flour (4 c)
400	g	(750 ml) flour (3 c)
300	g	soft brown sugar (1½ c)
250	g	(4x250 ml) All Bran breakfast flakes (4 c)
160	g	(2x250 ml) oats (2 c)
50	ml	baking powder (4 Tsp)
10	ml	bicarbonate of soda (2 t)
7	ml	salt (1 heaped t)

Live one day at a time, use it as much as you can, forget about yesterday, and live for tomorrow — Deon Viljoen.

500	g	margarine (melted)
750	ml	cold water (3 c)
30	ml	vinegar (white) (2¼ Tsp)
1	c	seedless raisins

Method:

Preheat oven to 180 °C (350 °F). Grease rusk pans. Mix all the dry ingredients and seedless raisins in a dish. Mix margarine, cold water and vinegar. Mix the dry ingredients with the liquid ingredients. The dough is reasonably soft. Put dough into pans. Flatten with your hand to approximately 4 cm high. Do not make rolls. Bake for 1 hr. Turn out on a cooling rack and leave for at least 12 hrs to cool; this is important as the rusks will crumble if not left for the required time. Slice lengthwise approximately 2½ cm and dry in the normal way. Makes about 5 dozen rusks. (You must try it.)
Joey Pienaar

Brown bread

Mixture:

4	Tsp	brown sugar
4	c	lukewarm water
4	t	dry yeast
4	Tsp	oil
5	c	Nutty Wheat
3	c	white bread flour or brown bread meal
3	t	salt
1	c	whole-wheat

Method:

Mix and knead. Let it rise for ± 2 hrs. Knead and place in greased pans. Let it rise again and bake for 1¼ hrs at ± 350 °F (180 °C).
Brenda Vlotman

One reaches a point in life where you cannot turn back and follow the foot tracks from where you came — A Welsh philosophy.

Coarse bread

4	c	whole-wheat meal
2	c	bread flour
1	t	salt
		wheat-germ (optional)
		sunflower seeds (optional)
1		cake or 1 t dry yeast
1	t	sugar
1½	c	lukewarm water
1	t	honey

Method:
Dissolve yeast and sugar in ½ c lukewarm water. Let it rise for 15 min. Mix all dry ingredients and knead with dissolved yeast until the mixture is elastic and no longer clings to your hands. Fill a pan half-full and allow to rise. Cover with a blanket. Bake for 1 hr at 180 °C (350 °F).

Joey Pienaar

Bitterness is the first step to a long and lonely journey.

White bread

1		yeast cake
4	c	lukewarm water, boiled and cooled until lukewarm
3	lb	flour (12 c)
1¼	Tsp	salt
1½	c	sugar

Method:

Soak the yeast in a cup of lukewarm water. Add the sugar and mix well. Add enough flour to form a liquid paste (about 1-1½ c). Beat with a wooden spoon until smooth and elastic, cover and leave overnight 9-10 hrs in a warm place. Put the remaining flour into a large mixing bowl the following day. Make a well in the centre and add the yeast. Dissolve the salt in 2 c of the lukewarm water and knead before using the last cup of lukewarm water. Knead the dough, i.e. flour, yeast and water, until smooth and till it no longer sticks to your hands. Add the remaining water if necessary and knead again until the dough is smooth and elastic. Put the dough into the mixing bowl, rub melted butter over the top and cover with plastic. Leave in a warm place to rise until double the volume. Knead lightly to spread the bubbles evenly. Place the dough in three large pans. Leave to rise again until double the volume. Bake about 1 hr at 350 °F (180 °C). Place brown paper over pans after 15 min. This will prevent the bread from browning too quickly.

Joey Pienaar

Everything worthwhile in life is worth fighting for.

Buttermilk rusks (self-raising flour)

1	kg	self-raising flour
5	ml	baking powder (1 t)
10	ml	salt (2 t)
2		eggs, beaten
190	ml	sugar (¾ c)
190	g	margarine, melted
500	ml	buttermilk (2 c)

Method:
Sift the flour, baking powder and salt. Beat eggs, buttermilk and sugar. Add the egg mixture to the dry ingredients. Knead lightly and add the butter, a little at a time, whilst kneading. Shape the dough into buns and place in breadpans. Bake immediately at 180 °C (350 °F) for 50 min. Turn out, break into portions and dry.
Joey Pienaar

Breakfast rolls

1,5	kg	flour
250	g	boiled, mashed potato
2		yeast cakes
125	g	butter (melted)
10	ml	sugar (2 t)
10	ml	salt (2 t)
2		eggs
1		small tin Ideal milk
		add lukewarm water to make up to 500 ml

Pride is something that causes you to laugh when deep inside you are actually weeping — Ena Murray.

Method:

Mix yeast, sugar, lukewarm water and 250 ml flour and allow to rise for 30 min. Add the rest of the ingredients and knead thoroughly. Allow to rise. Knead or roll dough into rolls. Allow to rise. Brush with beaten egg and bake for 10-15 min at 425 °F (220 °C).

Joey Pienaar

"Vetkoek"

(Delicious)

500	ml	lukewarm water (2 c)
2	t	sugar
2	t	dry yeast (level)
5x250	ml	flour (5 c)
10	ml	salt (2 t)
25	ml	oil (2 Tsp)

Method:

Stir sugar into lukewarm water and add yeast. Leave to rise until the yeast floats on top. Sift the flour and salt. Add oil to yeast, mix with the flour and knead thoroughly. Leave to rise for 50 min. Roll into vetkoek shape. Place on greased sheet (use oil). Cover with plastic and allow to rise for 20 min. Fry in hot oil till brown.

Joey Pienaar

No legacy is so rich as honesty.

Whole-wheat bread

450	g	whole-wheat meal (875 ml) (3½ c)
200	g	flour (375 ml) (1½ c)
7	ml	salt (1¼ t)
10	ml	dry yeast (2 t)
		or
1		(20 g) compressed yeast cake, crumbled
450	ml	lukewarm water (1¾ c)
50	ml	cooking oil (4 Tsp)
10	ml	golden syrup (2 t)
10	ml	vinegar (2 t)

Method:

Mix flour and salt in a large mixing bowl. Dissolve yeast in 60 ml (¼ c) of the lukewarm water. Mix the rest of the water with the oil, syrup and vinegar. Add the yeast mixture and mix well. Make a well in the centre of the flour mixture, add the liquid, mix and knead thoroughly. Cover while still warm and allow to rise to double the volume. Knock back and shape into a loaf. Place in a greased, medium-sized breadpan. Let it rise to the top of the pan. Bake ± 1 hr at 180 °C (350 °F).

Joey Pienaar

Laughter makes the world go round — An old American saying.

Salad and salad dressings

233

Banana candles
(Makes 6 helpings)

3		bananas
25	ml	lemon juice (2 Tsp)
6		pineapple rings
25	ml	mayonnaise (2 Tsp)
3		glacé cherries

Method:
Cut the bananas in half (crosswise) and dip into lemon juice. Arrange each piece upright in a pineapple ring. Spoon mayonnaise along the sides of the bananas. Fix a halved cherry onto each with a toothpick. It resembles a burning candle in a candle stick. Place each "candle" on a plate with lettuce leaves.
Joey Pienaar

Mixed salad
(Makes 2 helpings)

2		cooked potatoes, diced
1		small cucumber, diced
1	c	cooked peas
1		slice pineapple, coarsely chopped
		banana, sliced
		a pinch of cayenne pepper
1	t	salt
½	c	mayonnaise
		lettuce leaves
½	t	Aromat

Method:
Mix all the vegetables and fruit. Season with salt, pepper and cayenne pepper. Moisten with mayonnaise. Place a spoonful on each lettuce leaf. Garnish with slices of tomato and serve with more mayonnaise.
Joey Pienaar

Sometimes the hardest punishment of all comes from those who love us most — F.P. Koekemoer

Filled peach halves

8		canned peach halves
250	g	cooked ham, shredded
150	ml	mayonnaise (12 Tsp)
25	ml	finely chopped parsley (2 Tsp)
25	ml	finely chopped gherkins (2 Tsp)
5	ml	Aromat
		salt and pepper to taste
8		lettuce leaves

Method:
Drain the peach halves. Mix the ham, mayonnaise, parsley, gherkins, Aromat, salt and pepper. Place the mixture into the peach halves and refrigerate. Serve on lettuce leaves.
Joey Pienaar

Carrot and pineapple salad
(Delicious)

1	c	carrots
½	c	canned pineapple chunks, finely chopped
		or
½	c	fresh pineapple chunks, cut into small pieces
1		tomato, cut into pieces
1	pkt	orange jelly
		orange juice

Method:
Dissolve the jelly in ¾ c boiling orange juice diluted with water. Add other ingredients. Rinse a pyrex dish with cold water, pour mixture into it and allow to set. Turn out onto a platter and garnish with halved pinapple rings with a red cherry in the centre of each pineapple ring.
Joey Pienaar

Sometimes we travel so far in search of happiness when in actual fact it is right before our very eyes — Ella Marie.

Bean salad ("Sousboontjies")

1	c	sugar beans
4	Tsp	vinegar
2	Tsp	butter
2	Tsp	sugar
1	t	salt
½	t	pepper

Method:
Rinse the beans and soak overnight. Drain and boil in fresh water until nearly tender. Add other ingredients. Bring to the boil again and stir to a juicy mixture.
Joey Pienaar

Spiced beetroot

2	c	vinegar
2	c	water
½	t	ground cloves
		a stick of cinnamon
1	t	whole pimento
2		bay leaves
		salt and pepper to taste

Method:
Tie spices in a cloth and boil in the vinegar and water for 15 min. Pour the liquid over 1 pkt red jelly, pour mixture over grated beetroot and leave to set.
Mollie de Witt

Whether life crushes or polishes you, depends upon the material that you are made of.

Wheat salad

200	g	pearl wheat (250 ml) (1 c)
125	ml	mayonnaise (½ c)
3	ml	mustard powder (½ t)
1		medium onion
1		cooking apple
1		green pepper
410	g	peach slices (1 tin)
		salt and pepper to taste
1	t	Aromat

Method:
Boil wheat until tender. Pour into a strainer and rinse with cold water. Drain well. Mix mayonnaise and mustard. Chop onion, dice apple, slice green pepper and halve peach slices. Place all the ingredients into a salad bowl. Season with salt, pepper and Aromat and mix everything lightly with two forks. Can be prepared the previous evening.
Joey Pienaar

Curried pineapple salad

Cut 1 large pineapple into small pieces. Boil in 1 c sugar and water until tender. Mix 2 cups of white wine and 2 Tsp curry and bring to the boil. Thicken with 6 t maizena. Pour over the pineapple.
Joey Pienaar

Love is like a rose, the joy of all the earth.

Potato salad

6		potatoes, cooked
6		stuffed olives
		salt and pepper to taste
		parsley
8		rashers bacon
2		hard-boiled eggs
		salad cream
5	ml	Aromat (1 t)

Method:
Dice the potatoes. Fry bacon and cut into small pieces. Chop eggs finely, pour salad cream over and arrange the olives on top.
Joey Pienaar

Green salad

250	g	fresh or frozen green beans
250	g	fresh or frozen broccoli
1		onion, peeled and sliced
½		English cucumber, sliced
1		large Granny Smith apple, core removed and sliced
1		green pepper, seeded and sliced
		French salad dressing

Method:
String the beans if fresh beans are used. Boil in a little salt water until tender, drain and leave to cool. Wash broccoli and boil in a little salt water until tender. Drain, cut into pieces and cool. Mix beans, broccoli, onion, cucumber, apple and green pepper and add French salad dressing to taste. Chill well before serving.
Joey Pienaar

I never think of the future, it comes quick enough — Albert Einstein.

Carrot salad

1	kg	carrots
2		onions
1		green pepper, seeded and cut into rings

Method:
Boil carrots until half-cooked (not soft), rinse under cold water and allow to cool thoroughly. Place ingredients in layers ending with carrots.

Dressing:

82	g	tomato soup (1 pkt)
250	ml	water (1 c)
200	ml	vinegar (¾ c)
80	ml	Worcestershire sauce (⅓ c)
125	ml	cooking oil (½ c)
250	ml	sugar (1 c)
7	ml	mustard powder (1 heaped t)
		salt and pepper to taste
5	ml	Aromat (1 t)

Method:
Boil the ingredients for 2 minutes and whilst boiling pour over salad (allow to soak well). Cover and leave in refrigerator for at least 2 days before use.
Ina Steyn

When one shuts one eye, one does not hear anything.

Easy onion salad
(Makes 4-6 helpings)

750	g	onions, skinned
100	ml	condensed milk (8 Tsp)
5	ml	mustard powder (1 t)
100	ml	tomato sauce (8 Tsp)
100	ml	white vinegar (8 Tsp)

Method:
Boil onions in salt water until tender. Drain and cool. Mix condensed milk with mustard. Add tomato sauce and vinegar and whisk well. Place onions in a salad bowl and pour the sauce over.
Joey Pienaar

Bean salad

1	tin	beans in tomato sauce
1	tin	sliced green beans
1	tin	butter beans
½		chopped green pepper
1		chopped onion

Mix the above ingredients

⅓	c	sugar
⅓	c	vinegar
⅓	c	oil
3	t	sweet basil
1	t	mustard powder
½	t	Aromat

Mix well.

Method:
Drain the green beans and butter beans. Mix all ingredients thoroughly.
Joey Pienaar

Advice is like snow. The softer it falls, the deeper it sinks —
Samuel Coleridge.

Hot wheat salad
(Delicious — makes 6-8 helpings)

300	g	pearl wheat (375 ml) (1½ c)
3		large onions, chopped
25	ml	cooking oil (2 Tsp)
300	g	fresh mushrooms
1		chicken stock cube, crumbled
250	ml	boiling water (1 c)
		salt and pepper to taste

Method:
Rinse wheat and boil in sufficient salt water until tender. Drain well. Fry onion in cooking oil until tender. Wipe the mushrooms with a damp cloth, slice and fry with the onion until tender. Mix the wheat and onion mixture and pour into a medium sized, greased casserole (with a lid). Dissolve stock in the boiling water and pour over the wheat mixture. Season to taste with salt and pepper. Cover and bake for 40 min in a preheated oven at 180 °C (350 °F). Stir and serve hot.
Mollie de Witt

Sweet melon salad
(Delicious)

2	c	diced sweet melon
1	c	peach cubes
1	c	diced cucumber
190	ml	yoghurt (¾ c)
		a pinch of mustard and salt to taste

Method:
Mix all ingredients and serve on lettuce leaves.

Wrong doing is the worst misfortune that can befall a man —
Socrates.

Apple salad

2		red-skinned apples
1	c	grated cheddar cheese
1	Tsp	grated onion
1	Tsp	dried parsley
		salt and pepper to taste
		mayonnaise

Method:
Core apples after rinsing and dice (do not peel). Mix all the ingredients and moisten the mixture with mayonnaise. Serve cold. This salad is healthy and delicious with curry or a peri-peri dish.
Francis Schoeman

Curried peach or banana salad

Slice 3 large onions. Fry in 1 Tsp fat, add a ¼ or ½ green pepper, chopped (optional). Fry with the onion until pepper changes colour. Add 3 c water and boil until onion is tender and transluscent.

Take:

3	Tsp	flour (level)
12,5	ml	curry powder (or to taste) (1 Tsp)
6	Tsp	brown sugar

Method:
Blend flour, curry powder and sugar with ½ c water and add ½ c vinegar. Stir into onion mixture and boil for ± 3 min. Leave to cool. Add 1 medium tin sliced and drained canned peaches or 8 sliced bananas.
Ester Kleinhans

Our happiness in this world depends on the affections we are able to inspire.

Peach and rice salad

1		large tin canned peaches, chopped
2	c	cooked rice
¾	c	raisins
½		green pepper, chopped

Salad dressing:

2	c	mayonnaise
2	Tsp	chutney
1-2	Tsp	curry powder

Method:
Mix the salad dressing and blend with rest of the ingredients.
Joey Pienaar

French salad dressing

100	ml	salad oil (8 Tsp)
2	ml	pepper
5	ml	salt (1 t)
50	ml	vinegar (4 Tsp)

Method:
Place all the ingredients in a jar with a tightly fitting lid. Shake well.

Variations:
Use lemon juice instead of vinegar.
Add 5 ml (1 t) finely grated onion, or a crushed clove of garlic to the vinegar. Soak for 1 hr. Strain the vinegar through a sieve before using.
Add one of the following:
5 ml Worcestershire sauce, 12,5 ml chutney, 2 ml curry powder, a pinch of cayenne pepper, 12,5 ml sweet or sour cream, 12,5 ml cream cheese, 12,5 ml lemon juice or 12,5 ml orange juice.
Joey Pienaar

Life is not where you are but in the direction you move.

Dried fruit salad
(Delicious — 20 people)

1	kg	mixed dried fruit
100	g	chopped nuts
8		bananas

Method:
Soak the fruit in cold water for about 1 hr. Boil until tender and leave to cool. Cut the fruit into smaller pieces and place a layer of fruit, a layer of sliced banana, dressing and nuts until all ingredients have been used. Place in refrigerator before serving.

Dressing:

1		small tin evaporated milk (cold)
1		small tin condensed milk
		salt and pepper to taste
125	ml	vinegar ($\frac{1}{2}$ c)
10	ml	mustard (2 t)
125	ml	oil ($\frac{1}{2}$ c)

Method:
Whip the evaporated milk until stiff and fold into the condensed milk. Mix the vinegar, oil, mustard, salt and pepper and fold into milk mixture. Leave to set.

Joey Pienaar

Salad dressing
(With evaporated milk)

100	ml	evaporated milk (8 Tsp)
25	ml	vinegar or lemon juice (2 Tsp)
1	ml	pepper
5	ml	salt (1 t)
5	ml	sugar (1 t)
100	ml	salad oil (8 Tsp)

Economising for the purpose of being independent is one of the soundest indications of manly character — Sir Michael.

¼		garlic clove, chopped
50	ml	chutney (4 Tsp)
50	ml	finely chopped green pepper (4 Tsp)
20	ml	grated onion (4 t)

Method:
Place all ingredients in a jar with a tightly fitting lid and shake well.
Joey Pienaar

Moulded salad
(Sufficient for 6-8 people)

80	g	pkt lime jelly
125	ml	boiling water (½ c)
1		large cucumber (finely grated)
1		large gherkin (finely grated)
10	ml	onion juice (2 t)
12,5	ml	lemon juice (1 Tsp)
125	ml	Salanaise (½ c)
		salt and pepper to taste
10	ml	gelatine (2 t)
20	ml	water (4 t)
12,5	ml	thick cream (1 Tsp)
		few drops green food colouring

Method:
Dissolve jelly in the boiling water and cool. Add cucumber, gherkin, onion juice, lemon juice, Salanaise, salt and pepper and mix. Soak gelatine in 20 ml water and dissolve over hot water. Add to rest of the mixture with the cream and mix. If preferred, the colour can be improved with a little food colouring. Place into a large mould or small individual moulds and place in refrigerator to set. Turn out and serve.
Mollie de Witt

Look sometimes through your brother's specs and the world changes colour.

Boiled salad dressing

25	ml	butter (2 Tsp)
25	ml	flour (2 Tsp)
5	ml	salt (1 t)
5	ml	dry mustard (1 t)
12,5	ml	sugar (1 Tsp)
		a pinch of cayenne pepper
190	ml	milk, scalded (¾ c)
1	whole	egg
		or
2		egg yolks
50	ml	vinegar (4 Tsp)

Method:
Melt the butter in a saucepan and add the dry ingredients. Slowly add the milk and stir continuously until the mixture is smooth. Boil for about 3 min. Add a little of the boiling mixture to the beaten egg, stir well and pour back into the saucepan. Heat slowly to boiling point while stirring continuously. Remove from stove and add vinegar.
HINT: This dressing can be kept for a considerable time in a sealed jar.

Variations:
Add 50 ml full cream milk or fresh cream to the 250 ml salad dressing. Mix 250 ml mayonnaise with 250 ml salad dressing. Serve over potato salad.
Joey Pienaar

A fool may ask more questions in an hour than a wise man can answer in seven years — Madame Burnett.

Condensed milk salad dressing

1		egg yolk
1	tin	condensed milk (397 g)
5	ml	dry mustard (1 t)
3	ml	salt
1	ml	pepper
50	ml	vinegar (4 Tsp)
50	ml	salad oil or melted butter (4 Tsp)

Method:
Beat the egg yolks thoroughly. Add all the ingredients and mix well. Leave a while to thicken.
HINT: The salad dressing can be diluted with milk. More lemon juice or vinegar can be added.
Joey Pienaar

Potato salad
(hot)

6		medium sized potatoes, boiled and peeled
250	g	bacon, chopped
2		large onions, finely chopped
3		tomatoes, finely chopped
1	c	cream, slightly whipped
1½	c	grated cheddar cheese

Method:
Fry bacon, onions and tomatoes well. Slice potatoes and line an ovenproof dish with a layer. Add a layer of the bacon, onion and tomato over the potatoes and top with a layer of cheese. Repeat procedure ending with the cheese. Pour cream evenly over top and bake in oven at 180 °C (350 °F) until cheese and cream layer have baked through.
Joey Pienaar

A good mind possesses a kingdom — Seneca.

Salad dressing

1		egg
25	ml	sugar (2 Tsp)
2	ml	salt
3	ml	dry mustard
50	ml	vinegar (4 Tsp)
25	ml	thin cream (2 Tsp)

Method:
Beat the egg in the top half of a double boiler. Add the sugar, salt, mustard and vinegar and mix well. Heat over boiling water until the mixture thickens. Stir occasionally. Allow to cool slightly. Stir in the cream.
Joey Pienaar

Banana salad dressing
(Delicious with barbecue)

3		eggs
125	ml	white vinegar (½ c)
250	ml	sugar (1 c)
10	ml	mustard powder (2 t)
		a pinch of salt
250	ml	evaporated milk (1 c)

Method:
Beat the eggs, vinegar, sugar, mustard powder and salt in a saucepan until well mixed. Stir over medium heat until thick. Remove from stove when it starts boiling. Allow to cool. Add the evaporated milk and mix. Pour in a jar and store in refrigerator until needed. For a salad, slice a few bananas and pour the dressing over.
Joey Pienaar

Once a task has begun, half the work is done.

Moulded carrot and pineapple salad

1	tin	crushed pineapple (410 g)
1	pkt	lemon jelly (80 g)
100	g	white sugar (125 ml) (½ c)
1	ml	salt
200	g	finely grated carrots (500 ml) (2 c)
125	ml	cream (½ c)

Method:

Drain the pineapple and add water to juice to make up to 250 ml (1 c). Bring to the boil and dissolve jelly. Allow to cool till thick but not firmly set. Beat the jelly until frothy. Add the sugar gradually. Mix the pineapple and carrots and fold lightly into the jelly. Beat the cream until stiff and fold in. Rinse a salad mould with cold water. Pour in the salad mixture. Place in refrigerator to set.

To serve: Ease the edges of the salad away from the mould carefully. Place the mould into hot water for a few seconds. Unmould onto a wet salad platter. Garnish the salad as desired. Remove from refrigerator just before serving. Makes 6-8 helpings.

Joey Pienaar

When the going gets tough, the tough get going — Billy Ocean.

Macaroni salad with a beer dressing

(Delicious with barbecued meat or cold meat —
makes 8 helpings)

2	ℓ	water
10	ml	salt (2 t)
5	ml	cooking oil (1 t)
300	g	regular or elbow macaroni pieces (500 ml) (2 c)
1		small pineapple
3-4		bananas
1	tin	whole pitted litchis, drained (565 g)
1		small tin green peas, drained (225 g)

Beer dressing

125	ml	beer (½ c)
125	ml	mayonnaise (½ c)

Method:

Allow water to boil rapidly, add the salt and cooking oil. Slowly add the macaroni; water must continue to boil. Stir occasionally and let it boil rapidly for 12 min. Drain and cool. Peel the pineapple and dice. Peel the bananas and slice. Place macaroni, pineapple, banana, litchis and peas into a large salad bowl. Whip beer and mayonnaise until mixed. Pour over ingredients and mix lightly with two large forks. Refrigerate.

Joey Pienaar

Being is the great explainer.

Curried rice salad

750	ml	cooked rice (3 c)
125	ml	mayonnaise (½ c)
12,5	ml	chutney (1 Tsp)
1		red pepper
1		green pepper
1		onion (chopped)
125	ml	seedless raisins (½ c)
5	ml	curry powder (1 t)

Method:
Mix mayonnaise, curry and chutney. Seed peppers and chop finely. Add to first mixture and mix all ingredients thoroughly, cool in refrigerator before serving.
Mollie de Witt

Banana salad mould

1	tin	condensed milk
4		large bananas
1	t	dry mustard powder
1	Tsp	gelatine, soaked in ⎫
¼	c	cold water ⎬
½	c	boiled water ⎭
		(add to gelatine)
¼	c	vinegar

Method:
Slice bananas and mix all ingredients. Place in refrigerator.
Joey Pienaar

Do unto others what you would like done unto you.

Bread salad

Cut bread into 1½ cm cubes and fry in deep oil the previous day. Leave uncovered. Bread cubes can also be kept in the freezer.

Dressing:

4		eggs
375	ml	sugar (1½ c)
7	ml	dry mustard (1¼ t)
250	ml	white vinegar (1 c)
		salt and pepper
250	ml	cheese cubes (1 c)

Method:

Beat ingredients (except cheese) together for 5 min. Boil rapidly and stir continuously. Allow to cool. ± ½ hr before serving add 125 ml (½ c) fresh cream and 125 ml (½ c) mayonnaise. Mix bread and cheese. Pour dressing over just before serving.

Joey Pienaar

Moulded carrot salad

1	pkt	pineapple jelly
1		small tin crushed pineapple (410 g)
1	c	cream
1	c	finely grated cheddar cheese
2	c	finely grated carrots

Method:

Dissolve jelly in 1 c water and add the other ingredients. Rinse a salad bowl or mould with cold water or spray with a non-stick cooking spray. Pour the salad mixture in and place in refrigerator to set; preferably leave overnight in refrigerator.

Zena Conradie

Your path has been laid for you.

Cakes

253

Chiffon cake

250	g	flour (2 rounded c)
125	g	sugar (½ c + 2 Tsp)
8	ml	baking powder (1½ t)
4		eggs, separated
3	ml	salt (½ t)
1,5	ml	cream of tartar (¼ t)
125	ml	oil (½ c)
150	ml	water (½ c)
5	ml	lemon juice (1 t)

Method:
Sift the flour, 65 g of the sugar and baking powder. Make a well in the centre and add the oil, water, lemon juice and egg yolks. Mix until smooth. Beat egg whites, the rest of the sugar, salt and cream of tartar until stiff and fold into the batter. Pour mixture into an ungreased tube pan. Bake at 170 °C (340 °F) for 45-50 min. Invert to cool. Decorate with creamy white butter icing and toasted coconut.
Joey Pienaar

Chocolate cake

1½	c	water
4	Tsp	cocoa
½	c	oil

Boil and leave to cool.
Beat 4 eggs and 1½ c sugar thoroughly.

Add to egg mixture:

2	c	flour
4	t	baking powder

Add:
A pinch of salt and finally the cooled oil mixture. Bake at 180 °C (350 °F) for about ½ hr or test with a skewer.

Grace is the essence of charm.

White fruit cake
(Highest award — Pretoria Show)

4	c	flour (heaped)
500	g	margarine
3	c	sugar
12		eggs, separated
2	t	baking powder
1	Tsp	lemon juice
1	t	almond essence
1½	kg	blanched sultanas
125	g	mixed peel
125	g	flaked almonds
¼	t	ground ginger
250	g	cherries, finely chopped
250	g	glacé fruit, finely chopped
1	c	brandy
½	t	salt

Method:
Cream sugar and butter. Add salt and almond essence. Add egg yolks one at a time. Beat mixture well. Sift flour, baking powder and ground ginger. Wash the sultanas and drain well. Bake in a covered baking dish for 30 min at 130 °C (250 °F) until plump. Remove from oven. Cool until lukewarm. Now add all the fruit. Mix the flour with the butter mixture. Then add cooled fruit mixture and mix well. Then add the brandy and lemon juice, and finally fold in the stiffly beaten egg whites. Pour into two 23 cm pans lined with thick aluminium foil. Bake for 3 hrs at 150 °C (300 °F). After 3 hrs test the centre of the cake with a skewer, no raw batter must cling to the skewer. After the cake has cooled, pour ½ c brandy over and 2 days before use, another ½ c. brandy.

Mixture is enough for two 23 cm pans.

Joey Pienaar

Joyfulness is the sister of thankfulness.

Chiffon cake with oil

2	c	flour (500 ml)
1	c	milk (250 ml)
2	t	baking powder (10 ml)
1	c	sugar (250 ml)
⅓	c	cooking oil (80 ml)
¼	t	salt
4		eggs

Method:
Boil oil and milk. Sift the salt and flour (important not to add any other ingredients). Whisk eggs and sugar for 15 min. Add flour and salt. Mix well. Sprinkle the baking powder over the mixture and pour the hot milk over the top. Mix well. Bake ± 30 min at 180 °C (350 °F).
Dalene Jansen

Orange icing

2	t	grated orange rind
1½	Tsp	orange juice
¼	c	butter (60 ml)
		a pinch of salt
2½	c	icing sugar
1		egg yolk

Method:
Cream butter and margarine. Add egg yolk and salt and mix well. Mix the orange juice and rind. Add icing sugar and orange juice to butter and mix thoroughly. The mixture is sufficient for a large layer cake.
Joey Pienaar

What a better way of saying "I love you" than in a song — Nad.

Puff pastry jam tarts (p 274) attained the highest possible award at the Pretoria Show

Line your shelves with an array of delicious preserves – marmalade, fig, peach chutney, tomato preserve, etc (see from p 375)

This page was sponsored by Highveld Brokers tel
(012 – 325-2971)

Swiss roll
(Always a success)

4		eggs, separated
50	ml	cold water (4 Tsp)
250	ml	castor sugar (1 c)
250	ml	unsifted cake flour (1 c)
5	ml	baking powder (1 t)
		a pinch of salt
5	ml	vanilla essence (1 t)
150	ml	smooth jam (½ c + 2 Tsp)

Method:
Grease a swiss roll pan 30 x 45 cm, line with greaseproof paper and grease paper as well. Sprinkle with a little cake flour and shake the excess flour from the paper. Preheat oven to 200 °C (400 °F) and place shelf in the centre of the oven. Beat egg yolks, water and castor sugar until the mixture is pale yellow and has a spongy consistency. Sift the flour and baking powder and fold gradually with a wooden spoon into egg mixture. Beat egg whites and salt until it forms a peak when removing egg-beater. Stir a little of the egg whites into the yolk mixture and then fold the rest of the egg whites in. Pour batter into pan and spread evenly. Bake for 10 min. Turn out onto a damp cloth sprinkled with sugar. Remove the paper carefully and cut the short sides neatly with a sharp knife. Spread jam over the cake. Carefully roll the cake with the aid of the cloth. Cut the sides neatly and leave for at least 30 min on the cooling rack.

Mollie de Witt

Love should be as pure as the unspoiled beaches where we once first loved — Nad.

Dark fruit cake
(First prize — Pretoria Show)

4	c	flour, heaped (1 kg)
500	g	margarine
3	c	sugar (750 ml)
12		eggs, separated
2	Tsp	cinnamon (20 ml)
1	Tsp	instant coffee (10 ml)
2	Tsp	cocoa, heaped (20 ml)
1	t	bicarbonate of soda, dissolved in
1	Tsp	lemon juice just before it is added to mixture
1	t	almond essence (5 ml)
2	Tsp	apricot jam (20 ml)
1	c	brandy (250 ml)
½	t	salt
½	c	preserved ginger, finely chopped (optional)
250	g	dates, finely chopped
250	g	seedless raisins
250	g	currants
500	g	sultanas (1 lb)
125	g	mixed rind
125	g	flaked almonds
¼	t	ground cloves
¼	t	ginger
250	g	cherries, finely chopped
250	g	glacé fruit, ready-mixed (obtainable in boxes)

Method:
Cream sugar and butter. Add almond essence and salt. Add egg yolks one at a time. Beat mixture thoroughly. Mix all the spices with the flour. Wash sultanas, currants and raisins in water and drain. Bake in a covered oven dish for about ½ hr at 130 °C (260 °F) until plump. Remove and cool until lukewarm. Mix the fruit before adding to mixture. Mix dry ingredients with the butter mixture then add the cooled fruit mixture. Mix well. Add the brandy and lemon juice with the bicarbonate of soda. Finally, fold in the stiffly beaten egg whites. Pour into two 23 cm pans lined

---

Cherries are bitter to the surfeited bird.

with thick aluminium foil. Bake for 3 hrs at 150 °C (300 °F). Test the centre of the cake with a knitting needle or a skewer. There must be no raw batter on the needle. When the cake is cooked, leave to cool. Pour ½ c brandy over and add another ½ c brandy 2 days before eating.
(DELICIOUS MOIST FRUIT CAKE)
Joey Pienaar

Beat and bake cake

½	c	soft margarine
2		eggs
1	t	vanilla
2	t	baking powder (level)
¾	c	castor sugar
½	t	almond essence
1½	c	flour
½	c	milk

Method:
Beat all the ingredients together for 3-5 min. Pour into prepared pans and bake for 20-25 min at 180 °C (350 °F). Ingredients must be carefully measured. Delicious with various fillings and with whipped cream.
Badie Bloem

All creatures great and small. The Lord God made them all.

Orange syrup cake

250	g	margarine (1 pkt)
3		eggs
1	c	sour milk
1	c	dates
1	c	sugar
2	c	flour
1	t	bicarbonate of soda
½	c	nuts
½	c	cherries
½	c	mixed peel
		salt

Method:
Cream margarine, sugar and eggs. Mix bicarbonate of soda with sour milk. Fold into flour and salt. Add egg mixture and fruit. Bake for ± 1 hr in a tube pan at 180 °C (350 °F) and pour hot syrup over cake immediately as it comes out of the oven.

Syrup:
Mix juice of two oranges (¾ c), two t grated rind, one c sugar. Melt over low heat (boil a little).
Maxie Crafford

Orange ring cake

125	g	butter
2		eggs
2	c	flour
1	t	bicarbonate of soda — mixed with the milk
		salt
1	c	sugar
		grated rind of 1 orange
1	c	sour milk
1	c	finely chopped dates

---

*Take a moment of your time; it could be a moment of your life —
Jaya.*

Method:
Cream butter and sugar. Add eggs one at a time. Beat well. Add remaining ingredients. Beat well. Bake at 180 °C (350 °C) for 1 hr. Allow cake to cool in the cake pan. While the cake is still warm, pour the following syrup over:

¾   c   orange juice
½   c   sugar
Boil to a thick syrup.
Hester Naudé

Refrigerator fruit cake
(Delicious)

250	g	margarine
375	g	icing sugar
130	g	nuts, finely chopped
125	g	dates, pitted and finely chopped
60	g	seedless raisins, finely cut
125	g	glacé cherries, quartered
25	g	citrus peel
		whites of 2 eggs
12,5	ml	brandy (1 Tsp)
1½	pkt	Tennis biscuits

Method:
Cream the butter and sugar, add the brandy and fruit and mix thoroughly. Fold in the stiffly beaten egg whites and crushed biscuits. Place the mixture into a square dish and leave to set in the refrigerator.
Joey Pienaar

Beauty and deformity equally pass away.

Baked apricot cheese cake

Biscuit crust:
500	ml	Tennis biscuit crumbs (2 c)
80	g	sugar (100 ml) (8 Tsp)
5	ml	ground ginger (1 t)
5	ml	cinnamon (1 t)
180	g	butter, melted (200 ml) (¾ c)

Method:
Mix all the ingredients thoroughly. Press the mixture evenly into a 230 mm cake tin with loose bottom. Cover with aluminium foil and place in refrigerator to set while the filling is being prepared.

Filling:
240	g	sugar (300 ml) (1¼ c)
1	kg	cottage cheese
25	g	flour (50 ml) (4 Tsp)
2	ml	salt
15	ml	grated lemon rind (3 t)
5	ml	vanilla essence (1 t)
4		eggs
2		egg yolks
60	g	currants (100 ml) (8 Tsp)
1	tin	canned apricots (820 g)
		glacé cherries and angelica for garnishing
1	pkt	orange jelly
225	ml	fruit syrup or boiling water (¾ c + 3 Tsp)

Method:
Mix the sugar, cottage cheese, flour, salt, lemon rind, vanilla essence and 1 egg. Beat well. Add the rest of the eggs one at a time. Beat well after each addition. Finally add the egg yolks and beat well. Stir the currants into the cheese mixture and pour the filling into the crust. Bake for 5 min at 220 °C (425 °F), reduce the oven temperature to 100 °C (200 °F) and bake for 1 hr. Remove from

---

Once bitten twice shy.

oven and leave to cool. Arrange the canned apricots on the top and garnish with cherries and angelica. Heat fruit syrup and dissolve the jelly in the syrup or the boiling water. As soon as it thickens spoon the jelly over the layer of apricots. Leave to set.
Joey Pienaar

White layer cake

4		eggs
12,5	ml	milk powder (1 Tsp)
375	ml	sugar (1½ c)
½	t	salt
500	ml	flour (2 c)
250	ml	boiling water (1 c)
5	ml	vanilla essence (1 t)
125	ml	oil (½ c)
10	ml	baking powder, heaped (2 t)

Method:
Beat eggs and vanilla until frothy. Gradually add the sugar. Beat well until the mixture becomes a pale yellow. Sift the flour, salt, baking powder and milk powder twice. Mix the oil and the boiling water. Add egg mixture to the dry ingredients a little at a time while beating slowly. Lastly, add the oil and the boiling water and stir with a wooden spoon. Bake in two greased 23 cm pans for ± 30 min at 180 °C (350 °F). Ice after cooled.
Joey Pienaar

A watched kettle never boils.

263

Apricot cheesecake

Crust:

110	g	butter, melted (125 ml) (½ c)
70	g	sugar (85 ml) (⅓ c + 1 t)
375	ml	finely crushed corn flakes (1½ c)

Method:
Mix all ingredients, except 25 ml corn flakes and press into a greased loose-bottomed cake tin, 230 mm in diameter.

Filling:

12,5	ml	gelatine (1 Tsp)
125	ml	apricot syrup (½ c)
1	tin	canned apricots (820 g) (drained)
500	g	cream cheese
1	tin	condensed milk (397 g)
25	ml	lemon juice (2 Tsp)
125	ml	cream, whipped
		mint leaves for decoration

Method:
Dissolve the gelatine in the syrup. Melt over boiling water. Mash all the apricots except 5 and mix with the gelatine mixture. Whip cream cheese until smooth, then add the condensed milk and lemon juice. Fold in the apricot mixture, and then the whipped cream. Pour into the pie crust. Arrange the 5 apricot halves and mint leaves on top. Cover with glaze. Sprinkle crushed corn flakes around the edge.

Glaze:

125	ml	apricot syrup (½ c)
5	ml	maizena (1 t)

Method:
Mix ingredients and boil until thick. Leave to cool. Spoon over the cheese cake.

Joey Pienaar

Penny wise; pound foolish.

Syrup cake

75	ml	hot water
30	g	butter or margarine (37,5 ml)
120	g	flour (250 ml)
5	ml	baking powder
		a pinch of salt
2		eggs
100	g	sugar (125 ml)
5	ml	vanilla essence

Syrup:

50	g	butter or margarine (50 ml)
50	ml	golden syrup or honey

Method:

Melt the butter in the water and heat to boiling point. Place aside. Sift the flour, baking powder and salt. Beat the eggs until light and frothy. Gradually add the sugar and beat till dissolved. Add vanilla essence. Stir the dry ingredients into the egg mixture. Add the hot water mixture and beat for 1 min. Bake for 15-20 min in a greased oven-proof dish at 190 °C (375 °F). Meanwhile, melt the butter and syrup and pour over the cake immediately as it comes out of the oven. Loosen slightly round the sides and lift here and there to allow the syrup to run in underneath. Heat again for 1 min and serve hot with tea or as a dessert with cream or custard.

Joey Pienaar

Every day with Jesus is sweeter than the day before.

Chocolate cake
(First prize — Pretoria Show)

4		eggs
12,5	ml	milk powder (1 Tsp)
440	ml	sugar (1¾ c)
½	t	salt
500	ml	flour (2 c)
125	ml	cocoa (½ c)
5	ml	vanilla essence (1 t)
125	ml	oil (½ c)
10	ml	baking powder, heaped (2 t)
250	ml	boiled water (1 c)

Method:
Beat eggs and vanilla until frothy. Add sugar gradually. Beat well until mixture is a light yellow. Sift flour, salt, cocoa, baking powder and milk powder twice. Mix oil and boiling water. Add the flour mixture gradually to the egg mixture at a slow speed. Add the oil and boiling water mixture and stir with a wooden spoon until well mixed. Bake in two greased, 23 cm pans for ± 25-30 mins at 180 °C (350 °F)

Filling:

250	g	icing sugar
50	ml	butter or margarine (4 Tsp)
5	ml	vanilla essence (1 t)
25	ml	cocoa (2 Tsp)
2	Tsp	cold water

Method:
Cream the margarine and gradually add the icing sugar, cocoa and vanilla essence. Add 2 Tsp cold water and beat until light and fluffy.
Joey Pienaar

Learn by your foolish mistakes.

Feather cake
(First prize – Pretoria Show)

150	ml	milk
120	g	butter (130 ml)
200	g	flour (400 ml)
2	ml	salt
15	ml	baking powder
4		eggs
200	g	fine granulated sugar (250 ml)
		or
200	g	castor sugar (237,5 ml)
5	ml	vanilla essence

Method:
Bring the liquid and butter to the boil and stir to allow the butter to melt. Keep aside. Sift the flour, salt and baking powder. Beat the eggs and gradually add the sugar, beat until sugar is dissolved. Add vanilla essence. Add the dry ingredients to the egg mixture. Add the lukewarm milk mixture and mix. Pour the batter into two layer-cake pans, 220 mm in diameter. Only grease the bottom of the pan. Bake for 20-25 min in a moderate oven at 190 °C (375 °F).

Variations:
Chocolate feather cake: Add 20 g (50 ml) cocoa and 10 ml butter (2 t) to the milk and butter mixture. Bring to the boil.
Orange feather cake: Replace vanilla essence with 5 ml grated orange rind.
Joey Pienaar

Where there is love; there is God. Where there is God there is no need.

Sponge cake
(With hot milk — delicious)

3		eggs
250	ml	sugar (1 c)
500	ml	flour (2 c)
15	ml	baking powder (3 t)
2	ml	salt
250	ml	milk (1 c)
25	ml	margarine (2 Tsp)
5	ml	vanilla essence (1 t)

Method:
Beat eggs and sugar well. Sift the dry ingredients. Boil milk and margarine. Add the dry ingredients to the egg mixture. Mix well. Stir in milk mixture and vanilla essence. Bake in two pans for 20-25 min at 180 °C (350 °F). Delicious with coconut icing.
Joey Pienaar

Chiffon cake

240	g	flour (500 ml)
250	g	sugar (312,5 ml)
15	ml	baking powder
3	ml	salt
125	ml	oil
5		eggs, separated
180	ml	water
10	ml	lemon juice
5	ml	grated lemon rind
2	ml	cream of tartar

Method:
Use greaseproof paper to line the base of either 2 sandwich tins, 220 mm in diameter, or use a 250 mm tube pan. Sift the flour,

---

Count your blessings by smiles . . . not tears — Lady Falda.

sugar, baking powder and salt together. Make a well in the centre of the dry ingredients. Add the oil, unbeaten egg yolks, cold water, lemon juice and rind in this order. Beat until smooth. Add the cream of tartar to the egg whites and beat until stiff but not dry. Fold the egg whites lightly into the first mixture. Pour the batter into the tin(s). Bake in a moderate oven (180 °C — 350 °F) for 25-30 min for a layer cake or 40-50 min for one baked in a tube pan. When cooked, cake will feel springy to the touch. Invert when taken from the oven and leave until cold. Loosen sides of cake with a knife and remove from tin.
Joey Pienaar

Fruit ring

Boil:

3½	c	mixed fruit (fruit cake mixture) (500 g)
1½	c	cold water
1	c	sugar
1	t	bicarbonate of soda
125	g	margarine

Method:
Boil for 5 min and leave to cool. Whisk 2 eggs thoroughly and add 2 Tsp brandy. Sift 2 c flour, ½ t baking powder, ½ t salt, 2 t cocoa and 2 t mixed spices into egg mixture. Finally add the fruit. Bake at 180 °C (350 °F) for 1 hr in a ring cake pan. While still warm, pour 2-3 Tsp brandy over.
Ester Kleinhans

Count your age by friends . . . not years — Lady Falda.

Orange cake

3		eggs
1	c	sugar
3	Tsp	melted butter
¼	t	salt
1½	c	flour
1½	t	baking powder
¾	c	milk

Method:
Beat eggs until frothy, add sugar and beat for 4 min. Sift dry ingredients. Mix egg and flour mixtures and add milk. Add melted butter. Bake for 30-35 min at 180 °C (350 °F).

Syrup:

1	c	water
1	Tsp	butter
2	c	sugar
2	Tsp	grated orange rind

Method:
Boil all the ingredients and leave to cool. Add 1 c orange juice. Pour over hot cake.
Joey Pienaar

Honey cake .

1½	c	flour
3		eggs
3½	t	baking powder
		a pinch of salt
2½	Tsp	butter
1	c	milk
1¼	c	sugar
1	t	vanilla essence

Don't wait for the Last Judgement. It takes place every day —
Albert Camus.

270

Method:

Separate eggs. Beat yolks and sugar. Sift dry ingredients three times and add to egg mixture. Melt butter in milk and stir into egg and flour mixture. Bake for 20 min at 180 °C (350 °F).

Syrup:

4	Tsp	honey or syrup
2	Tsp	butter

Method:

Cut cake into squares while still warm. Melt the above ingredients and pour hot syrup over the cake.

Joey Pienaar

Coconut icing

(Delicious)

4	Tsp	margarine
3	Tsp	milk
½	c	sugar
½	t	vanilla essence
190	ml	coconut (¾ c)

Method:

Boil the margarine, milk and sugar. Remove from stove and add the rest of the ingredients. While still hot, spread over the cake. Turn oven on grill, place cake in oven and grill until mixture colours. Be careful, it burns easily!

Joey Pienaar

Welcome is the best cheer.

Biscuits

273

Puff pastry

(4½ doz)
(First prize — Pretoria Show)

4½	c	flour
1	t	salt
1½	t	cream of tartar (heaped)
1		small bottle ice cold soda-water (280 ml)
		yolks of 2 eggs and 2 Tsp white vinegar
500	g	butter (1 lb)

Method:

Place 4 c flour, salt and ½ t cream of tartar into mixing bowl. Mix ½ c flour in separate bowl with 1 t cream of tartar (for later use to sprinkle over grated butter). Grate ⅓ lb butter into the flour. Rub thoroughly into flour mixture. Whisk ice cold soda-water with egg and vinegar. Add to the flour mixture and mix until all the liquid has been absorbed. Place mixture into a plastic bag, and beat on the table for 30 seconds. Place in refrigerator for 2 hrs or longer. Roll lengthwise and grate ⅓ lb butter over ½ of the pastry. Sprinkle ½ of the cream of tartar and roll well so that the pastry is again flattened. Grate the last of the butter over and sprinkle the last of the cream of tartar on. Fold as before and again roll out well. Roll like a swiss roll, cut into 2 and place in a plastic bag. Place in refrigerator for at least 8 hrs. Now the pastry is ready for use. Roll out, cut in shapes and fold. Place in a dish with layers of plastic in between. Place in the freezer until ready for use. Preheat oven to 200 °C (400 °F). Place frozen tarts onto a flat baking sheet. Bake until light brown. (After 10 min, open the oven a few times, very quickly.) While the tarts are lukewarm, spread apricot jam over them.

Joey Pienaar

Leave the gossiping for the fools to do.

Cheese and bacon snacks
(Use pastry left over from jam tarts)

Roll pastry. Cut into 4 x 4 cm squares. Sprinkle squares with Aromat and cayenne pepper. Place a rasher of bacon onto one half of a square and place a piece of cheese on top of the bacon. Fold. Place in freezer until required. Do not thaw. Bake as for jam tarts.

Marie biscuit squares

3	pkts	Marie biscuits, crushed
500	g	margarine
1½	c	sugar
4		eggs
1	c	cherries, finely chopped
1	c	raisins, seedless
1	c	nuts
2	t	vanilla essence
1	c	Rice Crispies

Method:
Melt sugar and margarine. Beat eggs and vanilla essence thoroughly, stir in. Add fruit and nuts and then the crushed biscuits, flatten in the dish. Press Rice Crispies on top. Place in refrigerator to set. Cut into squares and place into a container and leave in refrigerator. Delicious.
Joey Pienaar

The difference between a man and a woman buying a hat is four hours.

"Tamboesies" (Custard slices)
(Makes about 60 "tamboesies")

500	ml	milk (2 c)
50	g	sugar (60 ml) (¼ c)
20	g	custard powder (30 ml) (6 t)
20	g	maizena (30 ml) (6 t)
		pinch of salt
5	ml	vanilla essence
		icing sugar, sifted
		lemon juice
		boiled water
		few drops almond essence
400	g	puff pastry
		or
		frozen puff pastry

Method:
Thaw the pastry. Preheat oven to 200 °C (400 °F). Roll out the pastry and cut into squares with a sharp knife, 4 x 4 cm. Do not roll the pastry too thinly. Place the squares on a large flat baking sheet and bake for about 12 min or until golden brown and puffed. Cool on a cooling rack.

Filling:
Blend the sugar, custard powder, maizena and salt with a little of the milk. Scald the rest of the milk and add gradually to the blended mixture. Return to the saucepan and stir until the mixture boils and thickens. Remove from heat, stir in vanilla and cover. Allow to cool. Split pastry squares. Sandwich together with cold custard. Mix icing sugar with lemon juice and boiling water to a spreading consistency. Flavour with almond essence and spoon over the top of the filled squares. Allow the icing to set before serving.

Joey Pienaar

The true meaning of religion is thus simply not morality, but morality touched by emotion — Arnold.

Custard biscuits
(Meat mincer — delicious)

250	g	margarine
8	Tsp	sugar
6	Tsp	custard
4	t	baking powder
3	c	flour
2		eggs
1	t	vanilla essence

Method:
Cream butter and sugar, add the beaten eggs, custard, flour, baking powder and vanilla essence. Mix well. Force the dough through a mincing machine with a biscuit attachment. Bake at 180 °C (350 °F) for 15-20 min.

Filling:

½	pkt	icing sugar
2	Tsp	margarine (heaped)
		pinch of salt
1	t	vanilla essence

Method:
Mix all ingredients well. Add cold water until the filling has the right consistency, ± 1 Tsp water. (This filling is sufficient for custard and coconut biscuits.)

If the doors of perception were cleansed, everything would appear as it is, infinite — William Blake.

Meringues
(Always a success)

1		white of an extra large egg
250	ml	castor sugar (1 c)
30	ml	boiling water (6 t)
15	ml	vinegar (3 t)
2	ml	baking powder

Method:
Place the egg white, castor sugar, boiling water and vinegar into a mixing bowl and beat well, until the meringue forms a peak when you remove the beater. Fold the baking powder lightly into the mixture. Place teaspoonfuls of mixture onto a baking tray lined with aluminium foil. Use a forcing bag with a meringue tube to pipe 4 cm meringues. Preheat the oven to 100 °C (200 °F). Bake for 1½ hr. Turn the heat off and remove when the oven is cold. Store in an airtight tin.
Joey Pienaar

Sweet pastry
(Makes 8 doz. shells)

4	c	flour
250	g	margarine
1	c	sugar
3		level t baking powder
1	Tsp	custard powder
2		eggs
1	t	salt

Method:
Cream sugar, butter and eggs. Add the dry ingredients to the butter mixture and mix well. Place in a plastic bag to keep moist.
Joey Pienaar

No man is an Island — John Donne.

Jan Smuts cookies

Use recipe for sweet pastry. Roll out between plastic sheets sprinkled with flour. Using a 6 cm biscuit cutter line patty pans with pastry. Put 2 ml apricot jam into each case and a spoonful of the filling on top. Bake the cookies for 15 min or until golden brown at 180 °C (350 °F) on the centre shelf of the oven. Remove carefully from pan and place on a cooling rack. Leave to cool.

Filling:

125	g	margarine
125	g	sugar (150 ml)
2		eggs, beaten
125	g	flour (225 ml, unsifted)
5	ml	baking powder
		apricot jam

Method:

Cream margarine and sugar. Add eggs and mix. Sift the flour and baking powder and mix with the creamed mixture.
Joey Pienaar

It is being afraid of the future that makes the future fearful —
Genl. Jan Smuts.

Hertzoggies (Hertzog cookies)
(First prize — Pretoria Show)

Use recipe for sweet pastry. Roll out between plastic sheets. Use medium biscuit-cutter — 6 cm. Line greased patty pans. Put ½ t apricot jam into each case. Bake at 180 °C (350 °F) until pastry is light brown. Cover with coconut filling.

Coconut filling:
5	c	coconut
125	g	margarine
2	t	vanilla essence
2	c	sugar
8		large eggs
		a pinch of salt

Method:
Cream butter and sugar. Add eggs, vanilla and salt and finally the coconut.
Joey Pienaar

Coffee biscuits
(No eggs — delicious)
(Meat mincer with biscuit attachment)
(First prize — Pretoria Show)

8	c	flour
1	lb	margarine (500 g)
2	c	sugar
1	lb	syrup (500 g)
3	t	bicarbonate of soda
1	t	vanilla essence
½	c	STRONG coffee

Goodwill and co-operation are the first principles necessary for the successful development of a sound national life — Genl. J.B.M. Hertzog.

Method:

Cream butter, sugar and syrup. Add bicarbonate of soda to coffee. Sift the flour into the mixture and mix well. Texture must be suitable to put through a mincer with a biscuit attachment. Bake at 180 °C (350 °F) for 15-20 min.

Filling:

½	pkt	icing sugar
2	Tsp	margarine, heaped
		a pinch of salt
1	t	vanilla essence
2	Tsp	very strong coffee

Method:

Mix well. Finally add the coffee. Place filling between two biscuits.
Joey Pienaar

Coconut Biscuits

(Mincing machine)

3½	c	flour
1¼	c	sugar
250	g	margarine
2		eggs
½	t	vanilla essence
½	t	bicarbonate of soda
½	t	baking powder
1	c	dessicated coconut
½	t	salt

Method:

Cream margarine and sugar thoroughly. Beat eggs and add coconut and then the remaining dry ingredients. (Mix bicarbonate of soda with a Tsp milk.) Mix ingredients thoroughly until ready to put through the mincer with the biscuit attachment. Bake at 180 °C (350 °F) for 15-20 min.
Joey Pienaar

Man is Heaven's masterpiece.

Condensed milk biscuits
(Very brittle)

12	c	flour
3	c	sugar
1½	lb	margarine (750 g)
4		eggs
1	tin	condensed milk
1	Tsp	syrup
3	t	bicarbonate of soda
3	t	cream of tartar
½	t	salt

Method:
Cream butter and sugar. Add eggs one at a time. Add condensed milk and syrup, mix well. Add flour, bicarbonate of soda, cream of tartar and salt. Mix to desired consistency and put through the mincer with the biscuit maker attachment. Bake at 180 °C (350 °F) for 15-20 min. Sandwich the biscuits with apricot jam or vanilla icing. The dough can also be shaped into balls.
Joey Pienaar

Traditional soetkoekies

2		eggs
8	c	flour
½	c	margarine
½	t	salt
2	t	cream of tartar
2	t	ground cinnamon
⅔	c	sweet wine
2	c	sugar
½	c	soft fat
1½	t	bicarbonate of soda
1	t	ground cloves
1	t	grated orange rind

Sow an act, and you reap a habit.

Method:
Sift the flour, bicarbonate of soda, salt and spices. Add the sugar and mix well. Rub the butter and fat into the flour mixture with your fingers. Beat the eggs well and add 2 Tsp wine. Add to the dry ingredients. Add more wine if the mixture is too stiff. Leave for 1 hr. Roll out and bake on a greased baking tray at 200 °C (400 °F) for about 15 min. Lift out and place on cooling rack. Place in an airtight tin to preserve the crispness.
Joey Pienaar

Jam squares

500	ml	flour (2 c)
25	ml	sugar (2 Tsp)
62,5	ml	water (1/4 c)
1		egg
125	g	margarine
5	ml	vanilla essence (1 t)
1	ml	salt
8	ml	baking powder (1 1/2 t)
		apricot jam

Method:
Sift dry ingredients and add sugar. Rub margarine in lightly. Beat egg and water and add. Mix to a stiff dough. Knead lightly and divide in half. Press one half on a greased baking tray and spread with jam. Grate the other half of pastry over the jam. Do not flatten. Bake for 20 min in a moderate oven at 180 °C (350 °F) until golden brown. Cut into squares once cooled.
Joey Pienaar

O what a tangled web we weave, when first we practise to deceive — Sir Walter Scott.

Ginger cookies
(First prize — Pretoria Show)

6	c	flour
1	c	margarine
2	c	sugar
2	Tsp	ginger
2		eggs
1	c	golden syrup
3	t	bicarbonate of soda
¼	t	salt

Method:
Cream butter and sugar. Add eggs to the mixture. Add syrup and ginger then bicarbonate of soda, mixed with 2 Tsp milk. Sift the flour and mix well. Shape into balls and flatten in pan (do not roll out).

Joey Pienaar

Sweet cookies

10	c	flour
3½	c	sugar
1	lb	margarine (500 g)
4		eggs
1	pkt	cream of tartar (3 t)
½	pkt	bicarbonate of soda (1 1/2 t)
½	t	salt
½	t	vanilla essence
1	c	currants (optional)

Method:
Cream margarine and sugar. Add eggs one at a time, then all the dry ingredients. Mix with milk. Roll and cut into required shapes. Bake at 180 °C (350 °F).

Ina Steyn

All that glitters is not gold.

Koeksisters
(This recipe is highly recommended)

3x250	ml	flour (3 heaped c)
12,5	ml	maizena (1 Tsp)
15	ml	baking powder (3 t)
12,5	ml	margarine (1 Tsp)
2		eggs
375	ml	milk (1½ c)
		a pinch of salt

Method:
Sift the dry ingredients and rub in the margarine. Beat the eggs and the milk. Mix to a soft dough. Knead for 12 min. Leave overnight in the refrigerator. Use part of the dough and leave the rest in the refrigerator. Roll the dough and cut into strips and plait. Fry in deep oil. Immerse immediately in ice-cold syrup.

Syrup:

16	c	sugar
¼	c	lemon juice
		grated rind of two oranges
1½	t	cream of tartar
2	c	orange juice
6	c	water

Method:
Dissolve sugar in water before water starts boiling. Add orange juice. Boil rapidly for 15 min. Add lemon juice and cream of tartar when the syrup is cooled. Leave overnight in the refrigerator. Do not use all the syrup at once. The syrup can be kept in the refrigerator for a considerable period.
Joey Pienaar

Beauty is not immortal.

Romany creams
(Delicious)

500	ml	flour (2 c)
5	ml	baking powder (1 t)
375	ml	coconut (1½ c)
60	ml	boiling water (¼ c)
250	g	margarine (½ lb)
250	ml	castor sugar (1 c)
25	ml	cocoa (2 Tsp)
		milk chocolate

Method:
Cream butter and sugar. Add flour, baking powder, salt and coconut. Dissolve cocoa in boiling water and add. Place teaspoonfuls on a greased baking tray. Bake in moderate oven for 6 min. Melt chocolate over boiling water or in a microwave oven at defrost. Spread between biscuits.
Joey Pienaar

Koeksisters

3	c	flour (heaped)
2	t	baking powder
2		eggs
1½	c	milk and water mixed
1	Tsp	margarine
		a pinch of salt

Method:
Mix dry ingredients and rub in butter. Beat the eggs and the liquids. Mix and knead for 10 min. Leave for 3 hrs.

A single word even may be a spark of inextinguishable thought — P.B. Shelley.

286

Syrup:

7	c	water
1	Tsp	cream of tartar
3		pieces of ginger
14	c	sugar
2	Tsp	syrup

Method:
Boil water, sugar and ginger for 3 min, remove and add cream of tartar and syrup (if desired also 1 Tsp lemon juice). Leave overnight in refrigerator.
Lettie Dempers

Jam tarts
(6 doz.)

6x250	ml	flour (6 c)
8	ml	salt
3		egg yolks, beaten
60	ml	white vinegar (¼ c)
5	ml	cream of tartar (1 level t)
190	ml	cold water (¾ c)
625	g	margarine (Yellow)

Method:
Sift dry ingredients. Rub in grated margarine. Add liquids and knead until pastry is soft. Leave overnight in refrigerator. Roll small pieces of dough out thinly. Cut with a round biscuit cutter of 8 cm in diameter. Put a small dab of smooth apricot jam on each surface. Fold and seal edges with a fork. Place on a greased baking tray. Brush beaten egg over tarts. Sprinkle with a little white sugar. Place pans in the refrigerator until all the pans are ready. Bake in oven at 200 °C (400 °F) for 10-12 min or until golden brown.
Joey Pienaar

It is better to die on your feet than to live on your knees —
D. Ibárruri.

Oatmeal biscuits
(Crunchies — delicious)

250	ml	margarine (1 c)
4x250	ml	coconut (4 c)
4x250	ml	oatmeal (4 c)
5	ml	cinnamon (1 t)
3	ml	salt ($\frac{1}{2}$ t)
50	ml	golden syrup (4 Tsp)
10	ml	bicarbonate of soda, dissolved in 80 ml ($\frac{1}{3}$ c) milk
250	ml	flour (1 c)
375	ml	sugar (1$\frac{1}{2}$ c)

Method:
Mix all the dry ingredients including the sugar. Melt butter and syrup. Add bicarbonate of soda and milk. Mix well. Press mixture into a swiss roll pan. Bake at 180 °C (350 °F) for 15-20 min. Cut into squares while still hot. Leave in pan for another 10-15 min then remove.
Joey Pienaar

Tasty dainty biscuits
(Delicious)

2	c	Post Toasties
2	c	oatmeal
2	c	sugar
2		eggs
2	t	baking powder
1	t	vanilla essence
$\frac{1}{4}$-$\frac{1}{2}$	c	chopped walnuts, optional
2	c	coconut
2	c	flour
2	Tsp	peanut butter

There never was a good war or a bad peace — Benjamin Franklin

½	lb	margarine (500 g)
2	t	bicarbonate of soda
		a pinch of salt

Method:
Cream the butter and the sugar thoroughly. Stir in the eggs. Add the peanut butter and mix well. Stir in the vanilla essence and bicarbonate of soda dissolved in 2 Tsp milk. Mix the remaining ingredients and add. Shape into small balls and bake at 180 °C (350 °F) for about 15 min.
Joey Pienaar

Oatmeal biscuits
(± 50 biscuits)

3	c	coconut
1	c	flour
4	c	oatmeal
1	c	butter or margarine
2	t	bicarbonate of soda
		dissolved in ¼ c milk
1½	c	sugar
½	t	salt
1	t	ground cinnamon
3	Tsp	golden syrup

Method:
Mix all the dry ingredients. Melt the butter and syrup and add. Stir in the dissolved bicarbonate of soda. Mix thoroughly. Press into baking tray ± 1 cm thick. Bake for 15-20 min in a moderate oven at 180 °C (350 °F). Cut into desired squares.
Mollie de Witt

It is better to win the peace and to lose the war — Bob Marley.

Coconut biscuits
(Round)

2	c	flour
2	c	coconut
1	c	margarine
1	t	bicarbonate of soda
		a pinch of salt
2	c	oatmeal
2	c	sugar
2	Tsp	syrup
4	Tsp	boiling water

Method:
Melt the butter, syrup, bicarbonate of soda and boiling water in a saucepan. Mix the flour, oatmeal, coconut and sugar and add to butter mixture. Mix well. Use a teaspoon, shape into balls and place on a greased baking tray. Flatten slightly with a fork and bake 15-20 min at 180 °C (350 °F).
Joey Pienaar

Brandy Snaps

2	Tsp	golden syrup
2	Tsp	butter
½	t	ginger
1		lemon rind
3	Tsp	sugar
½	c	flour
1	Tsp	brandy
		little lemon juice

The only way to have a friend is to be one — R.W. Emerson.

Method:
Melt the syrup, sugar and butter. Add the rest of the ingredients and mix well. Place small spoonfuls 10 cm apart on a greased baking tray. Bake for 12-15 min at 180 °C (350 °F). As soon as the top starts browning lift with the flexible blade of a knife and wrap round the handle of a wooden spoon. Work quickly as dough hardens easily. If too hard place back on the baking tray in oven until soft. Keep in an airtight container or bottle and before use fill with flavoured, firmly whipped cream or caramelized condensed milk and decorate with cherries.
Joey Pienaar

Refrigerated fruit biscuits
(Makes 21 cookies)

115	g	butter or margarine (125 ml)
100	g	soft brown sugar (125 ml)
1	tin	condensed milk (397 g)
5	ml	vanilla essence
75	g	seedless raisins (125 ml)
75	g	bleached sultanas (125 ml)
75	g	currants (125 ml)
100	g	glacé cherries, cut into quarters (125 ml)
50	g	nuts, chopped (125 ml)
2	pkts	Tennis biscuits of 200 g each, crushed

Method:
Melt the butter and sugar in a large saucepan over low heat. Stir in condensed milk and vanilla essence and remove from stove. Add remaining ingredients and mix well. Press mixture, with an egg lifter, into a greased 18 x 28 x 3 cm pan and leave in refrigerator for 24 hrs before serving. Cut into squares. Makes 21 4 x 3 cm squares.
Ina Steyn

Don't say: "I'll never drink of this water."

Coffee biscuits
(100 biscuits)

1	kg	flour
5	ml	bicarbonate of soda (1 t)
5	ml	salt (1 t)
500	g	butter or margarine
250	ml	golden syrup (350 g) (1 c)
200	g	sugar (250 ml) (1 c)
30	ml	coffee essence (6 t)
		or
30	ml	instant coffee dissolved in 30 ml hot water (6 t)
5	ml	vanilla essence (1 t)
2		eggs

Method:
Sift the dry ingredients. Melt the butter and stir into the syrup, sugar, coffee essence and vanilla essence. Leave to cool, add the beaten eggs and mix. Stir in the sifted dry ingredients and mix to a smooth dough. Roll and cut into strips or force through a mincing machine with the biscuit attachment. Bake until golden brown in a moderate oven at 190 °C (375 °F). Place the coffee icing between two biscuits.
Ina Steyn

God seems to have left the receiver off the hook and time is running out — Arthur Koestler.

Apricot biscuits

8	c	flour
1	c	smooth apricot jam
500	g	margarine
2	c	coconut (optional)
4	c	sugar
1	pkt	bicarbonate of soda (3 t) (dissolved in ½ c hot water or boiling milk)
4		eggs

Method:
Mix flour, sugar and coconut. Rub in margarine. Add unbeaten eggs to flour mixture and mix with a knife. Add water to bicarbonate of soda. Mix the dissolved bicarbonate of soda with the jam and add to flour mixture. Mix well, shape into balls and bake in moderate oven at 180 °C (350 °F).
Ester Liebenberg

Cream tartlets (Jam turnovers)

250	g	margarine
1	c	cream
3	c	flour (sifted)
		a pinch of salt

Method:
Beat butter and cream (does not mix well). Sift flour and salt into mixture and mix thoroughly (do not knead). Roll out thinly and cut into rounds — use a glass. Put a spoonful of firm apricot jam onto the centre of each round. Moisten round the edges with egg white and fold over to cover the jam. Secure the edges firmly and brush with beaten egg. Bake at 350 °F (180 °C).
Mollie de Witt

Never kill the goose that lays the golden eggs.

Coconut biscuits

1½	c	flour
125	g	butter or margarine
½	c	sugar
1	t	baking powder
1		egg

Method:
Sift the flour and baking powder, rub in the butter. Beat the egg and sugar and mix with the flour. Press the dough into a greased square dish. Spread apricot jam over and spread the coconut topping over the top. Bake for about 20 min in a moderate oven 180 °C (350 °F). Cut into squares and leave to cool in the dish before removing.

Coconut Topping:
Beat together 1 Tsp melted butter, ½ c sugar and 1 egg. Add 1 c coconut and mix. Spread over pastry and bake.
Ester Liebenberg

Ouma Hanna's koeksisters

Step 1:
4	c	flour
4	t	baking powder (heaped)
¼	t	salt
2	Tsp	margarine

Rub in thoroughly.

Step 2:
2		eggs
1	c	water

Mix with flour mixture and knead thoroughly. Leave for 8 hrs.

Service to others is the rent you pay for your room here on earth — Muhammad Ali.

Syrup:

| 2,5 | kg | sugar |
| 5 | c | water |

Stir until boiling. Add ½ lemon to boiling syrup and boil for 7 min. Remove from stove and add ¼ t cream of tartar, tartaric acid (¼ t) and juice of 2 lemons.

Method:

Roll pastry on a slightly greased surface. Cut into slices of 1 cm x 10 cm. Plait and place on a plate. Cover with plastic. Fry until nicely browned in deep, hot cooking oil. Remove from oil and plunge into ice-cold syrup. Drain on a rack. Place over a tray to allow excess syrup to run off.

Joey Pienaar

Continental truffles

100	ml	melted margarine
20	g	coconut
5	ml	instant coffee
397	g	condensed milk
30	g	cocoa
		salt
5	ml	vanilla
300	g	breakfast flakes

Method:

Mix all ingredients. Shape into balls and roll in coconut.

Joey Pienaar

It is not love that produces jealousy — it is selfishness — Justice Wallington.

Meringues
(60 meringues)

4		egg whites
2	ml	cream of tartar
		a pinch of salt
200	g	fine granulated sugar (250 ml) (1 c)
2	ml	vanilla essence

Method:
Whip the egg whites until very stiff (when removing beater it must form peaks). Add the cream of tartar and salt and beat again, but not too dry. Add the sugar gradually, about 20-25 ml at a time and beat until sugar has dissolved. Fold in the remaining 25 ml sugar with the vanilla essence. Grease a baking tray lightly. Shape the meringues neatly with two spoons or force the mixture through a large meringue tube. Small or large meringue cases can be made in the following way: Spread a base 10 mm thick, then pipe around the edge ± 25-30 mm high. Bake for 1 hr in a very cool oven (120 °C — 275 °F). Turn the oven off and leave for about two hrs in the oven to dry.

Note:
If the oven is too hot the meringue will discolour and be sticky in the centre. If they do not dry out well, they will shrink and have a soft centre. Store in an airtight container. Do not fill before serving because the cream or fillings make them soggy. Put two meringues together with firmly whipped flavoured cream. Fill meringues and tart shells with strawberries and cream or ice-cream or fruit fillings. Food colouring can be used to colour the meringues. The colour must be de':cate. Add the colouring carefully, a drop at a time to the firmly whipped mixture.
Mollie de Witt

In affairs consider what precedes and follows.

Pancake for beginners
(Recipes follow in pp 308, 313 and 315)

Pancake batter must be soft so that it can spread in a thin layer over the base of a hot frying pan. Mix the batter until smooth and leave for 30 min or longer in a cool place before using. Do not stir again. Use a pan with a heavy base, heat and spread with oil. Pour off excess oil. The pan must be very hot when the batter is poured in. Use a measuring cup or a soup ladle and use the same amount of batter for each pancake. Allow batter to spread quickly to cover the pan. If large pancakes are required, use 25 ml brandy or 50 ml lemon juice for a mixture of 2 kg flour. It keeps the pancakes soft. Keep pancakes hot by layering on top of each other in a dish and keep the dish warm over boiling water. Sprinkle with cinnamon sugar just before serving. The oven tends to make the pancakes tough.
Joey Pienaar

Love is an act of endless forgiveness, a tender look which becomes a habit — Peter Ustinov.

297

Brown tea biscuits
(80 biscuits)

2		eggs
80	g	brown sugar (100 ml)
200	g	golden syrup (150 ml)
125	ml	cooking oil (½ c)
480	g	flour
5	ml	bicarbonate of soda (1 t)
5	ml	salt (1 t)
10	ml	ginger (2 t)
10	ml	mixed spice (2 t)

Method:
Beat the eggs, add the sugar, syrup and oil and beat thoroughly. Sift the dry ingredients and mix with egg mixture to form a smooth batter. Refrigerate. Roll 3 mm thick and cut out into rounds or decorative shapes. Bake for 10-12 min on a greased baking tray in a hot oven (190 °C — 375 °F). Ice when cold.

Icing:

130	g	icing sugar (250 ml) (1 c)
		a pinch of salt
15	ml	(or slightly more) water or lemon juice (3 t)

Method:
Mix enough icing sugar and salt with water and lemon juice to a stiff enough consistency to use in an icing tube. Ice the biscuits and sprinkle with hundreds-and-thousands.
Ina Steyn

Love means never having to say you're sorry — Erich Segal.

Traditional soetkoekies
(Makes about 160 biscuits)

250	g	butter or margarine, at room temperature
600	g	sugar (750 ml)
5		eggs (extra large)
825	g	flour (6 x 250 ml, measured unsifted)
30	ml	baking powder
10	ml	ground nutmeg
2	ml	salt

To brush cookies:

1		egg, beaten
25	ml	milk
		sugar

Method:

Cream butter, sugar and 5 eggs. Sift flour, baking powder, nutmeg and salt. Add sifted ingredients to the butter mixture and mix to a reasonably soft batter. Cover and leave to rise for ½ hr. Preheat oven to 200 °C (400 °F). Grease baking trays lightly or spray with a non-stick spray. Roll the dough out thinly on a pastry board sprinkled with flour. Cut out rounds, 4-5 cm in diameter, with a biscuit-cutter. Place the round biscuits on the baking tray. Beat egg and milk and brush lightly over biscuits. Sprinkle a little sugar in the centre of each biscuit for decoration. Bake for 8-10 min or until golden brown. Remove from oven and leave to cool slightly. Place on a cooling rack to cool completely. Place in an airtight container.

Mollie de Witt

When love becomes a command, hatred can become a pleasure — Charles Bukowski.

"Skurwejantjies" (Rough oatmeal biscuits)

230	g	butter or margarine (250 ml)
50	ml	honey or golden syrup
10	ml	bicarbonate of soda (2 t)
400	g	sugar (500 ml)
275	g	flour (500 ml, unsifted)
250	g	oatmeal (750 ml)
150	g	coconut (500 ml)
100	g	chopped nuts (250 ml)
50	g	bran (250 ml)
2		eggs, beaten

Method:
Preheat oven to 160 °C (325 °F). Grease a baking tray of 40 x 27 x 2 cm or slightly larger. Melt butter and honey over medium heat. Add bicarbonate of soda and stir. (Mixture foams.) Let it cool slightly. Mix dry ingredients in a large mixing bowl. Add egg and butter mixture. Mix quickly and lightly to a stiff, crumbly dough. Place on baking tray and flatten with a spatula. Bake for 30-35 min. Cut into squares or triangles while still hot and leave on sheet until cold. Remove and place in an airtight container.
Joey Pienaar

Feather light scones
(With cream) (Makes 21 scones)

275	g	flour (500 ml measured, unsifted) (2 c)
10	ml	baking powder (2 t)
1	ml	salt
250	ml	sour cream (1 c)
2		eggs, slightly beaten

Friendship is tested rather in the thick years of success than in the thin years of struggle — Barry Humphries.

Method:

Preheat oven to 220 °C (425 °F). Grease a large baking tray lightly or spray with a non-stick spray. Sift the cake flour, baking powder and salt. Mix the sour cream and eggs. Add simultaneously to the flour mixture and mix with a palette knife until a pliable dough is formed; mix in more flour if dough is too soft or add a little milk if the dough is too stiff. Place the dough on a pastry board sprinkled with flour. Press out to thickness of 2 cm. Cut out rounds with a 5 cm diameter biscuit-cutter. Place on a baking tray. Bake for 12-15 min on third shelf from the top of the oven until light brown. Serve lukewarm.

Joey Pienaar

Coconut biscuits

(100 biscuits)

250	g	soft butter or margarine (275 ml)
300	g	sugar (375 ml) (1½ c)
2		eggs
80	g	coconut (250 ml) (1 c)
480	g	flour
5	ml	baking powder (1 t)
5	ml	salt (1 t)

Method:

Beat eggs, sugar and butter until light and creamy. Stir in the coconut. Sift the dry ingredients, add and mix thoroughly. Shape into small balls and flatten with a glass or force with a cookie press or roll the dough and cut into shapes. Bake for about 8 min until light brown in a moderate oven (190 °C — 375 °F).

Ina Steyn

It's the friends you can call at 4 am that matter — Marlene Dietrich.

Koeksisters
(Make the syrup and batter the previous night)
(Makes 5-6 doz)

1,75	kg	sugar (8 x 250)
1	ℓ	water
20	ml	golden syrup
2	ml	cream of tartar
1	ml	tartaric acid
		a pinch of salt
550	g	flour (4 ½ c, unsifted)
20	ml	baking powder
5	ml	salt
50	g	butter or margarine (60 ml)
375	ml	milk
1		egg

Method:
Heat sugar, water and golden syrup to boiling point, stir to ensure that the sugar melts before the syrup reaches boiling point. Boil syrup for 8 min, remove from stove, stir in cream of tartar, tartaric acid and salt and leave to cool. Place in refrigerator. Sift flour, baking powder and salt, rub butter into the dry ingredients until well mixed. Beat milk and eggs and add to flour mixture and make into a soft pliable dough. (Add a little flour if necessary.) Knead well. Cover and leave overnight in refrigerator. Roll dough out thinly on a slightly greased surface and cut into strips of 1 cm. Cut strips in 10 cm lengths, plait and place on a tray. Cover with plastic. Fry koeksisters until nicely browned in deep, hot cooking oil. (Brown both sides by turning the koeksisters. If the oil is too hot the koeksisters will brown only on the surface and will not be done in the centre.) Dip the hot koeksister immediately after removing from the oil, into ice-cold syrup. (Pour syrup into 2 dishes, keep one in the refrigerator and place the syrup in use in ice-cold water.) Place on a draining rack over a tray so that the excess syrup can run off.
Ina Steyn

Like fingerprints, all marriages are different — George Bernard Shaw.

Scones
(Enough for 8-10)

240	g	flour (500 ml) (2 c)
20	ml	baking powder (4 t)
3	ml	salt
25	ml	butter (5 t)
175	ml	milk (½ c + 4 Tsp)

Method:

STEP 1: Sift flour, baking powder and salt thoroughly in a mixing bowl. Rub in butter with the finger tips.

STEP 2: Cut in the milk with a spatula. The dough must not be smooth.

STEP 3: Place on a surface sprinkled with flour, press dough lightly together and roll out ± 20 mm thick. Cut with a biscuit-cutter.

STEP 4: Place on a greased baking tray and brush the top lightly with the beaten egg. Bake at 240 °C (450 °F) for about 12-15 min until golden brown and done. Remove from oven and leave to cool on a cooling rack.

Joey Pienaar

The moment you have protected an individual you have protected society — Kenneth Kaunda.

Choux pastry puffs
(Enough for 20)

250	ml	water (1 c)
100	g	butter (110 ml)
150	g	flour (310 ml) (1¼ c)
1	ml	salt
4		eggs

Method:
STEP 1: Place boiling water in a saucepan, add butter and melt over low heat. Stir flour and salt. Heat water and butter to boiling point and add flour mixture at once. Stir quickly with a wooden spoon so that the mixture forms a ball in the centre of the saucepan and does not cling to the sides. Remove from heat and let it cool slightly.
STEP 2: When cooled, add eggs one at a time and beat well with a wooden spoon after each addition.
STEP 3: Place spoonfuls of the mixture on a greased baking tray or place in a forcing bag with a meringue tube and pipe shapes, (long or round) as desired on the baking tray. Bake in a preheated oven at 200 °C (400 °F) for about 35-40 min until golden brown and done. Remove and prick on top with a skewer to allow steam to escape. Leave to cool.

For serving:
* Fill with cream and pour melted chocolate over or sprinkle chocolate vermicelli or grated chocolate on the top.
* A thick custard can also be made and used instead of cream as a filling.
* Any flavoured cream can be used as a filling. Whip cream with any liqueur and fill the puffs.
Joey Pienaar

When all think alike, then no one is thinking — Walter Lippmann.

Ginger bread
(Makes 1 medium-sized ginger bread or 2 small ones)

100	g	sugar (125 ml)
125	g	butter or margarine at room temperature
1		extra large egg
250	ml	golden syrup
325	g	flour (625 ml measured, unsifted)
5	ml	bicarbonate of soda
5	ml	cinnamon
10	ml	ground ginger (level)
2	ml	ground cloves
2	ml	salt
250	ml	hot water

Method:
Preheat oven to 180 °C (350 °F). Grease a medium-sized bread pan or two small ones and line with greaseproof paper, or spray with a non-stick spray. Cream sugar and butter or margarine. Add egg and mix well. Add golden syrup and mix thoroughly. Sift flour, bicarbonate of soda, cinnamon, ginger, cloves and salt three times. Add to creamed mixture and mix. Add water and mix to a smooth soft batter. Pour batter into pan carefully, fill ⅓ of the pan. Bake for 45 min on the centre shelf of the oven until done; test with a skewer. Allow to cool slightly in the pan(s). Then turn out onto cooling rack.
Joey Pienaar

Either men will learn to live like brothers or they will die like beasts — Max Lerner.

Oatmeal and nut biscuits
(120 biscuits)

130	g	butter or margarine (140 ml)
30	ml	golden syrup
2		eggs
200	g	sugar (250 ml)
300	g	flour (625 ml)
5	ml	bicarbonate of soda
3	ml	salt
5	ml	cinnamon
180	g	oatmeal (500 ml)
50	g	walnuts or pecan nuts, chopped (125 ml)
150	g	raisins or dates (chopped) (250 ml)

Method:
Melt butter and mix with golden syrup. Leave to cool. Beat eggs and sugar thoroughly and stir into the cooled butter mixture. Sift the flour, bicarbonate of soda, salt and cinnamon, add the oatmeal, nuts, and raisins or the dates and stir into egg and butter mixture. Mix thoroughly. Flatten to a thickness of 4 cm on a greased baking tray and bake for 8-10 min until light brown in a moderate oven (180 °C — 350 °F). Leave to cool before cutting into squares.
Mollie de Witt

Scotch shortbread

250	g	butter (275 ml) (1 c + 2 Tsp)
100	g	castor sugar (125 ml) (½ c)
240	g	flour (500 ml) (2 c)
60	g	maizena or rice flour (125 ml) (½ c)
1	ml	salt

Loneliness showed me desolation; Love showed me God's beautiful creation — Ella Marie.

Method:

Cream a ¼ of the butter and all the sugar. Add the rest of the butter gradually and cream the mixture. Sift dry ingredients and work into the creamed butter mixture until it is smooth but not greasy. Place in a greased baking tray ± 15 mm thick. Shape into an even round and with the thumb and forefinger decorate the sides, or place it firmly into a greased sandwich cake tin. Mark the top of the shortbread into wedges and prick evenly with a fork. Bake for 15 min in a hot oven (200 °C — 400 °F), lower the temperature to 160 °C (325 °F) and bake until a light straw colour (15-20 min).
Joey Pienaar

Fruit loaf

500	g	fruit cake mixture
1	c	water
125	g	margarine
2	c	flour
2		beaten eggs
1	c	sugar
1	t	bicarbonate of soda
10		cherries
1	t	baking powder

Method:

Boil fruit, sugar and water for 15 min. Remove from stove and add bicarbonate of soda and margarine. Stir to melt the margarine and leave to cool. Slice cherries and add. Add sifted flour and baking powder, and finally the beaten eggs. Bake in a greased tin lined with greaseproof paper for 30 min or until ready at 180 °C (350 °F).
Tina van Niekerk

Every day people are straying away from the church and going back to God — Lenny Bruce.

Quick scones

| ¼ | c | cooking oil |
| 1 | | egg |

Method:
Beat the cooking oil and egg thoroughly, add enough milk to make 1½ c of liquid.

Sift:

2	c	flour
4	t	baking powder
½	t	salt

Method:
Mix with egg mixture to a soft dough. Place spoonfuls on a pan sprinkled with flour. Bake for 10-12 min in a hot oven 200 °C (400 °F).
Badie Bloem

Pancakes
(20 pancakes)

240	g	flour (500 ml) (2 c)
10	ml	baking powder (2 t)
2	ml	salt
2		eggs
250	ml	milk (1 c)
250	ml	water (1 c)
12,5	ml	lemon juice or vinegar (1 Tsp)
25	ml	oil (2 Tsp)

Love is the reign of woman.

Method:

Sift the dry ingredients into a mixing bowl. Beat eggs until light and frothy and add the liquids and oil. Make a well in the centre of the dry ingredients, pour the egg and milk mixture in and beat or stir with a wooden spoon to a smooth batter. Heat a heavy pan; add 12,5 ml oil and pour off the excess. Allow the pan to get very hot. Pour just enough batter into the pan to cover the base with a thin layer. Heat. Shake to loosen the pancake after the edge looks set and dry. Turn over with a spatula or egg-lifter and allow the other side to brown. Place pancake on a warm plate; sprinkle with cinnamon sugar, dot with butter if desired and roll. Serve hot.

Joey Pienaar

Kisses

(75 biscuits)

500	g	soft butter or margarine
500	g	sugar (625 ml) (2½ c)
4		eggs
500	g	flour (4 c)
500	g	maizena (4 c)
5	ml	salt (1 t)
10	ml	baking powder (2 t)

Method:

Cream eggs, sugar and butter until fluffy. Sift dry ingredients and add to butter mixture. Mix to a smooth dough. Shape with a cookie press or roll into small rounds, flatten with a fork. Bake until golden brown in a moderate oven (190 °C — 375 °F). Put a vanilla filling between biscuits.

Ina Steyn

Kisses are keys.

Banana loaf

125	g	margarine
1½	c	sugar (375 ml)
3		eggs
5	ml	vanilla essence (1 t)
1	c	banana pulp (250 ml)
2	c	flour (500 ml)
2	t	baking powder (10 ml)
¼	t	bicarbonate of soda (1,5 ml)
¼	t	salt (1,5 ml)
2	Tsp	milk (25 ml)

Method:
Cream margarine and sugar until light in colour. Add eggs one at a time and beat after each addition. Add vanilla essence and fold in the banana pulp. Add the dry ingredients alternately with the milk. Bake at 180 °C (350 °F) for ± 1 hr. You can also add ½ c chopped nuts.
Joey Pienaar

A church is a hospital for sinners, not a museum for saints —
Abigail van Buren.

Date loaf with caramel sauce
(Makes 1 medium-sized loaf)
(Special)

5	ml	bicarbonate of soda
150	g	chopped dates(250 ml)
250	ml	boiled water
200	g	castor sugar (250 ml)
60	g	butter or margarine at room temperature (75 ml)
1		egg
200	g	flour (375 ml, unsifted)
5	ml	baking powder
		a pinch of salt
30	g	chopped nuts (75 ml)
5	ml	vanilla essence

Caramel syrup:

100	g	soft brown sugar (125 ml)
125	ml	fresh cream
40	g	butter or margarine (50 ml)

Method:
Heat oven to 180 °C (350 °F). Grease a medium-sized bread pan (23 x 13 x 5 cm) or spray well with a non-stick spray. Sprinkle bicarbonate of soda over dates. Add boiling water and mix. Leave to cool. Beat castor sugar and butter thoroughly. Add egg and beat. Sift flour, baking powder and salt over the mixture. Add nuts and vanilla essence and mix. Add dates and mix. Place in the pan. Bake for ± 1 hr or until cooked. Heat brown sugar, cream and butter over a low heat to boiling point. Boil for 5 min uncovered. Turn date loaf onto a platter and slowly pour hot caramel syrup over the top. Leave to cool.
Joey Pienaar

Shadow owes its birth to light.

Carrot loaf
(Makes 4 small or 2 large loaves)

450	g	grated carrots
1	pkt	stoned dates (250 g) cut fine
200	g	sugar (250 ml) (2 c)
		grated rind and juice of 1 orange
10	ml	bicarbonate of soda (2 t)
15	ml	cinnamon (3 t)
2	ml	ground ginger
6		eggs, beaten
1	pkt	seedless raisins (250 g)
1	pkt	glazé cherries (110 g, halved)
250	ml	water (1 c)
250	ml	cooking oil (1 c)
500	g	flour (4 c round)
10	ml	baking powder (2 t)
5	ml	salt (1 t)
2	ml	ground cloves
2	ml	ground nutmeg

Method:
Heat carrots, raisins, dates, cherries, sugar, water, cooking oil and orange rind to boiling point. Boil for 5 min and cool. Sift the dry ingredients. Stir in beaten eggs. Then add the dry ingredients. Add orange juice and mix well.

Place into pans and bake for 1 hr. To ensure that loaf is cooked, test with a skewer.

Joey Pienaar

There is no greater disloyalty to the pioneers of progress than to refuse to budge one inch from the positions they took.

Pancakes
(200-220 pancakes)

2	kg	flour
60	g	baking powder (75 ml) (6 Tsp)
20	g	salt (20 ml) (4 t)
16		eggs
4	ℓ	water
250	ml	vinegar (1 c)
1	ℓ	oil
50	ml	lemon juice (4 Tsp) (keeps pancakes soft)

Method:
Mix the dry ingredients in a large mixing-bowl. Beat the eggs, water, vinegar and oil and stir or beat into dry ingredients. Mix thoroughly. Grease a hot pan with a little oil, only for the first pancake. The rest of the batter is fried without adding oil to the pan. Pour the batter into the pan and fry on both sides till brown.
Joey Pienaar

Pancake fillings

Cocktail or Savoury fillings: Fry cocktail sausages, spread prepared mustard over and roll in small, hot pancakes.
Dice chicken livers and fry with a little chopped onion and mushrooms in butter. Mix with a little white sauce to form a soft mixture. Mix diced, fried chicken livers, a little sherry and seeded grapes with a cheese sauce.
For vegetarians, the following fillings are suitable:
Mix peeled, chopped tomatoes, lightly fried brinjal, fried chopped onion, fried chopped mushrooms with a cheese sauce.
Joey Pienaar

Learn to live, learn to laugh. This is the joy of everything.

Jan Smuts cookies
(Makes 4 doz)

Pastry:
425	g	cake flour (750 ml, unsifted)
10	ml	baking powder (2 t)
1	ml	salt
250	g	butter or margarine, at room temperature
200	g	sugar (250 ml)
2		eggs, beaten

Filling:
125	g	butter or margarine, at room temperature
125	g	sugar (150 ml)
2		eggs, beaten thoroughly
125	g	cake flour (225 ml, unsifted)
5	ml	baking powder
100	ml	smooth apricot jam

Method:
Sift flour, baking powder and salt. Rub in butter with fingertips. Add sugar and mix. Add eggs and mix all ingredients to form a dough. Roll out to a thickness of 3 mm and cut into rounds, 8 cm in diameter. Line greased patty pans. Cream butter and sugar. Add eggs and mix. Sift flour and baking powder and mix with egg mixture. Spoon 2 ml apricot jam into each patty pan and top with 2 ml filling. Bake approximately 15 min or until golden brown in a preheated oven at 190 °C (375 °F). Turn cookies out onto a cooling rack and cool.
Mollie de Witt

At some time in our lives, we all need to escape to some far-off island — Ella Marie.

Pancakes
(10 pancakes)

2		large eggs
200	ml	milk (¾ c + 2 t)
20	ml	oil (4 t)
5	ml	vinegar, lemon juice or brandy (1 t)
120	g	flour (250 ml) (1 c)
1	ml	salt
200	ml	water (¾ c + 2 t)

Method:
Beat the eggs. Add the milk, oil and vinegar. Add flour and salt and beat till free from lumps. Add the water and mix well. Leave the batter for ± 30 min. Pour a little oil into a frying pan and allow the pan to heat well. Pour the excess oil off and fry the batter.

Remarks:
It should not be necessary to grease the pan again.
Mollie de Witt

There is no better medicine for a broken heart than the words: "I love you" — Frans.

Cream scones

2	c	flour
4	t	baking powder
1	Tsp	sugar
½	c	cream (slightly sour)
1		egg
½	t	salt

Method:

Sift the dry ingredients. Beat the egg and mix it with the cream. Add to the dry ingredients and mix lightly with a spatula. Drop spoonfuls of batter onto a greased baking tray, if batter is too stiff add more cream. If the batter is too soft it will spread in the pan. Bake for 10-20 min in a hot oven 230 °C (450 °F).

Joey Pienaar

Some people learn from hurt; others never learn — Lady Falda

Tarts

317

Apple tart
(Delicious)

Pastry:
500	ml	unsifted flour (2 c)
250	ml	sugar (1 c)
10	ml	baking powder (2 t)
2	ml	salt
250	g	margarine

Filling:
1	tin	unsweetened pie apples, finely chopped (385 g)
125	ml	sugar (½ c)
75	g	dried fruit cake mixture (½ c) (125 ml)
2	ml	cinnamon
1	ml	ground cloves
		a pinch of salt
1	t	heaped custard powder mixed with a little water

Method:
Sift the flour, sugar, baking powder and salt. Rub in the butter or margarine with fingertips until it forms a dough. Cover the dough and leave aside. Preheat the oven to 180 °C (350 °F). Spread half the dough around the sides and base of an ovenproof pie plate. Mix the pie apples, sugar, dried fruit mixture, cinnamon, cloves and salt thoroughly. Put the mixture into a saucepan and warm slowly. Stir in the custard powder until it thickens. Leave to cool. Spread over the crust. Coarsely grate the rest of the dough over the top. Bake for 20 min or until the pastry starts to brown. Serve warm or cold. The tart freezes well.

Joey Pienaar

It is no weakness to admit a weakness.

Greek coconut tart
(Delicious)

Cream:
¼	lb	margarine (125 g)
1	c	sugar (250 ml)
3		eggs

Add 500 ml coconut (2 c). Sift 250 ml flour (1 c), 3 t baking powder, a pinch of salt. Mix ingredients with 250 ml (1 c) lukewarm milk. Pour mixture into 2 greased pie dishes and bake for 35 min at 180 °C (350 °F). When cooked pour the syrup over.
Boil for 5 min

1¼	c	sugar
1¼	c	water
1	t	vanilla essence

Can be served with cream.
Joey Pienaar

Ginger fridge tart

1½	pkt	ginger biscuits (crushed)
¾	c·	syrup
3	Tsp	custard powder
1½	c	boiling water

Method:
Boil syrup and water. Add 3 Tsp custard powder to the syrup. Break the biscuits. Mix all ingredients and pour into a greased mould. Leave to set. Serve with whipped cream.
Annamarié Strydom

I am a stranger and afraid in a world I never made.

Lollie's cheese cake

1	pkt	Tennis biscuits (crushed)
250	g	melted butter

Mix and press the biscuits into a pie dish.

Filling:

500	g	cream cheese
2		eggs
¾	c	sugar
1	t	vanilla
1		small tin evaporated milk (170 g)
2	t	custard powder

Method:
Mix all the ingredients thoroughly and spoon into the crust. Bake for 30 min at 180 °C (350 °F). It will taste delicious with whipped cream on top. Allow to cool completely before adding the cream.
Joey Pienaar

Brandy tart (Tipsy)
(Delicious)

250	g	dates
250	ml	boiling water (1 c)
5	ml	bicarbonate of soda (1 t)
250	ml	sugar (1 c)
60	ml	margarine (¼ c)
1		egg
375	ml	flour (1½ c)
3	ml	baking powder (½ t)
3	ml	salt (½ t)
125	ml	chopped nuts (½ c)

It's the friends you can call at 4 am that matter — Marlene Dietrich.

The children will love these jam tarts (p 287), Hertzoggies (p 280), coconut biscuits (p 281), coffee biscuits (p 280) and Romany Creams (p 286)

This page was sponsored by 'Strike Speelgoed Edms Bpk' tel (012 – 01480-3091)

Coconut ice and cheese cake topped with strawberries and cream (p 349) will satisfy the hunger of any sweet tooth

Method:

Chop dates finely. Sprinkle with bicarbonate of soda and pour boiling water over. Allow to cool. Cream butter and sugar, add eggs and beat. Add dates. Sift flour, baking powder and salt and add to date mixture. Mix well and pour batter into a greased dish and bake for 30 min in a medium oven at 180 °C (350 °F).

Syrup:

310	ml	sugar (1¼ c)
250	ml	water (1 c)
15	ml	margarine (3 t)
5	ml	vanilla essence (1 t)
100	ml	brandy (8 Tsp)
		a pinch of salt

Method:

Boil sugar, water, butter and salt for 5 min. Remove from stove and add vanilla essence and brandy. Pour over cooked tart. Decorate with cherries and nuts or whipped cream when cold.

Joey Pienaar

The longer you nurse a grudge, the longer it takes to heal.

Coffee caramel tart
(Delicious)

1	tin	condensed milk
1	c	strong black coffee (1½ Tsp. heaped Nescafé instant coffee mixed with boiling water)
2	t	heaped gelatine
1	Tsp	margarine
½	c	golden syrup
1	t	vanilla essence
3		egg whites
¼	c	cold water

Method:
Soak the gelatine in cold water and leave aside over boiling water. The water need not boil, but must be kept warm. Heat butter in a saucepan and stir in the syrup. Add the condensed milk and stir briskly to mix. Whilst bringing mixture to the boil, stir in the hot coffee. The coffee must be very strong. Boil the mixture for 10 min. Stir in the gelatine. Fold in the stiffly beaten egg whites and stir quickly. Remove and flavour. Pour into a pie shell. Leave in the refrigerator to set. Decorate with whipped cream.

Joey Pienaar

There is always room for a man of force.

Ginger tart
(Makes 1 medium-sized tart)

Crust:
150	g	¾ of a (200 g pkt) Marie or Tennis biscuits (crushed)
75	g	(80 ml) butter or margarine, melted (⅓ c)

Filling:
1	tin	evaporated milk, cooled overnight in the refrigerator (170 g)
125	ml	ginger syrup (½ c)
15	ml	gelatine (3 t)
30	ml	cold water (2 Tsp + 1 t)
1	tin	(397 g) caramelized condensed milk
30	ml	finely chopped ginger preserve (2 Tsp + 1 t)
		a pinch of salt

Method:
Crush biscuits and mix crumbs with butter. Line a deep pie dish ± 24 cm in diameter. Whip evaporated milk until stiff. Beat ginger syrup into mixture, sprinkle gelatine over cold water in a cup. Place the cup in a dish of boiling water to dissolve. Whisk the gelatine gradually into the milk mixture. Beat condensed milk, ginger preserve and salt into the mixture. Pour mixture into crust and leave in the refrigerator to set.

Joey Pienaar

We must correct a great deal; but not too much.

Coconut milk tart

Crust:
125	g	soft butter or margarine
100	g	sugar (125 ml) (½ c)
100	g	finely crushed (200 ml) Tennis biscuits
100	g	coconut (300 ml) (1 c + 4 Tsp)
60	g	sifted cake flour (125 ml) (½ c)

Filling:
4		eggs
25	g	flour (50 ml) (4 Tsp)
25	g	maizena (50 ml) (4 Tsp)
		a pinch of salt
1⅛	ℓ	milk (4½ c)
25	g	butter or margarine (25 ml) (2 Tsp)
200	g	sugar (250 ml) (1 c)

Method:
Mix butter and milk. Add the biscuit crumbs, coconut and flour. Mix well and flatten half of the pastry in an ovenproof dish ± 20 by 30 cm. Beat eggs thoroughly. Add flour, maizena and salt and beat thoroughly again. Boil milk, stir in butter then the sugar. Stir milk into egg mixture, pour back into the saucepan, stir constantly and boil over medium heat until thick. Spread over the crust, sprinkle the remaining crust over the top and bake for 35 min at 180 °C (350 °F).

Joey Pienaar

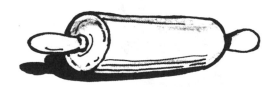

Home is where the heart is.

Tipsy tart
(Delicious)

¼	c	sugar
¾	c	boiling water
2	Tsp	butter
1	c	sliced dates
1¼	c	flour
¼	c	nuts
1	t	bicarbonate of soda
4	t	baking powder
¼	t	salt
1		egg

Method:
Pour boiling water over dates and keep hot. Cream butter and sugar and add egg. Beat well. Add hot date mixture then the dry ingredients. Bake for 20 min at 350 °F (180 °C).

Syrup:

1½	c	sugar
¾	c	water
1	Tsp	butter
1	t	vanilla essence
¼	c	brandy

Method:
Boil all the ingredients except the vanilla essence. Add vanilla. Pour slowly over hot tart.
Henda Gous

Behaviour is the mirror where one displays his image.

Corn flake meringue tart
(Makes 1 tart with a 27 cm diameter)

Crust:
50	g	butter or margarine, melted (60 ml) (¼c)
150	g	finely crushed corn flakes (250 ml) (1 c)
50	g	sugar (60 ml) (¼ c)
2	ml	ground cinnamon

Filling:
25	g	maizena (50 ml) (4 Tsp)
100	g	sugar (125 ml) (½ c)
3		egg yolks
500	ml	boiling milk (2 c)
5	ml	vanilla essence (1 t)

Meringue:
3		egg whites
		a pinch of salt
1	ml	baking powder
60	g	sugar (75 ml) (¼ c + 3 t)

Method:
Preheat oven to 125 °C (250 °F). Mix butter, corn flakes, sugar and cinnamon and press mixture firmly with a spoon, on the base and sides of a pie dish with a 27 cm diameter. Heat milk. Beat maizena, sugar and egg yolks in a medium-sized mixing bowl until light yellow. Add a little hot milk at a time. Pour back into saucepan, stir constantly and warm over medium heat until nearly boiling. Stir in vanilla essence and stir until the mixture boils. Lower heat and allow to simmer while making the meringue. Beat egg whites until stiff. Add salt and baking powder and gradually add the sugar. Pour hot mixture into the pie dish and cover with meringue. Bake 45-60 min. Turn oven off and leave tart in oven till completely cooled.
Joey Pienaar

He who doesn't love is not human.

Lemon meringue tart

1	tin	condensed milk (310 ml) (1¼ c)
125	ml	lemon juice (½ c)
		grated rind of one lemon
2		eggs (separated)
		a pinch of salt
1		pastry shell (p 335)

Method:
Beat the egg yolks and add to the condensed milk.
Add lemon juice and grated lemon rind and blend till thick and creamy.
Pour into baked pie shell.
Beat the egg whites and gradually add 6 t sugar. Beat till stiff.
Spoon beaten egg white over the filling.
Bake for 30 min in a moderate oven (325 °F — 160 °C) or until the egg white is golden brown in colour.
Serve chilled.
Marlene Heath

Rome wasn't built in a day.

Marshmallow tart
(Sufficient for 2 large tarts)

Filling:

1	tin	condensed milk (397 g)
2		containers fresh cream (2 x 250 ml)
750	g	marshmallows (cut in quarters)
1	pkt	cherries (large) (halved) (250 g)
3		lemons (squeezed)
1	tin	crushed pineapples (1 c) (strain to remove excess syrup)

Method:
Mix the condensed milk with the lemon juice. Add marshmallows and cherries. Add pineapple. Whip the cream until stiff and add to condensed milk mixture. Mix. Use Tennis biscuits to line a pie dish. Pour filling into pie crust and cool.
Joey Pienaar

Crustless milk tart

4	c	milk
1	t	baking powder
2	Tsp	margarine, level
4		eggs
1	c	sugar
		a pinch of salt
1	c	flour
1	t	vanilla essence
		or almond essence

Method:
Separate yolks and whites of eggs. Beat whites well. Melt margarine and add sugar and egg yolks. Add baking powder to flour and mix with margarine, sugar and egg yolks, as well as the milk and vanilla essence. Beat with an egg beater. Add stiff egg whites and

---

It is easier to keep holidays than commandments.

beat again. Pour into 2 pie plates and bake in a moderate oven for 30-35 min until cooked.
Joey Pienaar

Date tart

1	c	dates, finely chopped
½	t	bicarbonate of soda
1	c	boiling water

Chop dates, pour the boiling water and bicarbonate of soda over them and leave.

1		egg, beaten thoroughly
1½	c	flour
½	c	cherries, finely chopped
1	t	vanilla
		salt
1	c	sugar
¼	c	butter
1	t	baking powder

Method:
Cream butter and sugar, add egg, then the dry ingredients, cherries, vanilla and date mixture. Pour into a large pyrex dish. Bake approximately ½ hr at 180 °C or 350 °F.

Syrup:

1	c	sugar
1	c	coconut
6	Tsp	butter (level)
4	Tsp	milk

Method:
Boil the ingredients and pour over hot tart. Put back into oven for a few min.
Kotie Smit

Sweet is the nut but bitter is the shell.

Paraguayan tart

Serve in a fluted flan dish

6	Tsp	margarine
¾	c	(or more) self-raising flour
¼	c	cocoa
1	Tsp	cocoa (for syrup)
2	Tsp	instant coffee granules
6	Tsp	castor sugar
2		eggs
5	Tsp	brown sugar
		whole nuts for decoration

Method:

Cream butter and sugar and add eggs. Then add the cocoa and self-raising flour. Pour batter into flan dish and make a syrup from the following: Dissolve 1 Tsp cocoa, 2 Tsp coffee granules, 6 Tsp castor sugar and 1¼ c water, and pour over tart. Bake for 50-60 min at 160 °C (325 °F). When ready sift icing sugar over the top and decorate with the whole nuts. Serve with whipped cream — serve cream separately.

Mrs Jessie le Grange

Saratoga tart

(Something special)

3		egg whites
1	t	baking powder
14		cream crackers
		vanilla essence
1	c	sugar
⅛	t	salt
¾	c	peanuts
		whipped cream

Share not peas with the king and cherries with the beggar.

Method:

Beat egg whites until nearly stiff. Gradually add sugar and beat until firm. Add baking powder and vanilla. Stir in coarsely crushed cream crackers and peanuts. Draw 23 cm circles on the shiny side of aluminium foil, place on a flat baking pan and spray with "Spray and cook". Halve the meringue mixture and spread evenly over foil. Bake for 1 hr in a cool oven at 100 °C (210 °F). Cool, remove the foil carefully and place back on the oven shelf to allow the base of the meringue to dry. Fill with whipped cream and place two layers on top of each other. Top with the rest of the cream and sprinkle with flaked chocolate. Prepare the day before and place in refrigerator to keep meringue soft enough to cut.

Lena Colyn

Apricot cream cheese cake

1	tin	condensed milk (397 g)
80	ml	lemon juice (⅓ c)
2		medium eggs, separated
90	ml	cream cheese (⅓ c + 2 t)
250	ml	apricots (liquidized) (1 c)
		(can be substituted with strawberries)
25	ml	sugar (2 Tsp)
1		baked crust

Method:

Mix condensed milk and lemon juice. Stir until thick. Add beaten egg yolks, cream cheese and fruit. Pour into crust. Beat egg whites till stiff and add sugar. Pour over tart. Bake for 10 min or until browned at 180 °C (350 °F). Cool before serving.

Henda Gous

Where wine is not common, commons must be sent.

Cottage cheese cake

1	tin	caramelized condensed milk (397 g)
500	g	creamed cottage cheese
2		egg whites
1	t	vanilla
⅓	c	lemon juice
1		sachet gelatine (3 t)
		finger biscuits or sponge cake

Method:

Place finger biscuits or sponge cake in a pie plate. Cream the cottage cheese, condensed milk, lemon juice and vanilla. Dissolve the gelatine (3 Tsp cold water) and add. Stir in gelatine when syrupy. Beat egg white firmly and add. Pour mixture over the finger biscuits and decorate with finger biscuit crumbs. (Can also be decorated with flake (chocolate) or strawberries.)

Dalene Jansen

Cape gooseberry tart

2		swiss rolls
2		containers cottage cheese (natural) (2 x 250 g)
1	tin	canned gooseberries or apricots (385 g)
		juice of ½ lemon
1	tin	condensed milk (397 g)
2	Tsp	custard powder (level)

Method:

Drain fruit juice into a saucepan. Add ¼ c boiling water and ½ c sugar. Boil sauce and add 2 level Tsp custard powder blended with a little water. Boil until the custard thickens. Add fruit to cus-

---

All roads lead to Rome.

tard. Cut Swiss roll. Line the base of a rectangular pyrex dish with slices of cake. Spread cottage cheese mixture over the top. Finally pour the custard mixture over and allow to set.
Esther Liebenberg

Coconut tart

Crust:
Tennis biscuits

Filling:
1	Tsp	gelatine
½	c	sugar
1½	c	milk
¼	t	salt
1	c	coconut
¼	c	cold water
2		eggs, separated
1	t	vanilla essence
½	c	cream

Method:
Mix gelatine with water and leave. Mix ¼ c sugar and 2 egg yolks in a saucepan. Add milk slowly. Stir continuously over medium heat until mixture thickens. Remove from stove and add gelatine. Stir until dissolved. Now add vanilla essence. Place the saucepan in the refrigerator until the mixture thickens. Beat the egg whites with the salt until firm. Now add the other ¼ c sugar and beat thoroughly. Fold into mixture. Whip ½ c cream, add coconut and add to tart. Sprinkle a little coconut over tart and place in refrigerator.
Dalene Jansen

One swallow does not make a summer.

Triangle tart
(Frozen)

250	g	butter
1		container cottage cheese (250 g)
		a few marshmallows
½	c	castor sugar
2	pkts	Tennis biscuits
		a few cherries and nuts

Method:
Cream cottage cheese, butter, 1 t vanilla essence and castor sugar thoroughly. Place 3 rows of biscuits, 6 biscuits per row on a sheet of foil. Spread a layer of the above mixture over the biscuits. Place a second layer of biscuits on top. Mix marshmallows, cherries and nuts with the rest of the cream cheese filling and spoon onto the middle of the biscuits. Now fold the foil. The two edges must form a triangle. Secure edges and freeze. Thaw in refrigerator and remove just before serving.
Joey Pienaar

Cottage cheese cake
(Delicious)

Crust:
Cut a Swiss roll in slices and arrange in the base of a pie plate to form a crust.

Filling:

1		container cottage cheese (250 g)
½	c	lemon juice
1	tin	condensed milk (397 g)

Method:
Beat the above ingredients and pour onto swiss role base. Use a tin of canned fruit (your choice), drain and arrange over the filling. Thicken the drained juice with a little custard powder and when

---

Homekeeping hearts are the happiest.

cooled, pour over the top of the tart. Place in refrigerator to set. Gooseberries are delicious, but small halved apricots, youngberries and strawberries also look and taste delicious.
Mollie de Witt

Sweet pastry
(Does not shrink)

4	c	flour
1	c	sugar
1	Tsp	custard powder
1	t	salt
250	g	margarine
3	t	baking powder (level)
2		eggs

Method:
Cream sugar, butter and eggs. Mix the dry ingredients into the mixture with your fingers. Place between plastic sheets and roll. Sprinkle the plastic with flour to prevent the dough from sticking. Grease muffin pans, place rolled dough into them. Prick the base of the dough with a fork. Bake at 180 °C (350 °F) until light brown (± 15 min). Can be stored for a long time in an airtight container.

For large pastry cases:
Press dough into a pyrex dish. Prick the base of the dough with a fork. Bake at 180 °C (350 °F) until light brown. Can be stored for a considerable time in a plastic bag.
Joey Pienaar

When in Rome do as the Romans do.

Milk tart filling

(Delicious and creamy)
(2 milk tarts — 5 doz small tarts)

Boil together:

1	ℓ	milk
1	Tsp	margarine (heaped)

Beat:

3		eggs (large)
¼	t	salt
1	c	sugar

Sift:

1½	Tsp	flour (heaped)
1½	Tsp	maizena (heaped)
1	dsp	custard powder
1	t	vanilla essence

Method:

Add sifted flour mixture to already beaten egg mixture. Beat well until free of lumps. Stir some of the boiling milk into egg and flour mixture. Add the mixture to the rest of the boiling milk in saucepan. Stir until mixture thickens and starts to boil. Add vanilla essence. Lower heat, cover with the lid and allow to boil for 1 min. Pour immediately into prepared crusts. Sprinkle with cinnamon.
N.B. For tartlets, the mixture must cool for at least 2 hrs.
For something really special, sprinkle a layer of coconut in the large pastry case and then the filling. (See below.)

Coconut layer

(For 2 tarts)

125	ml	brown sugar (½ c)
250	ml	dessicated coconut (1 c)
60	ml	margarine (¼ c)
50	ml	milk (4 Tsp)

Tears bring relief, but they have never solved any problems.

10　ml　vanilla essence (2 t)

Method:
Mix all the ingredients in a saucepan, bring to the boil and spread over the base of the prepared pastry case.
Joey Pienaar

Hot apple cake

3	Tsp	margarine
1	c	castor sugar
3		eggs
1	c	flour
1	t	baking powder
		a pinch of salt
¼	c	milk
500	g	tin pie apples (410 g)

Sauce:

125	g	butter
1½	c	milk
¾	c	sugar

Boil for 10 min.

Method:
Cream butter and castor sugar. Add eggs, one at a time. Add dry ingredients and mix with milk. Place the batter in a greased pan or pie dish and place the pie apples on top. Bake in a moderate oven for about 35 min. On removing from the oven, pour the hot sauce over. Serve while still warm with whipped cream.
Joey Pienaar

Rejoice at your life; for the time is more advanced than you would think.

Milk tart
(Baked)

Pastry:

3	c	flour, sifted
1	t	cream of tartar
250	g	butter (cold)
1	c	cream (cold)
1		egg yolk
2	Tsp	lemon juice or vinegar
2	Tsp	brandy

Method:
Sift the flour and cream of tartar three times. Grate and rub in the butter. Mix the cream, egg yolk, lemon juice and brandy and beat lightly until frothy. Pour this mixture over the flour mixture and mix gently. All ingredients must be ice-cold. Line the pan or pie dishes with the pastry crust.

Filling:

6	c	milk (6 x 250 ml)

Boil the milk with pieces of orange rind and sticks of cinnamon. Mix 1 c flour, sifted, ½ small c maizena, 1½ c sugar and 1 c milk.

Method:
Remove the rind and cinnamon from the boiling milk. Stir in the flour mixture and boil until cooked. Beat 8 egg yolks mixed with a little of the hot mixture and stir in 1 heaped Tsp butter and a pinch of salt. Beat the egg whites until stiff but not dry and fold into filling. Pour into the lined pie dishes and bake for 5 min in a hot oven at 200 °C (400 °F). Reduce heat to 180 °C (350 °F) and bake another 10 min.
Joey Pienaar

Invest in ground; they stopped making it — Lady Falda.

Apple tart
(Fancy)

4½	Tsp	butter
1½	c	self-raising flour
½	c	milk
½	c	coconut
		salt
¼	c	currants
3		large eggs
1½	c	sugar
1		large tin pie apples (410 g)

Method:
Cream butter and sugar. Add eggs one at a time. Whisk thoroughly. Add salt, flour and milk alternately. Add coconut and currants. Spread half of the mixture in a rectangular greased pie dish. Cut apples into smaller pieces and spread evenly over the dough. Place remaining dough on top. Bake for 45 min at 350 °F (180 °C).

Syrup:

1	c	milk
1½	c	sugar
3	Tsp	butter
1½	t	vanilla essence

Method:
Boil all ingredients and pour over hot tart. Cool and decorate with cream.

Joey Pienaar

Don't waste time. It passes quicker than you think.

Green fig jam tart

Crust:
(Crumbed crust)

Filling

3		eggs, separated
¾	c	sugar
1	Tsp	gelatine
1	t	almond essence
1	tin	evaporated milk (410 g)
¼	c	cold water
1	c	chopped nuts
1	c	smooth green fig jam
		(can also be substituted with mixed fruit)

Method:
Beat egg yolks and sugar. Heat the milk and add. Place mixture into a double boiler over boiling water and stir until mixture thickens. Soak gelatine in the cold water for 5 min and stir into the hot mixture. Add nuts, almond essence and jam and leave to cool. Beat egg whites until stiff and fold into mixture. Pour into crumbed crust and cool.

Biscuit crust:

500	g	biscuit crumbs (2 c)
75	ml	white sugar (6 Tsp)
100	ml	melted butter or margarine (8 Tsp)

Method:
Mix the ingredients, if a little dry, add a little lemon juice. Press with a spoon and your hand into a dish ± 5 mm thick. Bake pie for 10 min at 180 °C (350 °F). The crust need not necessarily be baked. If not baked place it in the refrigerator to set. It is less crumbly if not baked.

Joey Pienaar

Loneliness is the severest form of punishment.

Brandy tart

1	t	bicarbonate of soda
1	c	dates (chopped)
1	c	sugar
1¼	c	flour
¼	t	baking powder
1	c	boiling water
2	Tsp	butter
1		egg
¼	t	salt
¼	c	nuts

Method:
Pour boiling water over dates and bicarbonate of soda. Stir until the dates are soft. Let the mixture cool. Cream the butter and sugar and add the well-beaten egg. Sift the flour, salt and baking powder. Add nuts. Add the date mixture and butter mixture alternately to the dry ingredients. Pour the batter into two 20,5 cm (8") ovenproof dishes (1 30,5 cm (12") dish). Bake for 20 min at 180 °C (350 °F).

What would have happened to us if we didn't have masks?

Syrup:

1	c	sugar
¼	t	salt
1	t	vanilla essence
¾	c	water
1	Tsp	butter
¼	c	brandy
¼	c	sweet wine
		or
½	c	brandy

Method:

Boil the sugar, water, salt and butter for 5 min. Remove from heat and add vanilla essence, brandy and wine. Pour while hot over tarts. Cool and decorate with cream.

Joey Pienaar

Nothing bonds people together more closely than grief.

A minute to smile; an hour to weep.

Sweets

Toffee apples

50		medium, red apples
50		suitable sticks
800	g	sugar (1 ℓ)
250	ml	water (1 c)
20	ml	vinegar (4 t)
200	g	golden syrup (150 ml) (12 Tsp)
		a pinch of salt
25	ml	butter (2 Tsp)
		red colouring

Method:
Wash and dry the apples and place a small stick firmly into the stem end. Heat all the other ingredients slowly, while stirring, to dissolve the sugar. Wipe the crystals from the sides with a brush. Boil the syrup to a light crack-stage. Remove from the heat and place the saucepan in boiling water over a low heat. Dip the apples, one at a time, into the syrup, covering the apples completely. Cool in an upright position.
Joey Pienaar

Sherbet

500	g	icing sugar
15	g	bicarbonate of soda
15	ml	tartaric acid (3 t)

Method:
Sift the ingredients three times. Store in an airtight container.
Ester Liebenberg

The roots of love do not lie in the bloodstream, but in the heart.

Fudge
(Makes 6 doz 2,5 x 2,5 cm squares)

165	g	butter or margarine (190 ml) (¾ c)
75	ml	golden syrup (6 Tsp)
1	tin	condensed milk (397 g)
325	ml	boiling milk (± 1¼ c)
1,2	kg	sugar (6 x 250 ml) (6 c)
140	g	flour (250 ml, unsifted) (1 c)
2	ml	cream of tartar
5	ml	vanilla essence (1 t)

Method:
Melt the butter and syrup in a large heavy based saucepan over low heat. Add condensed and boiling milk and mix. Mix sugar and flour and add to condensed milk mixture. Mix thoroughly. Stir constantly over a low heat and bring to the boil. Add cream of tartar the moment the mixture starts boiling. Boil 25 min (to the soft ball stage) over low heat and stir constantly with a wooden spoon to prevent burning. Remove from stove and add vanilla essence. Beat with a wooden spoon until mixture starts to thicken. Pour into a greased pan or dish (not smaller than 18 x 28 x 3 cm). Allow to cool. Cut into squares.
Joey Pienaar

Your father is your father, even though you are aware of his weaknesses.

Marshmallows

Boil 4 c sugar, 1½ c water. Switch oven plate on high and the moment the mixture starts boiling, reduce to low. Boil 6 min. Dissolve 3 Tsp gelatine, level, in 1 c boiling water. Remove syrup from stove and add the gelatine and 1 t vanilla essence. Cool. Pour into mixing bowl. Beat at high speed for 12 min. Grease a pan with margarine and pour mixture in. Cut into long strips. Roll in toasted coconut. Then cut into squares.
Joey Pienaar

Popcorn syrup
(To colour popcorn — enough for 1 bag of popcorn)

2½	c	sugar
½	c	golden syrup
½	c	water
1	Tsp	butter
¼	Tsp	salt
1	t	vanilla essence

Method:
Mix sugar, water, syrup, butter and salt and boil to the soft ball stage (240 °F — 120 °C). Separate syrup into three portions (work very quickly) and add 1 t colouring to each part. Pour over popcorn and stir the corn constantly. Spread the corn on waxed paper greased with butter.
Joey Pienaar

Every man is entitled to a second chance.

Coconut ice
(Makes 16 large pieces)

500	g	sugar (625 ml) (2½ c)
125	ml	milk (½ c)
250	g	coconut (780 ml) (3 c + 2 Tsp)
5	ml	vanilla essence (1 t)
1	ml	cream of tartar
		a pinch of salt
		few drops cochineal
		(red food colouring)

Method:
Grease a 20 x 20 x 5 cm pan or dish. Heat sugar and milk over medium heat to boiling point in a medium saucepan with a heavy base. Reduce heat, remove lid and boil for 2 min. Remove from stove, add coconut, vanilla essence, cream of tartar and salt and beat briskly until well mixed. Pour half of the mixture into a small pan and level. Stir a few drops of cochineal into remaining mixture to form a pink colour and spread while still hot over the white layer in the pan. Cut into squares and allow to cool.

Ina Steyn

Nothing in this world is free. Everything has a price.

Coconut ice
(Uncooked)

3¾	c	coconut
4½	c	icing sugar
1	tin	condensed milk (397 g)
¼	t	cream of tartar
¼	t	salt
1	t	vanilla essence

Method:
Mix thoroughly. Halve the mixture and add 1 t rosewater and a few drops of colouring to one half. Place layers on top of each other, cut into squares. Leave to set.
Joey Pienaar

Fudge
(Always a success)

1	tin	condensed milk (397 g)
1	tin	water (condensed milk tin)
6	c	sugar
3	Tsp	flour
¼	t	salt
¼	t	cream of tartar
125	g	margarine
3	Tsp	syrup

Method:
Boil syrup, condensed milk, water and margarine. Mix sugar, flour, salt and cream of tartar. Stir into syrup mixture (i.e. condensed milk, water, margarine and syrup.) Boil slowly for 20-30 min. Stir occasionally. Remove from stove, add 1 t vanilla essence, leave to cool and beat until creamy. Pour into greased pan. Cut when mixture starts to set.
Mollie de Witt

Turn over a new leaf today. It's still not too late.

Coconut ice

1	c	milk
4	c	sugar
2	c	coconut
		red food colouring
5	ml	rosewater (1 t)
		(obtainable from pharmacies)
		a pinch of salt

Method:

Bring milk and sugar to the boil in a saucepan, while stirring occasionally. Boil rapidly for 7 min. Remove and stir in the coconut. Mix well. Flavour with rosewater. Pour half into a greased pan. Colour the other half with red colouring to a light pink. Spread the pink layer over the white while still hot. The two layers must clearly be separate but must stick together and be reasonably thick. Cut into squares after it has cooled.

Love is only true and beautiful as long as it doesn't hurt anyone.

Those who weep recover more quickly.

Treat the children to marshmallows (p 348) and coconut ice (p 350)

This fudge recipe has always been a favourite particularly because it is quick and easy (p 354)

Microwave recipes

Fudge
(Delicious)

1	tin	condensed milk (397 g)
2	c	sugar
125	g	margarine (white or yellow)
1	Tsp	vanilla essence
¼	t	gravy browning for a darker caramel colour — for lighter colour only 3 drops

Method:
Mix all the ingredients in a mixing bowl. Microwave on high for 2 min. Stir well. Boil for 6 min on high. Stir every 2 minutes. Add vanilla essence and gravy browning and stir well. Grease pan with margarine. Pour mixture in and flatten. Cool and cut into squares.
Joey Pienaar

Bacon rolls

Roll bacon rashers around pieces of liver or apple, glacé cherries, pineapple, cheese, banana, dates and prunes filled with almonds. Secure with a toothpick. Place on a dish and cover with a paper napkin. Heat according to the quantity.
Joey Pienaar

One that loses before starting a project, is one that has lost already.

Corn bread
(Makes a medium-sized bread)

4		eggs
125	ml	milk (½ c)
100	g	sugar (125 ml) (½ c)
125	g	maizena (250 ml) (1 c)
25	ml	flour (2 Tsp)
7	ml	baking powder (1½ t)
		a pinch of salt
1	tin	creamed sweetcorn (410 g)
1	tin	whole kernel corn, drained (410 g) (optional)
30	ml	cooking oil (6 t)
		paprika

Method:
Beat eggs, milk and sugar. Sift the maizena, flour, baking powder and salt into the egg mixture. Stir until mixed. Add the sweetcorn, whole kernel corn and cooking oil and mix. Spray a microwave breadpan (28 cm) with a non-stick spray. Pour the mixture into the pan. Sprinkle a little paprika on top. Turn a saucer upside down in microwave oven and place breadpan on top of it. Microwave the bread for 15 min on medium (70 %) and a further 3-4 min on full strength (100 %). Leave for 10 min before turning out.
Joey Pienaar

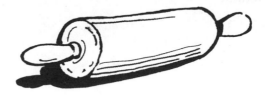

"I'm sorry." Those two little words are so easy, yet so hard.

Light fruit cake

250	g	blanched sultanas
50	g	mixed peel
75	g	ginger pieces
50	g	glacé fruit
250	ml	sugar (1 c)
125	ml	margarine (½ c)
2		eggs, beaten
500	ml	flour (2 c)
10	ml	baking powder (2 t)
3	ml	salt
250	ml	water (1 c)
15	ml	brandy (3 t)
5	ml	ginger (1 t)
125	g	cherries, chopped
125	g	nuts, chopped
100	ml	brandy

Method:
Line the base of a microwave tube pan with a piece of Superwipe towel. Place fruit, margarine and water in a large mixing bowl and cover with waxed paper. Microwave for 10 min at maximum strength and leave to cool. Add 15 ml brandy. Sift dry ingredients. Stir into fruit. Then add cherries and nuts. Mix. Pour into pan. Do not cover. Microwave for 40 min on defrost and then 3 min at maximum strength. Cool in pan. Turn out and pour the brandy over the top. Wrap in foil. Allow to mature. Pour ¼ c brandy over 2 days before use.
Joey Pienaar

Rather a diamond with a flaw than a stone without.

Buttermilk pudding
(Makes 6-8 helpings)

3	Tsp	margarine
1	c	sugar
2	c	milk
1	c	buttermilk
¾	c	flour
3		large eggs
1	t	vanilla essence

Method:
Mix all ingredients thoroughly with a beater till smooth. Pour into a glass dish. Microwave for 3 min at maximum strength and stir. Microwave a further 3 min and stir again. Microwave another 4 min and allow pudding to stand for 5 min.

Joey Pienaar

Chicken with mushrooms

250	ml	sour cream (1 c)
125	ml	dry sherry (½ c)
125	g	button mushrooms, sliced
1		x 410 g tin cream of mushroom soup
4		chicken thighs, boned

Method:
Arrange thighs in a glass dish. Mix rest of ingredients and pour over chicken. Chicken must be well covered with mushroom mixture. Cover with plastic clingwrap. Microwave for 20 min on 50 % strength (simmer or moderate). Serve on rice and garnish with Aromat and chopped parsley.

Never teach Grandma how to hold the porridge spoon.

Tomato sauce
(Makes about 500 ml)

This sauce can be made with great success, with tinned tomatoes if fresh tomatoes are unobtainable or expensive, or if ripe tomatoes are not available.

25	ml	cooking oil (2 Tsp)
2		medium onions, chopped
4		large, ripe tomatoes, peeled and sliced
15	ml	sugar (3 t) or to taste
5	ml	medium curry (1 t)
		salt and pepper
10	ml	maizena (2 t)
10	ml	tomato sauce (2 t)

Method:
Place the cooking oil and the onion in a fairly large microwave dish and microwave for 2 min on maximum (100 %). Stir the mixture and microwave another 3 min on maximum (100 %). Add the tomatoes, sugar, curry powder, salt and pepper and microwave on maximum for 5 min (100 %). Mix the maizena and tomato sauce, stir into the tomato mixture and microwave for 2 min on maximum (100 %).
Joey Pienaar

Apple dessert

65	g	soft butter (75 ml) (6 Tsp)
300	g	soft breadcrumbs (250 ml) (1 c)
4		apples
62	ml	soft brown sugar (5 Tsp)
4	g	grated lemon rind (5 ml) (1 t)
25	ml	lemon juice (2 Tsp)
60	ml	hot water (¼ c)

Smile and the whole world smiles with you. Cry and you cry alone.

Method:

Mix butter and breadcrumbs. Peel apples, slice and sprinkle with the lemon juice. Mix sugar and lemon rind. Place buttered breadcrumbs, apple slices and sugar mixture into layers in a greased dish. Pour the hot water carefully around the edges of the mixture. Bake for 15 min on high. Cover and leave for 5 min. Serve with whipped cream.

Joey Pienaar

Taiwanese meat dish

1 kg diced meat (beef, mutton or pork)
Marinade for 2 hrs in the following sauce:

Sauce:

1-2	t	soya sauce
4	t	dry sherry
1-2	t	oyster sauce (tabasco can also be used)
1½	t	sugar
½	t	garlic flakes
4	t	salad oil
1	t	Maigerd

Method:

Heat a browning dish for ± 9 min and fry meat. Stir frequently. Can be served with vegetables or on skewers with mustard sauce. If a microwave is not used, fry in deep fat on the stove. Freezes well.

Hester Zietsman

God sends meat; the devil sends cooks.

Fruit cake
(Makes 1 medium-sized cake)

125	g	butter or margarine
1	pkt	dried fruit cake mixture (500 g)
75	g	chopped dates (125 ml) (½ c)
75	g	mixed peel (125 ml) (½ c)
200	g	soft brown sugar (250 ml) (1 c)
5	ml	bicarbonate of soda (1 t)
180	ml	water (± ¾ c)
75	g	chopped glacé cherries (125 ml) (½ c)
75	g	chopped nuts (125 ml) (½ c)
50	ml	brandy (4 Tsp)
275	g	flour (500 ml unsifted, measured) (2 c)
5	ml	mixed spice (1 t)
5	ml	ground ginger (1 t)
5	ml	cinnamon (1 t)
		a pinch of salt
2		large eggs
5	ml	baking powder (1 t)

Method:
Microwave the fruit cake in a glass dish, about 21 cm diameter and 9 cm deep. Grease the dish well, cover the bottom with a reasonably large circle of greased greaseproof paper. Microwave the butter or margarine for 30 seconds in a large mixing bowl on maximum. Add the cake mixture, dates, peel and sugar and mix. Mix the bicarbonate of soda with the water and add. Microwave on maximum for 5 min. Add the cherries, nuts and brandy. Sift the flour, mixed spice, ginger, cinnamon and salt and fold into the fruit mixture. Add beaten eggs and stir well. Sprinkle the baking powder over the top and stir until mixed. Pour the dough into a glass dish. Microwave the cake for 20-22 min on 70% (medium or roast). Leave for a while and turn out. If there is a moist spot underneath, turn the cake over and microwave a further minute or two on 70% strength.
Joey Pienaar

Marry in haste and repent at leisure.

Christmas biscuits
(Makes ± 120 biscuits)

500	g	butter or margarine
400	g	soft brown sugar (500 ml) (2 c)
4		eggs
50	ml	milk (4 Tsp)
10	ml	vanilla essence (2 t)
300	g	chopped dates (500 ml) (2 c)
1	pkt	sultanas (250 g)
200	g	whole-wheat meal (500 ml) (2 c)
275	g	flour (500 ml measured, unsifted) (2 c)
20	ml	baking powder (4 t)
1	pkt	All Bran flakes (300 g) (=6 x 250 ml) (6 c)
		red and green glacé cherries for decoration

Method:
Microwave the butter or margarine for 2 min in a large mixing bowl on maximum. Add the sugar and mix. Beat the eggs and mix well into sugar mixture. Add the milk and vanilla essence and mix. Add the dates and sultanas and mix. Add the whole-wheat meal, flour and baking powder and mix. Add the All Bran flakes and stir in. Place teaspoonfuls of batter on greaseproof paper (the size of your microwave oven or the turn table). Place a halved glacé cherry on each biscuit. Microwave the biscuits about 3½ min on maximum.

Joey Pienaar

Marriages are made in heaven.

Crumbed mealie meal porridge (Putupap)
(Makes 4-6 helpings)

500	ml	cold water (2 c)
250	g	coarse mealie meal (500 ml) (2 c)
7	ml	salt (1½ t)
1	tin	whole kernel corn, drained (410 g) (optional)

Method:
Spray a microwave dish of 1,5 ℓ with a non-stick spray. Pour the mealie meal, water and salt in and mix. Cover with the lid or pierced clingwrap. Microwave on maximum for 5 min (100 %). Stir with a large fork until crumbly, cover again and microwave on maximum for 5 min (100 %) longer. Stir again until crumbly, cover and microwave it for 10 min on half strength (50 %). Add the whole kernel corn and stir with a fork.
Joey Pienaar

Cloths to wipe hands after dinner

Use 4 Superwipe towels. Dampen — do not soak. Place lemon slices in cloths. Wrap in clingwrap. Microwave for 1 min on high (100 %).

Chicken: cooking time

Use the weight of the chicken and multiply by 2 to determine the cooking time, eg. 1,40 kg = 28 min. Cook on roast or medium high (70 %).
Hester Zietsman

You can lead a horse to the drinking trough, but you cannot make him drink.

Brandy tart

¼	c	sugar
2	c	self-raising flour
1	c	brown sugar
1		egg, beaten
1	c	seedless raisins
1	c	dates
1	c	water
1	t	bicarbonate of soda
1	c	broken walnuts
		salt

Method:
Boil the dates, butter, brown sugar and 1 c water for 5 min in a large glass mixing bowl in the microwave. Leave to cool. Stir in the beaten egg. Stir in the sifted dry ingredients. Stir in the raisins and walnuts. Bake in microwave oven in a rectangular or round dish for 10 min on 70% (medium).

Brandy sauce:
Boil ¾ c sugar with 1 c water for 2 min on high (100%). Add 1 Tsp butter and ¼ c brandy. Pierce the cooked tart with a fork or a metal skewer and pour the sauce over. Serve with cream or custard.
Ina Steyn

What the eye doesn't see, the heart doesn't feel.

Rice

1	c	rice
2	c	boiling water
1	t	salt

Method:
Add 2 c boiling water to rice and cover. Soak for at least 20 min. Boil for 5 min on high (100 %) and then for 20 min on defrost (30 %). Leave in oven for 15 min.
Joey Pienaar

Romany creams

250	g	margarine
½	c	boiling water (125 ml)
2	c	coconut (160 g) (500 ml)
2	c	flour (240 g) (500 ml)
4	Tsp	cocoa (60 g) (heaped)
1	t	baking powder (5 ml)
1	c	castor sugar (200 g)
		salt

Method:
Cream margarine and sugar, add sifted dry ingredients alternately with the boiling water. Add coconut and mix well. Cover a glass plate with plastic wrap, place teaspoonfuls of the dough in a circle on the glass plate. Bake 10 biscuits for 2½ min on High. When cold, sandwich two biscuits with melted chocolate.
Joey Pienaar

The way you eat is the way you work.

Crisp baked fish

750	g	white fish fillets
		small tin cream of mushroom soup (270 g)
125	ml	grated cheese (½ c)
		a little Worcestershire or Tabasco sauce
		a pinch of garlic salt
10	ml	grated onion (2 t)
1		small pkt potato crisps, crushed

Method:
Arrange fish in a rectangular pyrex dish. Pour soup over, then sprinkle cheese on the top. Melt butter, add onion and microwave on High for 4 min. Remove and add sauce, salt and crisps. Spread over fish. Cook for 10 min on High. Serve with mixed peas and small carrots.
Rina van Niekerk

Potato dish
(Delicious with chicken and barbecues)

Medium potatoes (as many as required), white onion soup, margarine.

Method:
Wash or scrub potatoes thoroughly. Mix the onion soup with margarine. Cut the potatoes in ½ cm slices but do not cut right through. Spread the onion soup over the potatoes. Place in a covered glass dish in microwave oven for 8-10 min on High depending on the amount and size of the potatoes. Serve immediately. Normal oven: 375 °F — 400 °F (190 °C — 200 °C) for 1 hour.
Rina van Niekerk

A rotten fruit was once a beautiful blossom.

Porridge (stiff — "stywe pap")

3   c boiling water
1   c coarse mealie meal
       salt

Method:
Add boiling water to mealie meal, cover and place in oven for 3 min on High (100 %) — stir. Cook for another 3 min on High (100 %) and stir again. Keep covered. Now place on defrost (30 %) for 15 min. Use less water for a thicker porridge.
Joey Pienaar

Buttermilk rusks

625	ml	buttermilk (2½ c)
500	ml	sugar (2 c)
250	ml	butter (1 c)
10	ml	bicarbonate of soda (2 t)
10	ml	cream of tartar (2 t)
10	ml	baking powder (2 t)
10	ml	salt (2 t)
10	ml	oil (2 t)
1	kg	flour
1	t	lemon juice

Method:
Sift dry ingredients. Add sugar and rub butter in with fingertips. Add buttermilk and knead to a soft dough. Mixture is enough for 3 small glass breadpans. Microwave each pan for 12-15 min on High (100 %). Allow to cool and cut into rusk fingers. Dry in the warming drawer of a normal stove or on a very low heat in the oven.
Joey Pienaar

If you send somebody to hell, you're an agent for Satan and you'll surely get your commission.

Cheese cake

Crust:
¾	pkt	Tennis biscuits (crushed)
3	Tsp	butter
2	Tsp	soft brown sugar
½	t	cinnamon

Method:
Cream butter and sugar. Add other ingredients. Can be placed in microwave oven. The mixture is reasonably dry. Press the mixture firmly on the bottom and sides of a pie plate. Microwave for 1 min on High (100 %).

Filling:
250	g	cream cheese
¾	c	sugar
1		large egg
1	t	vanilla essence
		fruit pieces (peaches, apricots or orange)

Method:
Mix cream cheese, egg and sugar. Add vanilla essence. Pour into crust. Bake in microwave oven for 3 min on High (100 %).
Joey Pienaar

The man that loves his own wife, may come and visit mine — C.J. Langenhoven.

Baked avocado with shrimps

150	ml	milk (½ c + 2 Tsp)
¾	Tsp	margarine
1	Tsp	flour
1	tin	shrimps (212 g)
		a pinch of cayenne pepper
½	t	lemon juice
2	t	tomato puree
2		ripe avocados
2	Tsp	fresh breadcrumbs

Method:
Pour milk in a jug and warm for 30 seconds in microwave oven. Melt margarine, add flour, stir in milk gradually and return to microwave for a minute or until thick. Add shrimps, cayenne pepper, lemon juice and tomato puree. Mix well. Cut avocados in half and stone. Brush halves with lemon juice. Place mixture in avocado halves and sprinkle with breadcrumbs. Place avocados in a circle on paper in the microwave oven. Bake for 2 min on High. Serve hot with a slice of lemon.
Joey Pienaar

Chocolate fudge
(Makes ± 24 squares)

1	pkt	icing sugar (500 g)
50	ml	cocoa (4 Tsp)
50	ml	milk (4 Tsp)
5	ml	vanilla essence (1 t)
1	ml	salt
100	g	butter or margarine (110 ml) (⅓ c + 2 Tsp)

Honesty is the best policy.

Method:

Grease a 23 x 13 x 3 cm pan or spray with a non-stick spray. Sift the icing sugar and cocoa into an ovenproof glass jug, with a 2 ℓ volume. Add the rest of the ingredients with the butter on top. Cook for 2 min on High (100 %). Stir well and cook for a further 2 min on High, see that it does not boil over. Stir well and cook for a further 30 seconds on High. Pour mixture into a pan and cool slightly. Mark into squares and cut when cold. Keep in refrigerator until required. Turn out and break into squares.

Ina Steyn

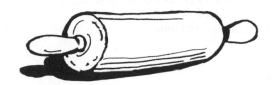

Cheese scones

(Makes 6 scones)

60	g	flour (125 ml) (½ c)
10	ml	baking powder (2 t)
2	ml	salt
		a pinch of cayenne pepper
		a pinch of mustard
50	g	grated cheddar cheese (125 ml) (½ c)
1		egg, beaten
25	g	margarine (30 ml) (2 Tsp + 1 t)
		milk for mixing

Method:

Sift the dry ingredients. Rub in margarine with fingertips. Add the cheese and egg. Mix with milk. Place spoonfuls on a browning dish preheated for 7 min. Bake for 1 min on High. Turn over and bake 1 min longer.

Joey Pienaar

Cheese digests everything but itself.

Bread rolls with a meat filling
(Light meal for 4 people)

4		large, round, fresh bread rolls
2		onions
2		eggs, beaten
1	Tsp	tomato puree
2	Tsp	freshly chopped parsley
4		thin slices of cheddar cheese
2	Tsp	butter
1		clove garlic
		salt and pepper (freshly ground)
1	t	mustard
2	Tsp	capers, optional
250	g	mince

Method:
Heat butter in browning dish, fry onion and garlic until translucent. Add meat and fry for 4 min on High. In the meantime, remove the top and the centre of the rolls and crumb. Add the crumbs to the meat, eggs, tomato puree, mustard, parsley and capers — mix well. Bake the mixture on High for 2 min. Fill the rolls with the mixture. Place the tomato slices and cheese on top. Bake in microwave for 40 seconds or until the cheese melts. Garnish with parsley. Serve with a crisp French salad.
Joey Pienaar

Beauty is not only skin deep.

Mutton curry with yellow rice and raisins

(4 helpings)

750	g	mutton thick rib, diced
1		large onion, chopped
15	ml	curry (3 t)
5	ml	turmeric (1 t)
10	ml	ground ginger (2 t)
3		cloves of garlic, crushed
40	ml	oil (8 t)
4		cooked potatoes, halved
1		large tomato, chopped
12,5	ml	lemon juice (1 Tsp)
40	ml	sultanas (4 Tsp)
50	ml	chutney (4 Tsp)

Method:

Marinade meat in curry, turmeric, onion, ginger and garlic in 20 ml oil. Preheat browning dish for 8 min on High (100 %). Add the rest of the oil to meat mixture and brown for 2 min. Stir and cook another 8 min on High (100 %). Add the rest of the ingredients, cover and boil for 15 min on medium (50 %). Stir and test meat. See recipe for yellow rice and raisins on p 374.

Joey Pienaar

A friend is a gift whose worth cannot be measured except by the heart — D. Dickason.

Cape Brandy tart

(Makes 1 tart)

STEP 1: Prepare ingredients.

250	g	dates, chopped
50	g	walnuts (125 ml, coarsely chopped) (½ c)
5	ml	bicarbonate of soda (1 t)
62,5	ml	margarine (¼ c)
250	ml	boiling water (1 c)
1		large egg
160	g	brown sugar (200 ml) (¾ c + 2 t)
180	g	flour (375 ml) (1½ c)
3	ml	baking powder
3	ml	salt

Sauce:

200	g	brown sugar (250 ml) (1 c)
		a pinch of salt
250	ml	boiling water (1 c)
125	ml	brandy (½ c)

Method:

STEP 2: Mix the dates, walnuts, bicarbonate of soda, margarine and boiling water and leave aside. Beat egg and sugar thoroughly and add to date mixture.

STEP 3: Sift the flour, baking powder and salt and fold into date mixture. Pour into a greased microwave tube pan and microwave for 12 min on maximum (High). Prepare sauce by mixing the sugar, salt and boiling water. Microwave for 2 min on maximum. Remove and stir in brandy. Pour over tart immediately when done and leave in the pan until the sauce has been absorbed. Turn the pan out onto a serving dish and fill the centre with whipped cream. Serve.

Joey Pienaar

It is no secret what God can do.

Mince rolls

1		French loaf
		or
6		whole-wheat bread rolls
1	pkt	Maggie Mince Fix (60 g) mixed with water according to instructions on the pkt
500	g	mince
25	ml	oil (2 Tsp)
1		red pepper, finely chopped
1		green pepper, finely chopped
100	g	Gouda cheese, diced

Method:
Cut loaf or rolls lengthwise and remove some of the contents to form a hollow. Fry mince in oil for 5 min in microwave oven. Add peppers and cheese to mince mixture. Fill the loaf or rolls with the mixture and place on a suitable baking dish. Place in microwave oven for 1-2 min on 70 %.
Joey Pienaar

Isn't it amazing how the rich get richer, and the poor get poorer.

Yellow rice and raisins

500	ml	water (2 c)
250	ml	rice (1 c)
5	ml	turmeric (1 t)
1	stick	cinnamon
		salt to taste
125	ml	seedless raisins (½ c)

Method:
Heat water for 6 min on high (100 %). Add the rice, turmeric, cinnamon and salt. Cover and boil for 10-12 min on high (100 %). Leave for 5 min. Drain. Remove cinnamon. Add raisins and stir. Warm on reheat (80 %).
Joey Pienaar

Depression is cancerous.

Preserves

Ripe fig preserve

Thinly peel the figs and leave in the sun for a while to harden on the outside. Prick well with a fork and leave overnight in a lime solution of 1 t lime in 4 ℓ water. Rinse the figs and place in the boiling syrup. For the syrup, use 2½ c water for every c sugar. Use 1 kg sugar for every kg of fruit. Add the juice of 1 lemon to every 2½ kg fruit. Add ½ t cream of tartar. Cover with the lid and boil rapidly for 1 hr. Remove from heat and leave for 6 hrs. Remove lid and boil until the syrup is thick and the figs are translucent. For flavour, crushed ginger can be added. Bottle and seal while still hot.
Joey Pienaar

Watermelon preserve

Cut into 50 mm slices, remove the soft part and peel the thin outer green peel. Prick each slice with a fork and cut into rectangular or square pieces, as desired. Weigh. Soak the watermelon pieces overnight but makatane watermelon pieces must soak for 2 days in the following solution: 2 Tsp lime per 3,5 ℓ water. Drain, rinse and soak for 2 hrs in fresh water. Boil the pieces until tender. Water must boil continuously. Make a syrup with 500 g sugar for every 500 g fruit and use 4 c water for every 500 g sugar. Add 3 Tsp lemon juice for every 1 kg fruit. Cover with the lid and boil the pieces in the syrup for 1 hr. Remove from heat and leave for 6 hrs. Remove lid and boil until the pieces are translucent and the syrup is thick. Place in sterilized jars, fill with syrup and seal.
Joey Pienaar

Dreams are good friends when you're lonely — Viki Leandros.

Peach slices

Peel the peaches and slice. Cover with 1-1¼ c water for every lb (500 g) fruit. Boil until the peaches are tender. Use the same water to make a syrup. Strain the water through a muslin or superwipe cloth. For every 500 g slices use 375 ml sugar (1½ c) and the water in which the fruit was boiled. Stir until the sugar has dissolved. Boil the syrup, add the slices, cover and boil for 1 hr. Remove from heat and leave for six hours. Remove lid, and boil until the syrup has thickened and the slices are cooked through.
Joey Pienaar

Canned peaches

Peel all the fruit thinly and neatly. Halve each peach. Stone. Prepare syrup with 1 part water and 2 parts sugar and heat until boiling. Place peeled peaches into boiling syrup and boil for 20-30 min. Bottle immediately in sterilized jars. Fill with the syrup and seal.
Mollie de Witt

Lemon marmalade

Rinse 5 large lemons thoroughly. Slice thinly without removing peel. Pour 5 ℓ water over them and soak for 24 hrs. Boil the mixture until the slices are tender — about 20 min. Leave for 24 hrs. Weigh and use 500 g sugar for every 500 g pulp. Halve 2 large apples. Add to fruit (high in pectin). Boil for 1 hr, with lid on and leave for 6 hrs. Remove lid and boil quickly until the mixture jells.
Joey Pienaar

Dreams are lies.

Peach chutney

2,5	kg	yellow peaches
1	Tsp	curry powder
1	t	ginger
25	ml	salt (2 Tsp)
2,25	kg	onions
1	t	whole cloves
1	t	turmeric
4½	c	white vinegar (1,125 ℓ)
750	g	sugar
10	ml	coriander (2 t)

Method:
Place spices in vinegar and bring to the boil. Stir in sugar, salt, curry powder and turmeric. Peel and slice peaches. Slice onions and add peaches and onions to vinegar mixture. Boil rapidly for 20 min. Bottle while hot and seal. Remember to remove the cloves.
Joey Pienaar

Sweep your own doorstep before you sweep that of your neighbours.

Orange marmalade
(Use oranges early in the season to ensure high pectin quality)

Finely slice 8 oranges without peeling. Seed. Measure 3 c water for 1 c of fruit slices. Soak overnight. Boil the following day until very soft. Leave overnight. For every 500 g pulp, measure 500 g sugar. Add the juice of 3 lemons. Boil rapidly and stir often. When the marmalade starts bubbling like lava, it is ready. Allow mixture to cool slightly before bottling in sterilized jars. If not slightly cooled the slices will rise to the top of the jar.
Joey Pienaar

Orange preserve

Early season navel oranges are preferable. Grate off rind with a fine grater. Rub salt into the oranges and leave for 30 min. Pour boiling water over and leave overnight. The following morning, rinse and cover with cold water. Leave for 8 hours and cover with cold water again. Halve oranges and boil until soft. Test with a skewer. Remove and drain on a cooling tray. Weigh the oranges. Prepare a syrup with 500 g sugar for every 500 g fruit and use 4 c water for every 500 g fruit. Add 3 Tsp lemon juice to every 1 kg fruit. When boiling add orange halves to syrup and boil, covered for 1 hr. Remove from heat and leave aside for 6 hrs. Remove lid and boil rapidly until the syrup is thick. The jam is ready if the syrup bubbles like lava.
Joey Pienaar

A love song is a key to happiness — Marius Barnard.

Green tomato preserve

Use unblemished tomatoes. Prick with a darning needle and soak overnight in a salt solution, 1 Tsp salt in 2,5 ℓ water. Rinse tomatoes and weigh. Boil syrup by using 500 g sugar for every 500 g tomatoes and 1 c water for every 2 c sugar. A few pieces of crushed ginger can be added to the mixture. Add the tomatoes to the boiling syrup. Cover and boil for 1 hr. Remove from heat and leave for 6 hrs. Remove lid and allow mixture to boil rapidly until the syrup thickens. Bottle and seal.
Joey Pienaar

Tomato sauce

3	kg	ripe tomatoes
4		large onions

Mince and boil

Add:

1		bottle white vinegar (750 ml) (3 c)
700	g	sugar
1	dsp	salt
1		clove garlic
2	Tsp	whole black peppercorns
3 level	t	cayenne pepper

Method:
Boil all ingredients until thick. Remove — add 2 dsp maizena to a small bottle of Tomango Tomato Sauce and stir thoroughly. Add to tomato pulp and boil until maizena is cooked. Bottle hot.
Brenda Vlotman

A man does not have to be an angel in order to be a saint —
Albert Schweitzer.

Cumquat preserve

2	lb	cumquats (1 kg)
2	lb	sugar (1 kg)
6	c	water (1,5 ℓ)

Method:
Make a small cut in each cumquat to remove the pips. Place in saucepan, cover with cold water, bring slowly to the boil and boil until tender enough to pierce with a match stick. Boil syrup with water and sugar, then cool. Drain fruit and place in cooled syrup. Reheat slowly to boiling point and boil until fruit is clear and the syrup thickens. Leave overnight and boil the following day before bottling in hot, sterilized jars. Seal.
Joey Pienaar

Apricot chutney

2,5	kg	stoned apricots
500	g	sultanas or seedless raisins
6		cloves garlic
750	g	onions
750	ml	sugar (3 c)
20	ml	salt (4 t)
20	ml	ginger (4 t)
10	ml	cinnamon (2 t)
7	ml	black pepper
2	ml	cayenne pepper
1,5	ℓ	vinegar

Method:
Mince the apricots, sultanas, garlic and onion. Add the rest of the ingredients, boil slowly until thick and pour into hot, sterilized jars. Seal.
Mollie de Witt

Never pick from the forbidden fruit tree.

Pickled yellow peaches (Atjar)

2	kg	sliced yellow peaches
4		large onions, chopped
1	c	sugar
750	ml	vinegar (3 c)
1	Tsp	curry powder
1	Tsp	turmeric
1	dsp	mixed spice
1	t	whole cloves
1	Tsp	salt

Method:
Boil all ingredients slowly over a low heat for 1½ hrs. Cool. Remove cloves and bottle in sterilized bottles.
Joey Pienaar

Apricot preserve

2,5	kg	apricots
2,5	kg	sugar

(NB. No water must be added)

Method:
Stone apricots and sprinkle with sugar. Allow to stand overnight or for at least 6 hours. Stir thoroughly and boil slowly till sugar has dissolved. Set heat on "high" and boil faster. Stir continuously till the mixture boils like lava. Bottle in sterilized jars and leave to cool. Seal.
Joey Pienaar

We should live our lives as though Christ was coming this afternoon — Jimmy Carter.

Ouma Hanna's green tomato chutney
(Delicious)

Step 1:

3	kg	green tomatoes
1½	kg	onions
2½		bottles vinegar (1,875 ℓ)
3	c	sugar
½	c	salt

Method:
Slice the tomatoes the night before, sprinkle with the ½ c salt. Pour the water off the following morning and add the finely sliced onion, sugar and vinegar. When boiling add the ingredients in step 2.

Step 2:

5		heaped Tsp flour
2	Tsp	curry
2	Tsp	mustard
1	Tsp	cayenne pepper
1	Tsp	turmeric
½	c	apricot jam
375	ml	vinegar (1½ c)

Method:
Mix well until free from lumps. Add about 1 c hot tomato mixture to the curry mixture and stir. Pour into boiling tomato mixture. Boil for 15 min. Stir constantly. Sterilize jars. Bottle hot mixture and seal.

Joey Pienaar

Most human beings have an almost infinite capacity for taking things for granted — Aldous Huxley.

One spark of hope can light a bonfire of joy.

Champagne breakfast

(The following recipes provide for 6-8 people)

STEWED FRUIT

*

YOGHURT

*

PANCAKE WITH TUNA FILLING

*

CHICKEN LIVERS WITH MUSHROOM
AND SHERRY SAUCE

*

MINUTE STEAKS WITH CHEESE

*

BAKED BANANAS

*

HOMEMADE WHITE BREAD

*

HOMEMADE BROWN BREAD

*

CRUMPETS

*

SCRAMBLED EGGS

*

SAUSAGES WITH BACON

*

Joey Pienaar

A song may end, but the melody lingers on.

386

Stewed fruit

300	g	mixed dried fruit
250	ml	water (1 c)
500	ml	fresh orange juice (2 c)
50	ml	medium dry sherry (4 Tsp)

Method:
Soak the dried fruit overnight in the water and orange juice. Place in saucepan, heat to boiling point, remove from heat and add sherry. Mix lightly and serve with yoghurt.

Pancake with tuna filling

120	g	flour (250 ml) (1 c)
5	ml	baking powder (1 t)
1	ml	salt
1		egg
190	ml	milk (¾ c)
12,5	ml	lemon juice (1 Tsp)
60	ml	melted butter (¼ c)

Method:
Sift dry ingredients into a mixing bowl. Beat egg until frothy, add remaining ingredients and beat thoroughly. Add to dry ingredients and beat until smooth. Fry in a little oil.

Tuna filling:

1 x200 g tin		tuna (drained)
1		hard-boiled egg, chopped
1		medium onion, chopped
25	ml	chopped parsley (2 Tsp)
125	ml	mayonnaise (½ c)

Method:
Flake the tuna, add rest of ingredients. Place a spoonful of filling on each pancake. Roll up and serve.

A tree is known by its fruit.

Chicken livers with mushroom and sherry sauce

500	g	chicken livers
2		large onions (chopped)
12,5	ml	butter (1 Tsp)
12,5	ml	oil (1 Tsp)
250	g	mushrooms (sliced)
		salt and freshly ground black pepper to taste
50	ml	medium dry sherry (4 Tsp)
5	ml	Aromat (1 t)

Method:

Thaw chicken livers and rinse under cold running water. Set aside. Sauté onion in oil and butter until translucent, add livers and sauté until light brown on all sides. Add mushrooms and seasoning, replace lid and simmer for about 20 min or until the chicken livers and mushrooms are cooked. Add sherry just before serving. Serve hot.

Minute steaks with cheese

6		minute steaks
		salt and pepper to taste
12,5	ml	butter (1 Tsp)
12,5	ml	oil (1 Tsp)
6		slices processed cheese

Method:

Season minute steaks with salt and pepper. Heat butter and oil in a heavy based frying pan until hot and fry meat until golden brown on both sides. Remove from pan, place in an ovenproof dish and place a piece of cheese on each portion of meat. Place under a heated grill and allow cheese to melt.

Better an egg today than a hen tomorrow.

Baked bananas

6   bananas
60   ml   butter (¼ c)
              a little brown sugar to sprinkle over bananas
              (optional)

Method:

Place bananas on a flat baking sheet and bake in preheated oven (160 °C — 325 °F) until skins discolour. Remove from the oven. Slit the skin on one side and dot with butter. Sprinkle with a little brown sugar (if preferred). Place under oven grill just before serving and grill until golden brown. Serve immediately.

I am a stranger and afraid in a world I never made — A.E. Housman.

Quick white bread
(Delicious)

2		cakes yeast
60	ml	lukewarm water (¼ c)
500	ml	milk (2 c)
50	ml	margarine (4 Tsp)
50	ml	sugar (4 Tsp)
10	ml	salt (2 t)
6	c	flour

Method:
Bring the liquid to the boil. Add margarine, sugar and salt and leave until lukewarm. Soften the yeast in the lukewarm water. Mix in about 750 ml flour with a spatula. Add rest of flour and knead well for 10 min. (The dough must be smooth and elastic and form bubbles under the surface.) Spread margarine lightly over the dough, cover well and leave in a warm place to rise to double the original size. Knead and place in 1 large or 2 small breadpans. Allow to rise again until double the original size. Bake for ± 50 min at 180 °C (350 °F).
Brown loaves: Use brown bread meal. Bake a little longer for 1 hour at 180 °C (350 °F).

Crumpets (flapjacks)

440	ml	flour (1¾ c)
10	ml	baking powder (2 t)
		a pinch of salt
25	ml	sugar (2 Tsp)
1x410g	tin	evaporated milk
1		egg
12,5	ml	oil (1 Tsp)

What the world needs is some "do-give-a-damn" pills — William Meninger.

Method:
Sift dry ingredients. Beat egg and milk. Add dry ingredients. Beat thoroughly. Leave for 25 min. Drop spoonfuls onto a hot greased frying pan. Turn once only. Place in a folded cloth and leave on cooling rack to cool. Place in a covered dish. Spread with butter. Keep in covered dish.
N.B. The secret lies in the cooling process.

Scrambled eggs

Scrambled eggs must be cooked over a low heat. They must be soft and creamy, not brown and crumbly.

Method:
Heat (60 ml) (4¼ Tsp) butter or margarine in a frying pan over a low heat. Stir together 8 eggs, 125 ml (½ c) milk, 2½ ml (½ t) salt, ½ t fondor or Aromat and a little pepper. (Scrambled egg is not whisked only stirred.) Pour into pan, stir and heat over a low heat until it starts to set. Remove from the stove: the heat in the pan is sufficient to complete the cooking process. Garnish with chopped parsley.

Don't put all your eggs in one basket.

Sausages with bacon

Use small Vienna or cocktail sausages. Cut sausages lengthwise but do not separate them. Spread a little prepared mustard in the sausage and place a strip of cheese in it. Roll in a rasher of bacon. Secure with a toothpick. Sprinkle with dry white wine. Place under a grill. Grill a few min. The cheese will not heat properly if placed too close to the grill.

All good things come to an end.

Alphabetical list of recipes

All bran rusks   221
Animelles   141
Apple
  -cake (hot)   337
  -dessert (microwave)   358
  -salad   242
  -tart   318, 339
  -toffee   346
Apricot
  -biscuits   293
  -cheese cake   262,264
  -chutney   381
  -cream cheese tart   331
  -pudding (baked)   190
Asparagus
  -soup (hot)   61
  -tart   44, 49, 50
  -tart (quick)   45
Atjar pickled (yellow peaches)   382
Avocado
  -and shrimp shells   37
  -baked with shrimps   368
  -dip   20, 23

Bacon
  -and cheese filling, potatoes
    with   175
  -and cheese snacks   275
  -and cheese tart   46
  -rolls (microwave)   354
  -sausages with   392
Baked
  -potatoes   178
  -pudding   206
  -tuna   66
Banana
  -and tuna starter   31
  -baked   389
  -candles   234
  -caramel pudding   186
  -ice-cream drink   12
  -loaf   310
  -pudding, upside down   212
  -salad (curried)   242
  -salad dressing   248
  -salad mould   251
Barbecues   127-146
Batter for fish   64
Beans
  -bredie, green   169
  -curried   177
  -garlic   131
  -grecian, green   169

  -green salad   145
  -salad   174, 177, 236, 240
  -stewed, green   168

Beef
  -curried   77
  -in puff pastry   82
  -slices with garlic butter   88
  -monkey-gland steak in beer   83
Beetroot
  -salad   178, 236
Biscuits   273-316
Blaauwkrantz dip   28
Bobotie   109, 111, 116
  -with a difference   110
  -waterblommetjie   118
Boerewors   104
Brandy
  -sauce for sago pudding   206
  -snaps   290
  -tart   342
  -tart, Cape   372
  -tart (microwave)   363
Braised
  -kidneys   96
  -snoek   68
Brawn   82
Bread
  -and rusks   220-232
  -brown   227
  -cheese   134
  -corn (microwave)   355
  -coarse   228
  -for a barbecue   145
  -green mealie, steamed   136
  -mealie, instant   143
  -milk   224
  -pot   128
  -pudding   181, 214, 215
  -rolls with meat filling
    (microwave)   370
  -salad   252
  -slightly coarse   224
  -whole-wheat   232
  -whole-wheat, quick   144
Brine   141
Brown tea biscuits   298
Butter, mustard   54
Buttermilk
  -pudding (microwave)   357
  -rusks   221
  -rusks, self-raising flour   230
  -rusks (microwave)   366

Cabbage, curried 168
Cakes 253-272
Canned peaches 377
Carrots
-and pineapple salad 235
-and pineapple salad,
    moulded 249
-salad 239
-salad, moulded 252
-soup 60
Caramel
-banana pudding 186
-dumplings 188
-pudding 204
-pudding, brown 203
-sauce, with date loaf 311
-tart, coffee 322
Caul, liver in 75
Caviar mock, potato slices in sour
    cream with 172
Champagne bréakfast 385-392
Cheese
-and bacon filling, potatoes
    with 175
-and bacon tart 46
-and ham tart 46
-bread 134
-cake, Lollies 320
-cake (microwave) 367
-cottage cheese tart 332, 334
-cream cheese Apricot tart 331
-dip, cheddar 26
-dip, cream 27
-fritters 54
-minute steaks with 388
-sauce, for lasagne 114
-scones (microwave) 369
-soup, quick 62
Chicken
-á la king 152
-baked portions 162
-chutney 149, 152
-curried 156, 163
-delicious dish 158, 160
-dip 26
-dishes 147-164
-economical dish 155
-fruit, chicken with 157
-Kentucky 149, 161
-livers with curry 93
-livers with mushroom & sherry
    sauce 388
-marinade for grilled chicken 140
-peri-peri 159, 160
-pie 151, 154
-Spanish 150

-Spanish paella 153
-sour cream pie crust for chicken
    pie 151
-with mushrooms (microwave) 357
Chiffon cake 254, 268
-with oil 256
Chitterling 146
Chocolate
-cake 254, 266
-fudge (microwave) 368
-pudding, baked 195
-sauce 208, 213
Chops
-curried 129
-mutton 80
-pork, roasted 86
Choux pastry puffs 304
Christmas
-biscuits (microwave) 361
-pudding, cold 180
Chutney
-apricot 381
-chicken 149, 152
-green tomato 383
-peach 378
Cloths to wipe hands after dinner
    (microwave) 362
Coconut
-biscuits 281, 290, 294, 301
-ice 349, 351
-ice (uncooked) 350
-icing 271
-layer for milk tart 336
-milk tart 324
-tart 333
-tart, Greek 319
Coffee
-biscuits 280, 292
-caramel tart 322
-liqueur 17
Condensed milk biscuits 282
Continental truffles 295
Corn bread 355
Corn flakes
-dessert 194, 199
-meringue tart 326
Corned meat 80
Cottage cheese tart 332, 334
Cottage pie 86
Cream
-liqueur 15
-pastry for Jam turnovers 293
-scones 316
Cream cheese dip 27
Croutons 60
Crumpets 390

394

Crustless
-milk tart   328
-savoury tart   52
Cumquat preserve   381
Curry
-and rice   106
-banana salad   242
-beef   77
-cabbage   168, 176
-chicken   156, 163
-chicken livers   93
-green beans   171, 177
-mutton and yellow rice   371
-peach salad   242
-pineapple salad   237

Dainty biscuits   288
Date
-loaf with caramel sauce   311
-pudding, traditional   193
-tart   329
Decoration for starters   30
Dessert for barbecue   134
Desserts   179-218
Dips   19-28
Dried fruit
-salad   244
-stewed   387
Dried sausage
-boerewors   103
-venison   124
Dumplings   98
-caramel   188
-cinnamon, traditional   208
-delicious sweet   212
-milk   195
-sweet   198

Eggs, scrambled   391
Entrées   29-39

Feather cake   267
Figs
-green, jam tart   340
-ripe preserve   367
Fish   63-72
-batter for   64
-cakes   64
-crisp baked (microwave)   365
-curried   71
-oven baked   72
-pickled, Grandma's   70
-salad   33, 66
-salad starter   31
Flapjacks   390
Fricadel, venison   126

Fridge tart, ginger   319
Fritters
-cheese   54
-green mealie   172
-minced meat   47
-pumpkin   142, 201
-sweetcorn - 144
Fruit
-biscuits, refrigerated   291
-cake (dark)   258
-cake (microwave)   356, 360
-cake (refrigerated)   262
-cake (white)   258
-chicken   157
-drink   10
-loaf   307
-pudding, baked   191
-pudding, ginger   204
-pudding, quick   217
-ring   269
-stewed   387
Fudge   347, 350, 354
-chocolate (microwave)   368

Gambas al ajillo   38
Garlic
-beans   131
-bread   131
-butter, beef slices with   88
-butter, snails in   33
-butter, mushrooms with
   shrimps   32
Ginger
-beer, traditional   11
-bread   305
-cookies   284
-fridge tart   319
-fruit pudding   204
-tart   323
Gooseberry Cape tart   332
Gourmet
-meat dish for the   74
-vegetable soup   58
Grecian green beans   169
Greek
-coconut tart   319
-leg of mutton   130
-punch   10
Green beans
-bredie   169
-curried   171
-Grecian   169
-salad   145
-stewed   168
-with vinegar sauce   179
Green fig jam tart   340

Hamburger, grilled   87
Ham
 -cheese tart   46
 -dip   21
Herb rice   167
Hertzoggies   280
Honey cake   270
Horseradish sauce   22

Ice-cream
 -banana drink   12
 -chocolate sauce for   213
 -pudding   182

Jam
 -squares   283
 -tarts   287
 -turnovers   293
Jan Smuts cookies   279, 314

Kentucky chicken   149, 161
Kidneys, braised   96
Kipper Kedgeree   32
Kisses   309
Koeksisers   285, 286, 294, 302
Kudu Stroganoff   123

Lasagne with cheese sauce   114
Lemon
 -drink   17
 -marmelade   377
 -meringue pie   327
Liver
 -cakes   115
 -chicken, with curry   93
 -chicken, in sherry and mushroom
    sauce   388
 -in caul   75
 -in gravy   90
 -paté   35
 -pie   97
 -rissoles   92
 -with sour sauce   91, 92
Liqueur
 -coffee   17
 -cream   15
 -Van der Hum   16

Macaroni salad with beer
    dressing   250
Marie biscuit squares   275
Marinade
 -for chicken   157
 -for grilled chicken   140
 -steak   137

Marmelade
 -lemon   377
 -orange   379
Marshmallow
 -pudding   209
 -sweets   348
 -tart   328
Mealie
 -dish, baked   173
 -pap tart   136
 -tart   146
Mealie bread
 -green steamed   136
 -instant   143
Mealie meal porridge
 -crumbed, Putu   143, 362
 -stiff   140, 366
Meat dish
 -for the gourmet   74
 -Taiwanese (microwave)   359
 -with mushroom soup   75
Meat filling for bread rolls (micro-
    wave)   370
Meat pie pastry   43
Meringues   278, 296
 -cornflake, tart   326
 -lemon, tart   327
Microwave recipes   353-374
Milk
 -bread   224
 -dumplings   195
 -filling   336
 -tart   324, 336
 -tart, coconut layer   336
 -tart, crustless   328
Minced meat
 -and noodle dish   112
 -dishes   101-120
 -fritters   47
Mince rolls (microwave)   373
Minute steaks with cheese   388
Mixed salad   234
Mocha dessert, frozen   186
Mock crayfish   34
Monkey-gland steak in beer   83
Montelimar pudding   195
Mushrooms
 -and sherry sauce for chicken
    livers   388
 -with chicken (microwave)   357
 -with garlic butter   36
 -with tuna, sour cream filling   39
Mustard
 -butter   54
 -sauce   21, 22
 -tongue   81

396

Mutton
  -chops   83
  -stewed   89
  -curry with yellow rice (micro-
    wave)   371

Noodle dish and minced meat

Oatmeal
  -and nut biscuits   306
  -biscuits   288, 289
  -rough biscuits   300
Offal   94
  -curry   95
Oil rusks   226
Omelette pizza   55
One dish evening meal   117
Onions
  -dip   20, 23
  -rings, fried   166
  -salad, cooked   142
  -salad, easy   240
Orange
  -cake   270
  -icing   256
  -marmalade   379
  -preserve   379
  -ring cake   260
  -sauce   184
  -sweet potatoes   167
  -syrup cake   260
Oven baked fish   72
Ox tongue, sauce for   78

Paella   148
  -Spanish chicken   153
Pancakes   308, 313, 315
  -fillings   313
  -for beginners   297
  -without eggs   184
  -with tuna filling   387
Paraguayan tart   330
Pastry
  -meat pie   43
  -plain   51
  -puff   274
  -sweet   278
Paté, liver   35
Paw paw wine dessert   183
Peach
  -and rice salad   243
  -canned   377
  -chutney   378
  -dessert   185

  -salad, curried   242
  -salad, filled halves   235
  -slices   377
  -yellow, pickled atjar   382
Pearl wheat   100
  -with raisins   99
  -salad   237, 241
Peri-Peri
  -chicken   159, 160
  -shrimp sauce   70
Pickled
  -fish, Grandma's   70
  -leg of pork with pineapple crust   90
  -yellow peach atjar   382
Pie crust, sour cream   151
Pig, roast suckling   84
Pineapple
  -and carrot salad   235
  -and carrot salad, moulded   249
  -pork chops with   79
  -pudding   200
  -salad, curried   237
Pizza
  -easy   42
  -omelette   55
  -quick   52, 53
Popcorn syrup   348
Pork chops
  -roasted   86
  -with pineapple   79
Porridge
  -crumbly, "Putu"   143, 362
  -stiff   140, 366
  -tomato sauce for   129
Potato
  -baked   178
  -dish (microwave)   365
  -in jackets   130, 174
  -salad   238, 247
  -slices with sour cream and mock
    caviar   172
  -stuffed, baked   173
  -with bacon and cheese filling   175
Pot bread   128
Poultry   147-164
Preserves   375-383
Pudding, baked   206
Puff pastry   274
  -beef in   82
Pumpkin fritters   142, 201
Punch   13, 15
  -alcoholic   14
  -easy   14
  -Greek   10
Putu porridge   143
  -microwave   362

Quick
-asparagus soup   61
-cheese soup   62
-dip   20
-pizza   52
-scones   308

Raisins
-pearl wheat with   99
-yellow rice with   374
Refrigerator
-fruit biscuits   291
-fruit cake   261
Rib of mutton, salted   133
Rice
-and peach salad   243
-boiled   99
-curry and   106
-dish, no effort   103
-microwave   364
-plain, herbed   167
-salad, curried   251
-steamed   107
-yellow with raisins (microwave)   374
Rissoles, liver   92
Romany creams   286
-dessert   182
-microwave   364
Roly Poly pudding   194
Rusks   220
-All Bran   221
-brown   226
-buttermilk   221
-buttermilk (microwave)   366
-buttermilk, self-raising flour   230
-oil   226
-sweet   223

Sabanang meat   113
Sago pudding   185, 187
-baked   216
-with brandy caramel sauce   206
Salads and salad dressings   233-252
Salad
-bean   174
-beetroot spiced vinegar   177, 236
-cooked onion   142
-easy onion   240
-fish   33, 66
-fish starter   31
-green bean   145
-instant beans   177
-tuna   71
Salad dressings   233-252

-banana   248
-beer   250
-boiled   246, 248
-condensed milk   247
-evaporated milk   244
-French   243
Salted rib of mutton   133
Samp   98
Saratoga tart   330
Sauce
-brandy caramel   207
-caramel   187
-chocolate   208, 213
-cucumber and yoghurt   24
-for grilled chicken   138
-for ox tongue   78
-horseradish   22
-mustard   21, 22
-orange   184
-red wine   203
-seafood   38
-sweet and sour dip   25
-tomato   129, 359, 380
Sausage   102
-dried   103
-dried venison   124
-Vienna, tart   48
-venison, frying   125
-with bacon   392
Savouries   44
-and snacks   41-55
-balls   45
-tart, crustless   52
Scones   303
-cheese (microwave)   369
-cream   316
-feather light   300
-quick   308
Scotch
-cream pudding   188
-short bread   306
Scrambled eggs   391
Sherbet   346
Slightly coarse bread   224
Shrimps
-garlic   32
-shells, avocado with   37
-with baked avocado (microwave)   368
-with peri-peri sauce   76
Skurwejantjies (oatmeal biscuits)   300
Snails in garlic butter   33
Schnitzel Wiener   78
Snoek
-braised   68
-roll   65

398

-tart 50
Sosaties 85, 132, 135
"Soetkoekies" 282, 299
Soufflé roll 67
Soup 57-62
   -asparagus (quick) 61
   -bean 61
   -carrot 60
   -cheese (quick) 62
   -vegetable, gourmet 58
   -vegetable pea 59
Sour cream
   -and mock caviar, potato slices
      with 172
   -pie crust, chicken pie with 151
Sour sauce with liver 91, 92
Spaghetti bolognaise 105
Spanish
   -chicken 150
   -paella 153
   -pie 151
Spiced
   -beetroot 236
   -minced meat 108
   -vinegar beetroot salad 178
Sponge cake 268
Steak
   -marinaded 137
   -minute, with cheese 388
   -monkey-gland, in beer 83
   -T-bone 87
Steamed
   -green mealie bread 136
   -rice 107
Stewed
   -fruit 387
   -green beans 168
   -mutton 89
Stroganoff
   -kudu/venison 123
   -with a difference 76
Stuffed
   -leg of venison 122
   -trout 69
Suckling pig roast 84
Sweetcorn fritters 144
Sweet
   -cookies 284
   -pastry 278
   -tart crust 335
Sweetmelon salad 241
Sweet potato
   -dish 170
   -glazed 170
   -orange 167
Sweets 345-351

Swis roll 257
Syrup cake 265

Taiwanese meat dish (microwave) 359
Tamboesies, custard slices 276
Tarts 317-343
T-bone steak 87
Tipsy
   -pudding 211
   -tart 325
Toffee apples 346
Tomato
   -dip 24
   -drink 12
   -chutney, green 383
   -preserve, green 380
   -sauce 380
   -sauce (microwave) 359
   -sauce for pap 129
Tongue
   -mustard 81
   -sauce for 78
Traditional
   -date pudding 193
   -nut dumplings 208
   -soetkoekies 282, 299
Triangle tart 334
Trout, stuffed 69
Truffles, continental 295
Tuna
   -and banana starter 31
   -baked 66
   -pancake filling 387
   -roll 65
   -salad 71
   -tasty starter 36
   -with mushrooms, sour cream
      filling 39

Upside down banana pudding 212

Van der Hum liqueur 16
Vegetables 165-178
   -gourmet soup 58
   -pea soup 59
Venison 121-126
Vetkoek 231
Vienna sausage tart 48
Vinegar pudding 189, 210
Vinegar sauce, green beans with 176

Waterblommetjie bobotie 118
Watermelon preserve 376
White

-bread quick   390
-layer cake   263
Whole-wheat bread   222, 232
-quick   144
Wiener schnitzel   78
Wine, paw paw dessert   183

Yellow rice
-and raisins (microwave)   374
-with mutton curry (microwve)   371
Yoghurt
-bread   225
-cucumber sauce   24